THE GROWTH DILEMMA

MANAGING YOUR BRAND
WHEN DIFFERENT CUSTOMERS
WANT DIFFERENT THINGS

ANNIE WILSON

RYAN HAMILTON

HARVARD BUSINESS REVIEW PRESS • BOSTON, MASSACHUSETTS

Library of Congress Cataloging-in-Publication Data

Names: Wilson, Annie (Lecturer in marketing), author. | Hamilton,
Ryan (Professor), author.
Title: The growth dilemma : managing your brand when different customers
    want different things / Annie Wilson and Ryan Hamilton.
Description: Boston, Massachusetts : Harvard Business Review Press, [2025] |
    Includes bibliographical references and index.
Identifiers: LCCN 2024047190 (print) | LCCN 2024047191 (ebook) |
    ISBN 9781647829735 (hardcover ; alk. paper) | ISBN 9781647829742 (epub)
Subjects: LCSH: Branding (Marketing) | Brand name products. | Selling.
Classification: LCC HF5415.1255 .W556 2025 (print) |
    LCC HF5415.1255 (ebook) | DDC 658.8/27—dc23/eng/20250217
LC record available at https://lccn.loc.gov/2024047190
LC ebook record available at https://lccn.loc.gov/2024047191

ISBN: 978-1-64782-973-5
eISBN: 978-1-64782-974-2

The paper used in this publication meets the requirements of the American National Standard for Permanence of Paper for Publications and Documents in Libraries and Archives Z39.48-1992.

CONTENTS

PART THREE

MANAGING SEGMENT RELATIONSHIPS OVER TIME

The Struggle Is Real

In 2015, Lands' End hired Federica Marchionni, the former US head of Dolce & Gabbana, with the goal of reviving its flagging brand and attracting new customer segments. Marchionni had a vision for moving Lands' End in a more fashion-forward direction, one intended to attract a younger, cooler set of customers to the brand.[1] Lands' End's core customer was primarily a middle-class but frugal suburban parent.[2] Then Marchionni arrived, in what we can only assume was an impeccably tailored Italian business suit. In an attempt to woo a younger audience, Marchionni introduced some daring changes to the Lands' End line, including spiked red heels, athleisure clothing, a pink cocktail jumpsuit, and a $600 evening jacket.[3] Items that were a far cry from the dowdy chinos, comfortable sweaters, and reasonably priced fleeces the brand was known for. From Marchionni's perspective, the changes were necessary if Lands' End had any hope of convincing millennials to empty their wallets at Lands' End's door. Marchionni herself apparently scoffed at the brand's classic clothing during internal presentations, asking, "Who would wear *that*?"[4]

But in its pursuit of growth, Lands' End alienated the customer base it had painstakingly built and nurtured over the preceding decades. The bold new designs and distinctly impractical lines strayed far from the brand's heritage. A former Lands' End creative director told the *Wall Street Journal* in 2016, "It doesn't look like Lands' End anymore." Instead of suggesting something approachable, Midwestern, or down-to-earth, the brand's new direction promised something much more upscale, less wholesome. Cape Cod instead of Lake Michigan. There was an implied lifestyle with the new styles and advertising "that if you wore Lands' End you'd be on a beach on Nantucket living the perfect life."[5] But, the vision of a perfect Nantucket life was not what had attracted the current base of loyal customers to the brand in the first place. They were looking to embody a very different lifestyle.

Lands' End became a house divided. The brand's core customers and the new customers Marchionni wanted to attract wanted divergent things from their clothes: form versus function; trendy versus comfortable; clothes for going out to brunch versus clothes for doing chores around the house. While it is possible for a brand to change its meaning over time, Marchionni implemented the changes to the brand's image and products at breakneck speed, resulting in confusion and frustration. The new customer segment Marchionni was courting never materialized. Meanwhile, existing customers abandoned the brand en masse. Lands' End went from generating $9.2 million in profit to clocking a $7.7 million loss within a year. To no one's surprise, Marchionni was out as CEO within just two years of her arrival.[6]

In hindsight, it's easy to see where Marchionni went wrong. She tried to attract new customers by trying to turn Lands' End into something it's not. She tried to make the brand more appealing to younger, more fashionable customers and, in the process, made it less appealing to existing customers. Lands' End tried to grow the way companies are supposed to grow, expanding its customer base by adding new customer segments to existing segments. But it lost more than it gained in the process of trying to grow. This type of misstep is not uncommon. Marchionni is hardly alone in her error.

Indeed, this general mistake is the subject of numerous business school cases and brand eulogies. Pursuing new customer segments without adequately considering how those customers will interact with existing segments is a mistake that brands make in pursuit of growth again, and again, and again.

The Growth Dilemma

Many managers today feel intense pressure to grow by attracting new customers. Consider how inescapable terms like "growth hacking," "growth marketing," and "growth engines" have become in today's corporate vernacular. An article in *Harvard Business Review*, aptly titled "Curing the Addiction to Growth," put it this way: "Wall Street and the capitalist culture celebrate—and demand—growth. Indeed, slow growth is regarded as something between a disease and a moral failing. When faced with declining growth, companies are urged to go back to the drawing board, rethink the business, and come up with a new strategy to pump up the top line."[7] In response to ratcheting expectations of growth, managers find themselves on a treadmill of constantly trying to attract new customers . . . *any* customers.

But this obsession with growth can be counterproductive when brands neglect the relationships between all the different customers they are acquiring. One common version of this problem occurs when managers overfixate on new customer segments they optimistically hope will bring in all those dump trucks full of additional money to the brand. In so doing, they often fail to consider any potential negative impacts these new customers might have on existing customers. Or they ignore how existing customers might dissuade those new customer segments from adopting the brand. This was the short, sad story of Marchionni's tenure at Lands' End.

Brands cannot simply treat their customers as a collection of independent groups they can just tack on to their customer base over time. Relationships between segments form an animate, dynamic ecosystem, where the value each customer derives from a brand depends, in part, on the other customers also buying that brand. It is only by acknowledging the interdependences between customer segments and managing customers as part of a brand ecosystem that firms can facilitate sustainable growth.

New customers bring their own values, behaviors, and symbolic meanings to brands. So, any time new customers start using a brand, decision-makers must consider the impact of those customers on the entire brand system. Sometimes, the effects of a new customer segment on a customer ecosystem are neutral. Customer segments are often unfazed by the existence of the other segments buying the brand. Sometimes, the effects of serving new customer segments are positive. There are segments that other customers aspire to because they are cool, or fashionable, or expert. Attracting those segments to a brand can indirectly attract other customers who want to be like them. And sometimes the effects are negative. Just as introducing a new plant or animal to an ecosystem can risk disrupting the balance, new customer segments can influence brand dynamics, both directly and indirectly. In the wild, the impact of an invasive species is rarely felt immediately. Often, it is only later—often too late—that the damage to other plants and animals in the ecosystem is fully realized. The same can be true for new customer segments within a brand's ecosystem.

This is the growth dilemma: as brands grow, they must acquire more customers. As the customer base grows, those customers will be increasingly diverse in terms of their preferences, identities, and values. As the brand changes its offerings to better serve one part of its customer base, it becomes increasingly likely that it will make those offerings less appealing to another part of its customer base. As it embraces the values important to one customer segment, it risks offending the sensibilities of another customer segment. As some customers embrace the brand as an identity marker, they alienate other customers who don't want to signal membership in that group. The result is often conflict within the customer base over how the brand should be used, what it stands for, and whom it should and shouldn't serve. Growth multiplies the thicket of divergent customer preferences, increasing the complexity of managing the relationships between customers to the point where conflict feels almost inevitable.

How This Book Can Help

This book is designed to help brands navigate the perilous waters of growing through the acquisition of new customers. At the heart of this book is the Segment Compatibility Matrix, a framework that maps out the various ways customer segments can interact with one another. This matrix is designed to help managers better understand the dynamics of their customer ecosystem. In particular, the matrix can help brands more strategically target new customer segments and better manage their customer bases over time. The matrix can also be used to diagnose sources of conflict between customer segments, so they can be addressed or, ideally, avoided.

In the pages that follow, we will provide you with strategies and tactics for managing the interactions between customer segments to maximize value, for you and your customers, and minimize conflict between segments. The stories and advice we will share come from our research, consulting engagements, and conversations with dozens of marketing theorists and practitioners.

In part 1, we will explain the different ways in which customer segments can interact with one another and introduce some of the perils and opportunities that come from these interactions. We will introduce the Segment Compatibility Matrix (chapter 1) and discuss the four primary relationship dynamics between customer segments: Separate Communities (chapter 2), Connected Communities (chapter 3), Leader-Follower Segments (chapter 4), and Incompatible Segments (chapter 5).

In part 2, we will dive deep into what makes segments incompatible and how to avoid or resolve conflicts that result from that incompatibility. We will discuss the four most common sources of conflict between customer segments: functional conflict (chapter 7), brand image conflict (chapter 8), user identity conflict (chapter 9), and ideological conflict (chapter 10). Then, we will explain how brands can assess the risks of conflict when deciding whether or not to target a new customer segment (chapter 11), and how to avoid and escape conflict between customer segments (chapter 12). We will also examine the rare occasions when brands can benefit from knowingly embracing conflict, and what factors to take into account when considering this as a growth strategy (chapter 13).

In part 3, we explore the process of managing customer segment relationships over time. First, we show how brands can combine and layer relationship strategies to create more value for customers within and across segments (chapter 14). Then, we discuss why the job of customer segment relationship management is never done, and why it is crucial for brands to continuously monitor, maintain, and update relationships between customer segments, lest their hard-won gains slip away from them (chapter 15).

We wrote this book to be a field guide to help brands navigate the obstacles and uncertainties involved in growing by attracting new customer segments, not an abstract dissertation to sit forgotten on the bookshelf once read. Throughout the book, we have included tables and diagrams detailing the types of conflict that can develop between customer segments and the ways in which brands positively combine relationship strategies to maximize value for customers. These tables and charts can be used as a quick desk reference. We also included questions and exercises throughout the book that brand managers can use to begin to understand the dynamics between their customer segments and evaluate whether inviting a new customer segment into the fold might bring conflict or not.

As practical as we have tried to make this book, we want to be clear that managing customer relationships is not a matter of simply checking off a few tasks on a list. What we are proposing is a wholesale reevaluation of the way brands think about growth marketing. The conventional view of customer segments as independent growth targets is outdated. So, we propose a new business discipline: *segment relationship management* (SRM). SRM involves examining and managing the various ways customer segments create and destroy value for a brand's users because of how they relate to one another.

SRM is designed to span the marketing and strategy functions within an organization. It takes an ecosystem view of managing the relationships between customers and the brand. It's about seeing the customer base as an interconnected system rather than a collection of discrete parts. One of the primary benefits of implementing SRM is identifying and avoiding the growth-killing conflicts likely to erupt between various customer segments. Had Lands' End taken an SRM approach, it would have quickly realized that the two segments it was trying to serve would inevitably pull the brand apart by requiring fundamentally different products and brand images. Further, the very presence of each segment was likely to turn off the other in using the brand as a self-expressive signal. The fashionista attracted to a sleek pink cocktail jumpsuit doesn't want to be associated, via the brand, with the suburban mom looking for a comfortable cable-knit sweater for the elementary school's fall fair. And vice versa.

But SRM isn't just about avoiding land mines. The relationships between customer segments can also provide opportunities, if brands are diligent in looking for them. Lands' End had seemingly set itself up with an impossible challenge by trying to transform its casual, comfy brand into something more fashionable, with more upscale appeal. The path it took was doomed to fail because—through the brute-force introduction of stilettos and sequined evening wear—it tried to convince customers that Lands' End was something it wasn't. The result felt jarring and desperate. But what if Lands' End had instead offloaded some of that change in brand image to a new segment of customers? One that could convince other customers that the relatively unexciting brand was actually a fashion statement? What if they had instead attracted customers who could change the brand's image just by being customers of the brand, reducing the need for Lands' End to invest enormous amounts of time, money, and effort into forcing it through a stilted marketing strategy?

In fact, let's make the challenge harder. What if instead of a reliable but unobjectionable brand like Lands' End, we instead choose a brand that was at one point widely agreed on as being the least fashionable brand imaginable. Could an SRM approach allow Crocs to reinvent itself from the dowdiest, least fashionable footwear imaginable to something . . . cool? Yes. Yes, it can. And we'll tell you how in the next chapter.

Meet the Authors

Annie is a senior lecturer of marketing at the Wharton School, University of Pennsylvania. She teaches courses on introductory marketing, consumer behavior, advertising and communications, and the wellness industry. Annie has received teaching awards across Wharton's undergraduate, MBA, and executive MBA programs. She has published case studies on the marketing strategies of companies such as Crocs, Athletic Brewing Company, Liquid Death, Cann, the Philadelphia Eagles, MilkPEP, Allbirds, and Headspace and Calm. Collectively, these cases are currently taught at over two hundred universities worldwide.

Annie's academic research focuses on how people perceive the behaviors, communications, and actions of other consumers and brands. Annie also studies consumer minimalism and its implications for product marketing and status signaling. She received a BA in psychology and English from Georgetown University and a PhD in marketing from Harvard Business School. Before joining

Wharton, she worked as a behavioral scientist for the Vanguard Group. Annie is also a certified personal trainer and a former Division I athlete.

Ryan is a marketing professor at the Goizueta Business School at Emory University. He has taught classes on marketing management, marketing strategy, consumer psychology, and the use of humor in business. He is an award-winning teacher and researcher, and has been asked on several occasions to deliver the "last lecture" to his students at graduation. He has produced two lecture series on marketing and decision-making for the Great Courses, a company that produces educational and entertaining college-level lectures by professors selected exclusively for their ability to teach.

Ryan has more than twenty years of experience as a consumer behavior researcher. He mostly studies how consumers make judgments and decisions, with a particular interest in the psychology of branding and pricing. His research findings have been covered in the *Harvard Business Review*, the *New York Times*, and the *Wall Street Journal*, among other outlets. He has an undergraduate degree in applied physics. He received his PhD in marketing from Northwestern's Kellogg School of Management. Ryan has an eclectic background that includes a job running a proton accelerator and time spent performing stand-up comedy.

Between us, we have taught thousands of undergraduates, MBAs, and executives on topics related to consumer psychology, customer decision-making, growth marketing, branding, advertising, and marketing strategy. We have also consulted with dozens of organizations on these topics, including Walmart, Vanguard, FedEx, Visa, Home Depot, Estée Lauder, Sony, Cigna, Ipsos, and Visa.

This book was born out of our belief that diligent management of the dynamics between customer segments isn't just a nice-to-have but a must-have for any business that wants to grow successfully. In our work as professors, executive trainers, and consultants, we've seen too many companies struggle, either because they have attracted incompatible customer segments or because they have blinded themselves to opportunities for high-velocity growth by failing to understand how certain segments can bolster or collaborate with other segments. So, we set out to define a systematic approach for understanding the various ways customer segments interact with each other within the context of a brand. The resulting Segment Compatibility Matrix simplifies and codifies the learnings we've derived from the many firms we've studied that have struggled with the growth dilemma, as well as those that have beautifully navigated their way through it.

Ultimately, successfully growing and maintaining a customer base is about creating a balanced ecosystem. Every segment should have a purpose and a place, and the connections—or separations—between them must be thoughtfully designed to support the overall success of the business. Brands should evolve as they add new customer segments, and managers must constantly monitor signs of tension or erosion. Resolving the growth dilemma requires keeping the forest in mind as you grow with each new tree.

This book will help you do that.

So, let's start.

PART ONE

THE DYNAMICS OF CUSTOMER SEGMENT RELATIONSHIPS

1

The Segment Compatibility Matrix

When Crocs bestowed its Classic Clog upon the world in 2002, it emphasized the shoe's supreme utilitarian functionality. Made from a specially formulated foam material called "Croslite," Crocs were comfortable, lightweight, durable, and easy to clean. Predictably, Crocs's initial customers were primarily people who appreciated the practicality: boaters, gardeners, health-care workers, service workers, and kids (or, more specifically, the parents who had previously watched their kids trudge through mud moments after getting new sneakers). Crocs called this core customer segment, who valued the shoes because of how comfortable they were, the "feel goods." Owing mostly to the feel-goods segment, global sales of Crocs increased from $1.2 million to $850 million between 2003 and 2007.[1]

But with growing popularity came increased criticism from everyone else. Despite Crocs's obvious utility—or perhaps because of it—many people thought they looked hideous. Even the least fashion-forward could appreciate the social costs of wearing the squishy foam clogs in public. Crocs were mercilessly mocked by fashion influencers, talk show hosts, and comedians. One viral meme pictured an orange Croc with the caption: "See those little holes? That is where your dignity leaks out."[2] Crocs were even a part of the plot of the 2005 satirical comedy *Idiocracy*. In the movie, Luke Wilson's character awakes from a five-hundred-year hibernation to encounter a future society in which intelligence and good taste have declined to practical nonexistence. Absolutely everyone wears Crocs.

Because of Crocs's aesthetic, few customers outside of the feel goods were interested in buying them. At some point, even the feel goods started to feel reluctant to wear them in public. The fear of social ridicule started outweighing their functional superiority. "But they're so comfortable!" can only shield one's self-esteem for so long.

At the same time, the people who bought Crocs generally weren't buying multiple pairs. Their durability was a virtue for the feel goods, but it also meant that Crocs did not need to be replaced often. The feel goods were also not interested in the other styles of shoes made by Crocs—despite the brand's best efforts to sell new silhouettes like rain boots, golf shoes, and flats. For the activities the feel goods were using Crocs, other designs just didn't suit them as well as the clogs they already owned. And just as all these factors were conspiring to dampen demand for Crocs, the 2008 global financial crisis hit. By 2009, things looked bleak for Crocs. The company was stuck with excess inventory and was forced to cut jobs. Its stock price, once nearly $75, plummeted to a little over a dollar.

Crocs desperately needed to turn the brand around. One way to do that would be to target a new segment of customers. But what group of customers should it target? Really, which new customers *could* it target? And what new source of value might it offer to entice customers beyond the squishy, slip-resistant comfort that had been failing to excite interest for years? The growth strategy Crocs ended up pursuing was one that, from the outside, looked like a delusional fever dream. Crocs turned its hideous clogs into a cutting-edge fashion trend. It accomplished this by acquiring a new target segment: cool, hip, fashion-forward young people it called "explorers."

The transition from ugly symbols of indignity to hip drip was partly attributable to good luck. From the late 2010s into the early 2020s, "ugly luxury" gained traction as a mainstream fashion trend. Traditional aesthetics were out. Unconventional and ostentatious styles were in, particularly in the footwear space. For trend-setting explorers, oversized jeans, baggy shirts, prairie dresses, and bum bags were popular, as were chunky sneakers, Birkenstocks, and Uggs.

But ugly luxury wasn't just about ugly. Much of the appeal was that it was ugly in a way that was self-aware, attention-grabbing, and intentionally outlandish. As a fashion writer at *Vogue* explained, "Most of these [ugly luxury footwear] are aestheticised, cartoon versions of ugliness that seem to have been designed with the specific intention of travelling long distances on the [social media] feed."[3] Academic researchers also tried to account for the appeal of ugly luxury. In a series of laboratory and field studies, Lehigh University professor Ludovica Cesareo and colleagues discovered an "ugly luxury premium" for profoundly ugly fashion. But not just any ugly. "A luxury product that is mundanely ugly, or just a little ugly, is not enough to generate social status or benefit the wearer," Cesareo told us. "It must be distinctively ugly—horrifically, unforgettably ugly."

"Horrifically, unforgettably ugly," you say? Crocs, are your ears burning?

The brilliance of the Crocs management team was in seizing the moment. The brand created a narrative that the ugliness of Crocs was exactly what made them "one of a kind." The shoes, unlike conventional clogs or slip-ons, were unique, bold, and self-aware.

Everyone knew they were ugly, and that was the point. They were instruments of self-expression and rebellion against boring, traditional fashion.

The brand released a flood of new designs and collaboration clogs made with celebrities and brands that offered new takes on the original Classic Clog silhouette. Crocs teamed up with a mélange of high-fashion brands, stylish celebrities, and symbols of kitschy camp: Balenciaga, KFC (yes, that KFC), Hidden Valley Ranch, Hello Kitty, Post Malone, Peeps, 7-Eleven, Luke Combs, Christopher Kane, Bad Bunny, KISS, Salehe Bembury, and General Mills. Shoe drops, limited-edition clogs, and outlandish designs drove media buzz and added hype around releases. Explorers ate it up. The scarcity of unique collaborations and styles made them even more attractive to trendsetters, who were willing to pay a premium. Limited-edition lines of Crocs clogs sold out in minutes, then immediately resold on secondary markets for many multiples of the retail price. Pairs of the Post Malone collaboration clogs were going for $4,000 from resellers. And those KFC collaboration clogs? They were reselling for over $400 after they sold out within a half hour of launching. The brand also continued to expand its line of Jibbitz, charms that plug into the holes on the shoes and give customers the ability to personalize their Crocs. Want a pizza-slice charm for your clogs? Crocs has you covered. Need a Keith Haring icon accessory on your shoe? Or a NASCAR logo? Look no further.

The strategy worked. The Crocs clog—against all the laws of nature and good taste—became the "it" shoe. Crocs appeared at Paris and London Fashion Weeks, were worn by artists, designers, and celebrities like Margot Robbie, Heidi Klum, and David Hockney, and became a preferred footwear brand among US teens. Importantly, explorers were a segment of customers that could drive fashion trends. As explorers flocked to the brand, they didn't do so quietly. They were active social media users and content creators, spreading the gospel of Crocs to new customers. As a result, a third segment, whom we will call "fashion followers," suddenly wanted Crocs because the cool and fashionable explorers wore them. Fashion followers would have never been bold enough to set this trend themselves, but if the explorers said Crocs were cool, then that was enough for them. Crocs must be cool.[4]

When Crocs set out to grow internationally, the brand prioritized markets with large populations of explorers. Reaching the explorers first was the most efficient way to grow, because the explorers pulled in the fashion followers.

At the same time, Crocs continued to attract and serve the feel goods with separate tactics that appealed to them—emphasizing their practical value and posting more wholesome, community-oriented content on social media, including posts celebrating health-care workers or asking Crocs fans to talk about what they love about their Crocs shoes. The company had to ensure that explorers didn't drive away the brand's core segment. Crocs marketers cleverly redefined their key benefit of "comfort" to refer to both the physical comfort of the shoes, for the feel goods who cared about orthopedic support, and the emotional comfort of expressing oneself, for the explorers and fashion followers. Unlike many fashion brands, Crocs's new framing also made the brand explicitly inclusive, which reduced the likelihood of conflict between customer segments. To be judgmental about another type of Crocs customer would contradict the brand ethos.[5]

By 2022, Crocs was one of the fastest-growing brands in the United States, and its Classic Clog was a best-selling item of clothing on Amazon. The next year, annual revenue reached $3.96 billion.[6]

The brilliance of Crocs's turnaround strategy lay not just in its decision to target the explorers, but also in how it managed the *relationships* between customer segments to facilitate cooperation and avoid conflict. Crocs's marketing tactics attended to two

factors central to understanding the relationships between customer segments:

- The source of value each customer segment derives from
  the brand

- The extent to which each segment influences or is influenced by other customer segments using the brand

By expanding the meaning of "comfort" to include both utility
and self-expression, Crocs cultivated the belief that the brand could
serve multiple segments simultaneously without undermining the
authenticity or identification value of the brand. By targeting the explorers, Crocs also cozied up to a segment of customers with a huge
amount of cultural influence, particularly with fashion followers.
This allowed for a more efficient use of Crocs's marketing dollars:
outreach to explorers would be multiplicative, driving engagement
and interest that would trickle down beyond both the explorers and
the feel goods to the large segment of fashion followers. Crocs didn't
just avoid potential problems between different groups; it leveraged
the relationships between segments as a strategic asset. It facilitated
high-velocity growth by attracting customers who would make their
offerings more valuable to other customers.

We will teach you to do what Crocs did: to effectively manage
your brand when different customers want different things from
you. You will learn how to manage existing customer segments
and attract new ones in ways that create multiplicative growth, and
how to reduce the risk of conflict between the customer segments
who want different things from your brand. And because you won't
always be able to avoid conflict, you'll also learn what to do when
your customer segments go to war with each other.

To adeptly manage the relationships between customer segments,
it is first important to understand the potential relationships they
can have with one another. We've created the Segment Compatibility Matrix to explain these relationship types and explain how

FIGURE 1-1

The Segment Compatibility Matrix

The value that segments get from the offering

	Divergent	Collaborative
Indifferent	Separate Communities	Connected Communities
Influenced	Incompatible Segments	Leader-Follower Segments

Orientation toward other segments

they relate to one another. The matrix can be used as a tool for diagnosing the relationship status of current customer segments, identifying which customer segments a brand should (or should not) target next, and developing strategies that maximize value for the brand and its customers. (See figure 1-1.)

Understanding Relationships between Customer Segments

We have organized customer segment relationships along two axes. The horizontal axis defines the nature of the value that customer segments derive from the offering and each other. It distinguishes between groups of customer segments that get significantly unique and nonoverlapping value from an offering (divergent) and groups of customer segments for whom some of the value of an offering is created jointly or in conjunction with other segments (collaborative). On the vertical axis, we consider the extent to which customer segments are affected by the other customers who are also using the brand. Some groups of customer segments are largely unaffected by the other customers who happen to also be using a brand's products or services (indifferent). In contrast, some customer segments are highly sensitive to which other customers are also using the brand (influenced).

The intersection of these two axes (source of value and degree of influence) creates four possible relationship types between customer segments:

- **Separate Communities.** Separate Communities tend to want different things from a brand, but also tend to be unbothered by the divergent tastes of those other segments. For example, parents of sick kids and partygoers nursing hangovers buy Pedialyte for very different reasons. But evidence suggests they are largely indifferent to the fact that the other segment is also buying the hydrating electrolyte drink. Each segment gets what it wants out of the brand and is unfazed that other segments are also using the brand, even if for different reasons or toward different ends. Because Separate Communities are self-contained and have minimal influence on one another, a growth strategy built on Separate Communities has the advantage of compartmentalization: brands can grow simply by courting each new segment independently, in a serial fashion. The disadvantage of Separate Communities is that growing in this way can be relatively costly, and it limits the potential for organic growth beyond each respective community.

- **Connected Communities.** For Connected Communities, the brand's offering becomes more valuable as more people use it via network effects. These customer segments seek similar benefits from the product or service, and—within reason—care more about whether other customers are using the offering than they do about who those other customers are. Social media platforms like Instagram, two-sided markets like eBay, and shared platforms like Microsoft Office are all common types of Connected Communities. Some segments want to use Instagram primarily to post vacation selfies, while others want to use it to discover new recipes, and others are just seeking mindless meme scrolling. Instagram is a more valuable network for every segment the more users are present and active because it creates a virtuous cycle: more content draws in more users, which spurs more content and more connections, which draws in more users. Similarly, different segments of customers use Venmo as a payment platform for different use cases—receiving payments for work, sending money to a loved one, or paying someone back after a night out. But regardless of what segment one falls into, the presence of other segments on the platform makes it more valuable for any user as it increases the chances that someone they need to pay or receive money from is also on Venmo. So, while each individual segment might want different things from the brand (that's what makes them different segments, after all), they benefit from each other in making the offering more valuable to all. Hence, they create value collaboratively.

- **Leader-Follower Segments.** The dynamic between Leader-Follower Segments is hierarchical, with Leaders sitting above the Followers in status. Follower segments often see Leader segments as trusted experts, trailblazing role models, or aspirational exemplars. Just by using the brand, Leaders attract Followers to use it too. In the case of Crocs, fashion followers bought clogs because they saw them worn by explorers, whom they admired as cool and fashion-forward. This is how they collaborate to create value. The Leaders imbue legitimacy onto a brand or its offerings, which draws in the Followers. And in many cases, the use of the brand by Followers to emulate Leaders can feed into the perceived (and often self-perceived) legitimacy of the Leaders. A Leader-Follower strategy can be more efficient relative to the costs of acquiring multiple segments independently. It can also increase the Follower segment's willingness to pay. The trick for Leader-Follower Segments is to keep the offering attractive to Leaders—and to keep the brand primarily associated with the Leaders, not the Followers—to maintain that perceived credibility and legitimacy.

- **Incompatible Segments.** As the title suggests, Incompatible Segments do not mix well with one another. They want divergent value from the brand, and unlike Separate Communities who can coexist or ignore each other's differences, the presence of one segment negatively influences another, usually by interfering with the latter's ability to get what they want from an offering. The upscale fashionistas Lands' End was trying to attract were incompatible with the middle-aged suburban parents Lands' End had traditionally served—at least, those segments would have been incompatible if Lands' End had managed to actually attract any of the former. In this case, the incompatibility between the segments is driven by differences in preferred product offerings, preferred brand image, and in the use of the brand as an identity marker for each segment. Serving—or trying to serve—Incompatible Segments often results in conflict between them, leading to the possibility of brand crisis and mass customer churn.

The relationships between segments are not fixed or static. Nor are they inherent to the segments. Brands can change their offerings, and customers can change the way they use offerings. These changes can cause segments to better align, sometimes resulting in more collaborative value, or to misalign, leading to divergent preferences and incompatibility. And strategic changes by the brand or natural evolutions in customer tastes can make segments more or less sensitive to the influence of other customers too.

Consider the relative indifference of Pedialyte's customer segments toward each other. As of this writing, these segments peacefully coexist as Separate Communities. But that indifference is likely more contextual than dispositional. One could imagine Pedialyte deliberately changing its brand to better align with the hungover segment by introducing innuendo-laden ads and products designed to appeal to the hangover-prone. In trying to increase the brand's popularity with drinking adults, it might shift the parents-of-sick-kids segment from indifferent to influenced. These customers might start to think less of the brand as a safe and wholesome remedy for their young children and may become sensitive to being associated with a segment of rowdy partiers through the brand. If Pedialyte got careless, it could easily drag its main customer segments from the Separate Communities quadrant down into the Incompatible Segments quadrant. If the brand became known as a hangover drink you could give to your kids versus a children's remedy that also helps with hangovers, it could create problems for the brand's parent segment who might reasonably not want to buy a product for their child that is too strongly associated with partying.

It is also possible for a brand's customers to have different relationship types across its various segments. Crocs's explorers and feel-goods segments related to each other as Separate Communities: they valued the shoes for different reasons (utility versus self-expression), and were largely peaceably indifferent to one another wearing Crocs. But explorers were in a Leader-Follower relationship with fashion followers. The latter was drawn to Crocs because they wanted to emulate the same self-expressive coolness of the explorers. Explorers have a different relationship with the other two major Crocs segments.

Managing the relationships between customer segments requires understanding the nature of those relationships. So let's start by digging into those four relationship types, their pros and cons, and how to best manage each.

2

Separate Communities

Timberlands: For Laying Bricks
and Dropping Beats

Separate Communities are like different neighborhoods in a city. New York City is made up, collectively, of all of its constituent boroughs, and there is a shared attitude and identity of the city as a whole. "It will always be New York or Nowhere," as hardcore New Yorkers put it. But each neighborhood also has its culture and shared preferences specific to that area. People tend to move to Brooklyn, Manhattan, Queens, and the Bronx for specific reasons. In this analogy, each neighborhood coexists with the other neighborhoods in the city, but everyone in New York is probably generally happier with the clustering of preferences, values, and identities cultivated in each borough or neighborhood than they would be if they were all uniformly distributed across the city, or if the boroughs didn't have their own distinct personalities and culture.

When brands create Separate Communities, providing value to each segment does not undermine the brand's ability to provide value to other segments. (See figure 2-1.) Likewise, the growth of

FIGURE 2-1

Segment Compatibility Matrix: Separate Communities

The value that segments get from the offering

	Divergent	Collaborative
Indifferent	**Separate Communities**	**Connected Communities**
Influenced	**Incompatible Segments**	**Leader-Follower Segments**

Orientation toward other segments

one segment does not affect the growth of the other segments. Separate Communities want different things from a brand—they value different aspects of it or use it in different ways or for different purposes—but they are indifferent toward and unaffected by the other segment(s) using the brand in their own way too. For example, Garmin serves hikers, golfers, anglers, and scuba divers with GPS-enabled watches and devices. Zoom serves organizations and individual consumers with its videoconferencing software. Spotify streams content for music lovers, podcast listeners, and audiobook fans. Athletic Brewing Company sells nonalcoholic beer to health-conscious former drinkers, young parents, and athletes. In each case, these segments peacefully coexist. Podcast fans on Spotify don't conflict in any way with the billion Swifties using Spotify to stream Taylor's versions over and over . . . and over and over. These brands can serve each segment without creating problems for the others.

Some brands start out serving separate communities of consumers at launch. Warby Parker launched as a discount eyewear brand, cutting costs by eliminating middlemen and competing with the high-margin monopolies that sell the majority of eyeglasses in the United States.[1] It attracted a segment of customers looking for quality glasses at a reasonable price. But the brand simultaneously attracted a segment of style mavens, who liked the hip, fashionable designs coming from a cool startup brand. While targeting multiple segments out of the gate is possible, it's more common for brands to start by targeting one segment and then adding additional customer segments over time. Like Crocs, which started by serving the feel goods, then added explorers and fashion followers as it grew.

In our experience, when brands target multiple segments—either simultaneously or by adding customers to their portfolios over time—they tend to give little thought to how these segments might interact with one another. They often *assume* these customer segments will naturally and happily operate as Separate Communities. They neglect to consider that, sometimes, multiple segments will not actually be indifferent to each other when they are buying the same brand. Serving new segments can make the brand less valuable to other customers, especially if they are not adequately managed as Separate Communities.

Attracting and Managing Separate Communities

Sometimes Separate Communities of customers start consuming a brand organically, without coaxing or targeting. In these cases, brands must decide whether or not to explicitly market to and serve this new segment, particularly when it wants something different than the brand's original customer base. This is what happened when LEGO noticed that it had a nontrivial segment of adult consumers who were buying these children's toys for their own enjoyment.

Paal Smith-Meyer, a former LEGO employee, told *National Geographic* that when senior leadership first found out that adults were buying LEGO in large quantities for themselves, "they thought it was very strange."[2] It did not occur to the brand that there was a real economic opportunity in embracing its adult consumers. As

Smith-Meyer put it, "The company didn't think their adult fans had value. Leadership actually thought [adults] were detracting from the brand." So, LEGO did not make any special effort to attract or retain the segment, despite the fact that it kept making some sets that fortuitously appealed to older customers as much as or more than younger customers. Adults ended up buying significant percentages of products targeted at children and teens, including licensed sets inspired by movies like *Star Wars* and *Harry Potter.*

But this incidental success with the nontargeted adult segment was not enough to overcome an overall decline. By the early 2000s, the brand found itself $800 million in debt and on the verge of bankruptcy. Everything was *not* awesome at LEGO. Desperation forced LEGO to reconsider its previous dismissiveness of the adult segment.

LEGO started working with adult fans to create new models deliberately intended to cater to adult tastes and skill levels. New sets designed for adult consumers included detailed architectural models of well-known buildings like Frank Lloyd Wright's Taliesin, a botanical series, representations of famous artwork, and sets of nostalgic television shows, including *Seinfeld* and *Friends.* It also established official online communities and conventions for adult builders. The brand was delighted to discover that these adult-targeted products could be sold at higher price levels than many of its other lines.

LEGO continued to serve its younger customer segments alongside its adult fans of LEGO (AFOL) segment. Sure, some of its model sets—particularly those based on video games like *Super Mario Brothers* and entertainment properties like Marvel movies—have crossover appeal to both kids and adults. But the adult and kid segments largely exist as Separate Communities, each using the bricks for their own purposes without stepping on each other's toes. The company doesn't split out revenue numbers on sets sold to adults versus children, but one executive recently admitted to a more than four times increase in the adult market in the last decade alone.[3] LEGO's strategy of (1) identifying sales coming from a small group of customers outside of its current target segments, and (2) getting behind that segment to grow and support it, is a common way for brands to develop Separate Communities.

LEGO's new segment emerged somewhat serendipitously, and only when a crisis forced the company to acknowledge and target AFOLs. Not all customer segments will patiently wait around for years to be explicitly acknowledged and served by a brand. It is usually better for brands to build Separate Communities by identifying and targeting underserved segments for growth *before* the brand is on the brink of bankruptcy. For example, when Timberland started selling its iconic waterproof boot in 1973, the brand targeted blue-collar workers who needed tough work boots for factory or outdoor jobs. The boots proved successful with this audience. But they later became popular with another segment too: rappers and hip-hop artists. Tupac, Biggie Smalls, Nas, and Jay-Z were notable early fans, and their influence spread the boots' popularity to others in the community. It was thanks to hip-hop lyrics that Timberland boots earned the nickname "Timbs." Where Timberland's original worker community cared most about the function of its boots, the hip-hop audience sought them out as a fashion statement. As Nas said, "Suede Timbs on my feets makes my cipher complete."

Like LEGO, Timberland initially hesitated to embrace the new segment. According to brand representatives, they were unsure whether it would make sense to cater to a group who was interested in its shoes for fashion, when the core value of the product was intended to be function. Consumers and journalists outside the brand suspected Timberland was trying to strategically keep its distance from Black and urban consumers. The *New York Times* quoted fashion editors saying, "I think that they [Timberland] think that if their clothes are celebrated by the black, urban community, with all its ills, that it will cheapen their brand names." Timberland representatives denied this. Regardless of the explanation for why,

Timberland overlooked the strength and spending power of the hip-hop segment.

By the mid-1990s, however, the brand realized the opportunity and decided to actively embrace hip-hop fashion and grow the segment as a separate user community, independent of its worker segment.[4] Today, Timbs are known as much for their associations with hip-hop culture as they are for their utility as work boots. The brand continues to create new styles and colors for its more fashion-oriented audience, including boots in shades more appropriate for the club than for work like purple and gold. Meanwhile, it continues to serve its factory-and-construction-worker audience with the Timberland PRO product line.[5] At this point, the workers segment and the hip-hop segment are both core to the brand. The brand runs separate social media accounts for the two segments and creates distinct advertisements intended to resonate with one group or the other, too. The brand means something different to each segment, and each wants different things out of their Timberland boots. But crucially, they operate as Separate Communities; each segment is aware of the other segment but largely indifferent to the fact that the other group views the brand differently and derives different value from its products.

For both LEGO and Timberland, the brands grew segments of consumers that had already organically adopted the brand. This is a common and advisable growth strategy. But sometimes, brands are also wise to look for nonuser segments as growth opportunities. Crocs did this when targeting the explorers as an additional segment to add to its base of feel goods. The food and beverage container brand Stanley also did as much when it targeted moms on the go (nonusers) to complement its existing workers, outdoorsmen, adventurers, and military personnel segments. Stanley decided to target moms on the go after a small group of female influencers proved through an affiliate marketing partnership that this segment was indeed hungry (or thirsty) for the Quencher bottle. But when Stanley committed to targeting the segment, it committed fully, releasing new styles of cups and social media marketing geared toward moms on the go. This new segment expanded the brand's audience significantly, ultimately elevating the water bottle to cultural icon. (Yes, late capitalism is weird.) A new range of colored tumblers and collaboration cups brought in stampedes of moms and young women to the brand. Literally. Crowds of women caused chaos when they stampeded displays in Target stores to snap up limited-edition Starbucks collaboration water bottles. Stanley's revenue grew from $73 million in 2019 to over $700 million in 2023.

For Separate Communities to be successful, it's important that they are kept apart. Separate Communities ideally need separate marketing plans, separate communication channels, and separate messaging. When possible, they should get separate products, even if they're similar. Stanley sells different water bottles to its moms on the go and outdoorsmen segments; Timberland creates different shoes and ads for workers and hip-hop fans; LEGO connects with adults and kids via different sets.

A brand that identifies distinct segments within its customer base but then attempts to reach them all with a single, uniform, undifferentiated marketing plan is doing the marketing equivalent of carefully separating out laundry into lights, darks, and delicates, then tossing them all into the same washing machine together. Separate Communities should have some soft, and occasionally hard, boundaries around them. The risk of conflict is reduced when each segment feels it has an independent space—sometimes a physical space, but often a metaphorical, conceptual space—within which to access the brand.

Pros and Cons of Separate Communities

A Separate Communities strategy can help brands diversify their customer bases, reducing risk should one segment suddenly find itself drawn to another brand. Another benefit of Separate Communities is that brands can cater to the specific wants and needs of each segment. Timberland, LEGO, and Stanley can sell different products, use different distribution channels, and create unique messaging to best suit the preferences of the different segments they serve. Sometimes brands even deliberately exaggerate the differences between customer groups or draw bright lines around them so that they can create more resonant offerings and brand worlds for each group. This can make offerings more attractive and brands more meaningful to each respective segment, driving customer acquisition and loyalty.

The biggest downside of managing Separate Communities is that it can be expensive, particularly when it requires creating and managing different marketing mixes to serve each community optimally. It is more costly for Timberland to create different products and communications for workers and hip-hop fans than to standardize its marketing mix for all segments. Also, by definition, Separate Communities tend to be indifferent to what other segments are doing, so it is hard to use success with one group to ignite growth with another. Growing Timberland in the hip-hop audience is unlikely to be a primary driver of interest among blue-collar workers. Instead, growth tends to be constrained within each community type, which means there can be significant costs related to acquiring and cultivating subsequent new segments.

It can be tempting to assume that growing through Separate Communities is an easy growth path. Simply add a segment to your customer base to serve a new community, right? Not really. Brand managers can mistakenly assume that customer segments will be indifferent to each other only to later find they are very much not. Brands must ensure that the multiple segments they want to serve as Separate Communities are truly indifferent to and unbothered by each other.

Moreover, providing truly differentiated value to serve Separate Communities often requires significant talent, resources, and discipline to serve each community well. In many cases, it also requires that the brand be able to stretch its purpose or positioning in a way that is believable to all customers and resonates with each community's preferences and needs. The overarching Timberland brand stands for durability, authenticity, and heritage, which rings true to both the workers and the hip-hop fans but comes to life for them in different ways through products, distribution channels, and brand communications. For LEGO, the brand encourages creative play for all ages, even if the assembly kits are designed to be more or less difficult or center on different themes for kids versus adults.

3

Connected Communities

Why Horizon World Collapsed.
Well, One of the Reasons

Think of Connected Communities as a bazaar. Or a mall. Or *Fortnite*. Various groups of people wandering around under a shared roof, seeking a similar source of value—exotic bargains, a Nordstrom and a Cinnabon, a battle royale while dressed in a digital banana costume. There are many different types of people and customer segments looking to fulfill consonant wants and needs, and they are not terribly bothered by sharing the space with others. In fact, up to a certain point, having more people tends to improve things: more customers means more vendors, stores, and newbies to merc. The more users seeking value from the brand—that is, the more segments that are networked together by the brand—the more attractive the brand becomes to all of them. It's a self-fulfilling value proposition.

Social media platforms and large multiplayer games with a shared universe are prototypical examples of offerings that generate and benefit from Connected Communities. (See figure 3-1.) The value

FIGURE 3-1

Segment Compatibility Matrix: Connected Communities

The value that segments get from the offering

		Divergent	Collaborative
Orientation toward other segments	Indifferent	Separate Communities	**Connected Communities**
	Influenced	Incompatible Segments	Leader-Follower Segments

LinkedIn provides for its users—facilitating connections to find new jobs, serving as a source of wisdom and inspiration from peer- and thought-leader-generated content, being a forum for shamelessly bragging about your latest professional accomplishment—would be severely diminished if the network consisted of only you and a few friends or colleagues. Different segments may not pay attention to or interact with each other on the platform, but they benefit from the fact that they are both on LinkedIn. A greater number of users, even if from very different industries or with very different professional perspectives, enhances the platform's value as a broad-reaching and expansive professional networking site. And metaverse worlds without any creators or players are typically quite lame, as Meta proved with the failed launch of its social virtual reality experience, Horizon Worlds, in 2022.

Two-sided marketplaces are another common place to find Connected Communities. Airbnb is only valuable if the brand can attract a substantial number of both hosts and renters. eBay got more useful to everyone when it attracted more people listing their items for sale and more people bidding on goods. Roblox must continue to attract both players and game developers to thrive.

From the perspective of the customers using the brand, growth is good in the context of Connected Communities. As long as new users remain indifferent to other users and don't generate conflict, more is better.

Attracting and Managing Connected Communities

Brands can try to create Connected Communities at launch or create them later in pursuit of growth. Platforms, such as social media sites, dating apps, and marketplaces, typically must enter the market with a Connected Communities strategy because their value depends on the presence of many users.

Brands that sell products that depend on a minimum viable network need to grow aggressively out of the gate. If they don't, they risk a swift death. Imagine if, when people first heard about Uber, they downloaded the app but the first few times they tried to request a ride no drivers were available. Or imagine an eager driver who signed up for Uber and did not receive any ride requests during their first few hours on the app. Dating apps with few options for matching leads to frustration, sometimes even forcing people to take drastic actions, like trying to meet people in real life.

Common strategies for quickly establishing a minimum viable network include making it really easy to start using the product, or offering promotions that encourage consumers to want to use the offering and refer it to their friends. To grow its network of drivers quickly in new geographies, Uber offered strong financial incentives to drive, particularly in its first year after launch. It gave aggressive options for financing and leasing cars, which kept drivers in the network, by establishing minimum driving participation to keep a leased car. Uber also used surge pricing—charging riders more during times of peak demand—to attract more drivers onto the roads at busy times. Advanced data analytics systems predicted where riders would be, allowing drivers the maximum opportunity to generate revenue.

On the passenger side, Uber used financial incentives to entice riders to download the app, making the first ride free, and offering ride credits. Uber also drew customers by subsidizing the service so that prices were artificially low for riders, often well below competing services. One big draw for new riders was how the app seemed to remove the friction prevalent with car services and taxis. Word of mouth—"It's so much easier than a cab"—drove more growth on the rider side. The fact that "Ubering" became a verb is evidence of the strategy's success. Uber also launched first in cities with high concentrations of restaurants, nightlife, and major sporting events. These strategies paid off. From approximately 2010 to 2012, Uber grew from a thousand to more than a million users.

Uber created its own network, but tapping into existing networks is another way for brands to pursue a Connected Communities strategy. When the online social gaming company Zynga launched *FarmVille* in 2009, much of its success was credited to leveraging Facebook's network. By integrating the game into the social networking site, Zynga was able to tap into a large and highly connected network of potential players immediately. The brand deliberately built social connections into the game. As Facebook users of that era might remember, players received in-game rewards for inviting friends to play, incentivizing an avalanche of invitations to join the game from people you barely remembered from high school. *FarmVille* became the number one game on Facebook, topping out at more than 80 million active monthly users, and it stayed in the number one spot for more than two years.[1] When Airbnb launched in 2008, the company hacked its way into the Craigslist community to drive fast and early growth, particularly growth of the number of hosts, which was crucial for quickly building up the network. And when the craft marketplace Etsy was founded in 2005, the founders announced it to community forums of crafters. They also attended art and craft shows across the United States and

Canada to find influential artisans with established followings to sell on the site. By 2010, Etsy boasted 6.7 million product listings for handmade goods. None of these successful Connected Community brands built their own network from scratch; rather, they leveraged existing networks to cultivate a customer base.

While volume is paramount for Connected Communities, drawing in segments that are divisive or controversial, or overindexing on one segment, usually inhibits expansion. The volume of users should not come *entirely* at the expense of the *quality* of users, particularly in two-sided markets. Sure, Airbnb and Uber are only valuable if there are sufficient hosts and guests and drivers and riders, but a large number of low-quality hosts or rude riders would threaten user retention and long-term stability. Relative indifference between customer segments can become a situation of negative influence if they stop collaborating with each other.

Brands must also consider the quality of the network they are cultivating. Airbnb, for example, offers a professional photography service for hosts that ensures listings look good for prospective renters. Meanwhile, Etsy created internal tools for processing orders and contacting customers, sponsored third-party apps for easier store management, and published a "Seller Handbook" to make it easy for sellers to run their stores and keep buyers satisfied. And both Airbnb and Uber use rating systems for a transparent view of satisfaction for both sides of the market. Because low scores can result in someone getting booted from the platform and high scores make users more desirable to other parties, the rating system encourages good behavior and keeps the overall quality of the network high.

Pros and Cons of Connected Communities

Orchestrating Connected Communities is particularly appealing because they can result in a self-perpetuating growth engine. When the value of a product or service is determined by the size of its network, scale begets scale. The result can be multiplicative or even exponential growth. Moreover, businesses and platforms that leverage Connected Communities can reduce their marginal costs because they typically rely on the assets, relationships, or expertise of their users versus creating them in-house. Once built, Connected Communities can become self-reinforcing as users contribute more relevant and resonant content to connect other users, and customers feel reluctant to leave networks for fear of missing out.

But there are also several ways a Connected Communities strategy can go wrong. Brands pursuing a Connected Communities strategy must thread the needle between being buried in debt before acquiring a sufficiently large network and not investing enough in rapid growth, strangling the network before it can be established.

Creating a network is often expensive. Fast growth typically requires creating low barriers to entry, which can be costly for brands. Brands need to be able to support low-cost access or non-revenue-building activities long enough to build a minimum viable network. Only after a sufficient network exists can a brand start to significantly monetize or profit from products and services, just hoping there is still time to outpace all that network-creation expense. WeWork had a vision of shared coworking spaces where part of the draw was the vibrant community of people sharing the space. It signed up customers rapidly, but not as rapidly as it accumulated losses in pursuit of its network of users. After several years of multibillion-dollar losses, almost $20 billion in debt, and another $100 million in unpaid rent and lease termination fees, WeWork filed for bankruptcy.[2]

On the other hand, spending too little can also be a risk. What are some examples of this phenomenon? All the social media platforms you've never heard of because they ran out of money before growing to a viable size. Networks can also get lost in their purpose if customer segments can't agree on a use case and platform owners don't guide the network toward a particular use case. This seemed to be the fate suffered by the social audio app Clubhouse.

A final potential downside of Connected Communities is the nature of networks themselves. They can be fragile. Just as networks allow a brand to scale quickly, they can implode just as fast. Technical glitches, cultural shifts, or a shiny new competitor can cause users to defect en masse. The short-form video sharing platform Vine surged in popularity after it was released in 2012. But Vine died a quick death after top creators left the platform for other opportunities, and competitors like Instagram and Snapchat lured away many of its users. It was shut down for good in 2017. Connected Communities are both explosive engines of growth and fragile ecosystems. Live by the network, die by the network.

Just as with Separate Communities and Leader-Follower Segment strategies, growth itself can also pose a threat to the integrity of Connected Communities. As more—and more diverse—customer segments adopt a service or join a platform, the likelihood that they'll all remain indifferent to each other diminishes. When the segments on the platform start to have conflicting values or interests, the benefits of network effects can rapidly turn to disadvantages.

4

Leader-Follower Segments

Real Chefs Know It's Pronounced
"Luh Croo-zay"

Leader-Follower relationships are like when the cool kids start wearing a certain brand, and all of the wannabe cool kids follow suit. By using a brand, Leaders bestow perceived credibility, authenticity, quality, or social status on that brand, which attracts Followers like iron filings to a magnet. This is the relationship between the explorers and fashion followers in the story of Crocs's turnaround. Similarly, the fact that Harley-Davidson is a preferred brand for hardcore bikers makes it attractive to the workaday accountant who wants to feel like a rebel outlaw on the weekends, after brunch with the in-laws.

Apple's Final Cut Pro (FCP) editing software benefited for years from a Leader-Follower relationship. (See figure 4-1.) Every aspect of making a movie is expensive: cameras, lenses, tripods, gimbles, trucks, boom mics, lighting, sets, locations . . . plus all the humans one needs to pay to work their magic both in front of the camera and behind it. Low-budget productions are forced to use cheaper alternatives for all the necessary equipment and talent relative to what is

FIGURE 4-1

Segment Compatibility Matrix: Leader-Follower Segments

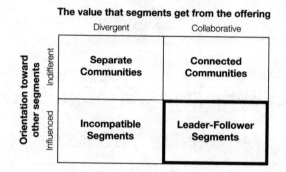

available to major studios—with one notable exception: editing software. As productions moved from film to digital in the early 2000s, the same software that major Hollywood studios were using to produce blockbuster films was suddenly available, at a reasonable price, to anyone willing to drive down to Best Buy and get it.

Apple's Final Cut Pro was powerful enough to gain wide adoption among established filmmakers who viewed it favorably compared to six-figure proprietary hardware and software systems like Avid's Media Composer. Auteurs like David Fincher, Zach Snyder, and the Coen Brothers switched to this over-the-counter software that could be run on a MacBook. Oscar nominees for Best Editing were edited using Final Cut Pro: *Cold Mountain* (2003), *No Country for Old Men* (2007), *The Curious Case of Benjamin Button* (2008), *The Social Network* (2011), and *Parasite* (2019).

Amateur filmmakers found it easy enough to learn that they started using it too. As Steve Jobs, then Apple's CEO put it, "Final Cut Pro has democratized professional video editing by bringing the capabilities of a $50,000 editing bay to everyone for under $1,000."[1] And because of its association with a segment of Leaders (established filmmakers), Final Cut Pro also became popular with Followers (aspiring filmmakers) who used the software in the hopes of refining their skills and fulfilling their dreams of one day joining the established filmmakers' segment. The established filmmakers gave Final Cut Pro credibility. The aspiring filmmakers derived value from Final Cut Pro's capabilities, but also from the psychological benefit of knowing they were using the same powerful tools as Oscar winners.

Unfortunately, when Apple released Final Cut Pro X in 2011, it made a hard pivot toward catering to a third segment of customers: video specialists. This customer segment also consisted of professional editors, but unlike the established filmmakers, they focused on lower-quality, lower-stakes productions: wedding videographers, editors at local TV stations, people making corporate and government office training films. Video specialists were not a Leader segment. They did not win Academy Awards. They just needed better editing software than entry-level tools like iMovie, but they did not need or want the bells and whistles required for a Hollywood production.

Apple saw this segment as an opportunity. To cater to the video specialists, Apple redesigned the FCP interface, automated more functions, and simplified the workflow. The changes made editing easier, especially for less skilled editors. But left out in this update were some key features established filmmakers relied on, such as "edit decision lists," the ability to import video files from third-party hardware, use of multi-cam editing, and backward-compatibility with previous releases of Final Cut Pro. The Leader segment gave the update scathing reviews and even started a petition begging Apple to continue supporting the previous version of the software, FCP7, since the new one was so bad (for them). The petition gathered 1,600 signatures in a week.

Apple slowly added back most of the missing features to appease the established filmmakers segment, but the brand lost market share in the meantime to competitors like Avid and Adobe that capitalized on the moment. Filmmakers who continued to use Final Cut Pro tended to stick with the older, discontinued version. Famously, in 2019, the Academy Award– and Palme d'Or–winning film *Parasite* was edited on the nearly decade-old Final Cut Pro 7, not Final Cut Pro X. This had a trickle-down effect on the aspiring filmmakers who stopped using FCPX because it didn't feel like the "real deal" anymore. In a Leader-Follower strategy, when you lose the Leaders, you often lose the Followers.

Attracting and Managing Leader-Follower Segments

Managing Leader-Follower Segments requires fostering the belief in Followers that they can genuinely access or recreate the skills, feelings, or experiences of the Leaders they want to emulate. The brand (Crocs, Final Cut Pro) becomes their entry to the cool kids' club. It's a passport to status, or at least, a passport to the feeling of status. Leaders influence Followers when both want to use a brand's product or services for similar ends.

Providence is a seafood restaurant in Los Angeles with two Michelin stars, favored by Hollywood elites like Melanie Griffith, Sarah Jessica Parker, and Brad Pitt. The chef and owner is Michael Cimarusti, a James Beard Award winner, whose tasting menus have been praised as "intricately orchestrated," his cooking as "sensitive and exacting," and his restaurant as "consistently turning out the best seafood cooking in Los Angeles—and some of the best in the country."[2] Chef Cimarusti works his magic in a professional kitchen, with state-of-the-art equipment. But when he's making food at home, just for himself and his family? "I use a Le Creuset Dutch oven pretty much every time I cook at home," he told *Food & Wine* magazine.[3]

Le Creuset has been selling its premium line of handcrafted, French-manufactured, enameled cast-iron cookware for a hundred years. Its brightly colored skillets, fryers, and Dutch ovens are designed to be beautiful enough to earn a pride of place on permanent display in the kitchen—not hidden away in a cupboard. Its cookware is durable enough to last for years, and versatile enough to service almost any cooking needs. The company's marketing explicitly calls out both the Leader and Follower segments, even if it flips the order: "Le Creuset has been trusted by home cooks and master chefs for generations."[4]

World-renowned, Michelin-starred chefs are a tiny Leader segment but a crucial one for the brand. Importantly, enameled cast iron is not designed to stand up to the rigors of a professional kitchen, where pots and pans can sometimes be under constant heat for hours at a time. The brand is not making products for professional kitchens but for cooks—both professional and amateur—who want to make professional-grade food at home.

Brands do not pursue a Leader-Follower strategy by simply hiring some influencers to promote their offerings. Leaders attract Followers because the Followers believe there is a genuine segment of aspirational customers that use the brand's products, and that by using the same stuff, they can perform like, live like, or feel like the Leaders. Influencer strategies, on the other hand, usually work by generating positive associations between the celebrity and the brand, or by raising awareness. But even when influencer campaigns work, fans are typically not fooled into thinking the celebrity actually uses the brand themselves in real life (or "IRL," as the influencers put it), that they weren't paid large sums of money to endorse the brand, or that they represent an actual segment of users. Fiat hired Jennifer Lopez in 2011 to support the launch of its 500 car model. The campaign featured a television ad, purportedly showing "Jenny from the Block" driving a Fiat around the Bronx. It was later revealed that Lopez never traveled to New York for the shoot and instead used a body double. There was also a disastrously cringey performance at the American Music Awards in which a part of Lopez's song-and-dance number involved her getting behind the wheel of a Fiat 500 on the stage. By our count, there were approximately zero people who believed Lopez was actually a Fiat customer.

In contrast, when Crocs leveraged the power of influencers like Justin Bieber and Post Malone, they were true representatives of the explorer segment Crocs was trying to reach. The brand chose these influencers in part because they were known Crocs fans. They repped Crocs because they wanted to. They wore them long before they profited from their affinity for the clogs. Crocs used influencers to draw in explorers, some of whom were famous celebrities and some of whom were just the coolest people in their personal social circles, who subsequently served as a Leader segment for the fashion followers. Cultivating a Leader segment requires serving an aspirational segment of customers—or creating the belief that there is a nontrivial segment of aspirational consumers—that Followers want to emulate.

Beats versus Bose, the great noise-canceling headphones battle of the 2010s, illustrates this point well. Bose pursued an influencer strategy. It partnered with the National Football League to become the "Official Headphone and Headset of the NFL." Coaches and staff for all thirty-two teams were required to use Bose headsets for in-game communication. Bose also partnered with professional golfer Rory McIlroy and NFL players J.J. Watt, Russell Wilson, and Larry Fitzgerald Jr. for a series of expensive ads. While this campaign boosted brand awareness, it had limited influence on potential customers. We believe, in part, this is because Bose used these influencers in a way that did not create the impression that they were representative of a Leader segment. When Bose put celebrity athletes in ads, they were often shown using the headphones in entirely unrelatable situations, such as to drown out a coach describing football plays in a smoothie shop, or to relax while sitting alone around a swanky backyard swimming pool at their McMansion.[5] The scenes felt contrived and certainly not reflective of situations in which a customer—or even the athletes in the ads—might actually use the headphones. Moreover, the limited number of celebrities using Bose contributed to the feeling that these were obviously paid sponsorships or influencer relationships rather than people who reflected an actual customer segment for Bose.

Beats by Dre, on the other hand, used a much more effective Leader-Follower strategy to grow its headphones market share. Beats partnered with more than twenty professional athletes at the top of their game, including Serena Williams, Simone Biles, Conor McGregor, and Michael Phelps. Many other A-list athletes soon also started using Beats on their own. Advertisements showed athletes preparing for matches or games by listening to music on their Beats headphones. For the 2012 Olympics, the brand skirted sponsorship rules and sent custom headphones to high-profile athletes, who were seen wearing them ahead of and between events.[6] That same year, LeBron James gave everyone on the US Olympic basketball team a pair.[7]

Amping oneself up for a high-pressure event was a more relatable usage occasion for many consumers—even if the occasion was more likely to be a varsity track meet or a marketing lecture than the Olympic trials. The sheer number of professional athletes sporting Beats cultivated the feeling that there was a Leader segment that preferred Beats. People saw athletes actually wearing Beats during their actual warmups before actual competitions on the field, on the court, or by the pool, and not just in highly produced commercials. Ironically, Beats became so popular among NFL players that the league had to ban them because their use risked violating its contract with Bose.[8] Followers, who aspired to be like this segment of hardcore celebrity athletes, snapped up Beats. By cozying up to the professional athlete Leader segment, Beats turned itself into a status symbol. The brand used a similar strategy in the music world to attract high-profile artists to the brand too. (It probably wasn't too hard for Beats to get A-list artists and athletes on board given that the brand was founded by Dr. Dre and Jimmy Iovine, the chairman of Interscope Records.)

By 2014, Beats (which was founded forty-two years after Bose) held 62 percent of the dollar share within the premium headphones market, compared to Bose's 22 percent share, despite Beats consistently receiving worse product reviews than Bose.[9]

When managing Leader-Follower Segments, it is imperative that the brand remain associated with the Leader segment and not become overly associated with the Follower segment. Typically, this requires elevating the Leaders (e.g., showcasing them in communications) and continuing to serve them so that they stay with the brand. This is clearly where Apple went wrong with Final Cut Pro X when it stopped providing sufficient value for its established filmmakers segment. In some cases, it also requires limiting access to products or services for Follower segments or downplaying their association with the brand. To continue to attract Followers, Le Creuset needs to be considered the preferred home cookware for professional chefs, not wannabe chefs.

Likewise, creating Leader-Follower Segments requires establishing and maintaining hierarchy within the brand, such as via different products or services as Home Depot does with its Pro line; via demarcations of status such as badges or credentials as is often seen in social media platforms and loyalty programs; or via communications such as by showcasing Leaders and Followers in their separate elements. Home Depot even offers delegated parking spaces for its Pro members. Sometimes brands maintain hierarchy simply by ignoring the Followers entirely in marketing and communications. Harley-Davidson doesn't ever acknowledge the middle-aged accountants who buy most of its motorcycles. Neither the Leaders nor the Followers want that. Creating and maintaining hierarchy ensures Leader segments feel recognized for their status and Followers have a clear aspirational segment to follow.

Pros and Cons of Leader-Follower Segments

Leader segments elevate the image of a brand generally, by providing compelling evidence of the brand's coolness or authenticity or exacting performance. The influence of a Leader segment can create marketing efficiencies in acquiring Follower segments. Sometimes, just by cultivating and serving a small Leader segment, brands can attract a trail of Followers into the brand without spending much. Sometimes, with particularly powerful or influential Leader segments, this happens accidentally.

Pabst Blue Ribbon (PBR) was serendipitously adopted by a Leader segment in the early 2000s, reversing a twenty-year decline. While sales were busy cratering nationwide, Pabst noted one remarkable, accidental exception. Sales in Portland, Oregon, were exploding, doubling month-over-month.[10] Some clever market research identified this mysterious group of PBR enthusiasts. They were anticorporate, antimarketing, nostalgia-loving, authenticity-seeking culture makers. Or as they soon came to be known: hipsters. The hipster segment was a Leader segment, setting the trends for a much wider group of Followers that shared some of the same values, if not exactly the same penchant for knitting, rockabilly, and aggressively curled mustaches. By the mid-2000s, many of the initially derided hipster eccentricities had bled their way into mainstream fashion and culture, where they were picked up by much larger hipster-adjacent segments of Followers.[11] Some of these trends included the increased prevalence of facial hair and tattoos, skinny jeans, beanies, man buns, plaid flannels, chunky, thick-rimmed glasses—and, of course, Pabst Blue Ribbon. From 2003 to 2009, PBR enjoyed double-digit annual growth every year. It went from selling less than 1 million gallons in 2000 to more than 92 million in 2012.[12]

The use of a brand by Leader segments can also create opportunities for brands to sell tokens or souvenirs of the brand to Followers who cannot access the same products as Leaders. Luxury brands often sell perfumes, keychains, or other tchotchkes so that Followers can buy a piece of the brand without diluting its prestige. In the case of Ferrari, the brand emblazons its logo onto shampoos, T-shirts, sunglasses, computers, and more to sell to fans (Followers) who want to be like Ferrari owners and drivers (Leaders) but definitely can't afford the cars themselves.[13] Like Connected Communities, growth through Leader-Follower Segment relationships tends to be multiplicative, as growth in Leader segments can result in proportionally larger growth in Follower segments.

However, creating and maintaining Leader-Follower relationships isn't easy. First, attracting genuine Leader segments to the brand means convincing them that the brand is sufficiently premium or exclusive or cool or professional grade. This can be difficult for new brands and sometimes even harder if your brand already has a reputation for being more pedestrian. Reebok has tried several times to gain traction among elite runners. One attempt, the Premier Road Plus DMX shoe in the early 2000s, was met with limited success. Leaders weren't interested in Reebok because they didn't think the brand was in the elite category of running shoe. For this reason, it is typically easier to start premium—whether it's luxury, quality, performance—and move down market rather than the other way around.

Crocs is a notable exception. It was able to move upstream by attracting a more fashionable and cooler Leader segment, years after establishing its reputation with the feel goods. But Crocs also got a bit lucky, riding the tailwinds of an unexpected fashion trend, a global pandemic that left many people working from home and more interested in comfortable versus fashionable footwear, and the popularity of playful social media channels like TikTok and Instagram. Without taking anything away from the brand's bold and successful strategy, Crocs may have had a much harder time attracting the explorer segment without these favorable market conditions.

Managing Leader-Follower Segments also usually requires building the brand so that it will stay attractive to other segments if the Leaders move on. For example, as Crocs capitalized on its explorer segments to grow, it never neglected its feel goods audience. It also continued to diversify its product portfolio—offering new SKUs of much less Croc-y looking sandals—to stabilize demand and keep the brand healthy even when inevitably fashion changes and the explorers move on. Crocs could try to keep the fashion-forward segment interested in Crocs indefinitely, but it knows fashion rarely works that way, save for the most iconic luxury brands. It needs to milk the fad while it has the Leaders on board but build the brand for a more general audience once they move on to the next (hopefully less head-scratchingly bizarre) fashion trend.

5

Incompatible Segments

LinkedIn, a Site for Networking and Trauma Dumping

If Separate Communities are like neighborhoods in a city, and Connected Communities are like a bazaar, and Leader-Follower Segments are like the cool kids and wannabes, Incompatible Segments are like Thanksgiving dinner with your extended family when someone brings up politics. Whether it results in just a tense, awkward silence or actual fisticuffs over the mashed potatoes, no one is having a good time. Incompatible Segments exist everywhere, all the time, usually with minimal problems. But when brands force Incompatible Segments into contact, the result is conflict. Your liberal aunt and your conservative uncle peaceably coexist in separate states for most of the year. It is only when they are compelled to sit across the table from each other that one will end up tearfully and hastily repacking the Jello salad they brought so they can leave early, while the other is berated by Grandma for ruining Thanksgiving. Again. So too can Incompatible Segments exist within markets but only become a problem when they are forced together. (See figure 5-1.)

FIGURE 5-1

Segment Compatibility Matrix: Incompatible Segments

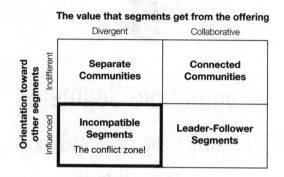

One of the key points in this book is that when deciding to serve multiple segments, brands need to make clear-eyed evaluations of the likelihood that each segment will care about the presence of other segments also using the brand, and whether they create value collaboratively or will conflict with each other. As we will explore in the next few chapters, there are a lot of ways for customer segments to fall into conflict over a brand. The indifference of two segments to each other should *not* simply be assumed but should be actively assessed based on what is important to them and based on what value they are seeking from the brand.

Incompatibility does not mean that the segments necessarily dislike each other or are motivated by antagonism or hate. Incompatible preferences between customer segments can simply be rooted in disagreement over how a product or service should be used, or over the meaning of the brand, what it stands for, or who it represents. Segments become incompatible when the presence or behavior of one segment impedes another segment's ability to get what it wants from the brand.

Old Navy spurred conflict among its customers when the brand tried to create a more size-inclusive shopping experience. As part of this "bodequality" initiative, the brand eliminated unique plus-size styles and special sections. Instead, it started carrying all sizes, from 00 to 30, in stores and on the same displays. This gave plus-size customers the ability to shop in exactly the same way as everyone else, not forcing them to go to separate plus-size areas within the store or to shop exclusively online. Generally, this initiative was well received. Friends of different body types could now shop together, and consumers generally saw the value and moral imperative of greater inclusivity. Old Navy was celebrated for the idea. The problem was that Old Navy did not properly adjust its in-store inventory to meet size demands appropriately. This error, combined with the fact that all sizes were presented on the same racks, meant that stores sold out of middle sizes and were stuck with way too many very small- and very large-size options. Midsize customers were frustrated by having to dig through piles of outlier-sized clothing only to find out their size was not in stock. Sales began declining soon after the program began and dropped by about 19 percent year over year, causing the brand to scale back on its size-inclusivity initiative.[1]

Or take the example of Etsy. For nearly a decade, Etsy positioned itself in opposition to companies like Amazon that sold mass-manufactured products. What made Etsy special was its celebration and support of artists and artisans. Early on, Etsy prioritized independent crafters, small businesses, and hobbyists. Conscious consumers could purchase items on the platform knowing they were handmade by sellers. However, as part of a plan to drive growth and profits, Etsy started allowing sellers to use third-party manufacturers as production partners for goods. Conflict ensued between sellers who saw the new policy as a means to make a lot more money and those who thought the company was betraying its core principles and values. In the 2020s, the site introduced additional changes that prioritized sellers who fulfilled orders faster and more efficiently versus creating a positive experience between the buyer and the seller. Drop shippers started crowding out artists. Etsy's core seller audience felt jilted by the company, a number of whom left the platform to sell their goods elsewhere.[2]

The heat of any resulting conflict often depends on the source of the incompatibility. When not rooted in political, religious, or moral ideology, the conflict between Incompatible Segments typically looks more like a tug of war, wherein each segment tries to pull the brand in the direction of the value it seeks, rather than a clash of aggression or hostility.

Managing Incompatible Segments

Conflict between Incompatible Segments doesn't have to emerge from a single, explosive event. Sometimes it grows like mold behind the walls, slowly eroding the value of a brand's offerings for customers. Cory Doctorow of *Wired* argues this is how most social media platforms deteriorate. Doctorow poetically refers to this phenomenon as "enshittification." The process of enshittification, he says, is as simple as it is nearly inevitable: "First, they [platforms] are good to their users; then they abuse their users to make things better for their business customers; finally, they abuse those business customers to claw back all the value for themselves. Then, they die."[3]

Doctorow's process is rooted in an understanding of Incompatible Segments. The process starts with quickly growing the user base—typically a requirement for a Connected Communities strategy. Platforms incentivize growth by providing content that users will find valuable, such as posts by family and friends or media relevant to their hobbies or interests. But when the network grows sufficiently large, the platforms attract another segment: business customers—sellers and media companies—who want to tap into this big audience to advertise or drive traffic to their sites. Users and business customers are Incompatible Segments. They seek divergent, often conflicting types of value from platforms, and the presence of the business customers on the platform negatively affects the platform experience for users.

As the platform inevitably turns its attention toward creating value for its business customers—because it wants to make money—it starts to make changes that degrade the user experience, peppering user feeds with advertisements, ramping up creator content and irrelevant paid media. Initially, users tolerate some of this annoying content. Users might feel OK scrolling past a few ads or the posts of some random professional creator during their mindless scrolling. But conflict has already started to build. As the platform increasingly focuses on hitting quarterly earnings numbers, the content that users actually want gets crowded out. As commentators have increasingly noted, social media networks are now less "social" and more means for users to follow influencers and brands.[4] For the user, the platform becomes an endless feed of infomercial, advertorial, and junk advertising that users don't find valuable. The platform then enters end-stage enshittification. When users finally decide, after months or years of conflict with the brand's business customers, that they are no longer getting sufficient value from the platform, they stop visiting, causing the platform to wither.[5] At this point, the platform owners sometimes make desperate attempts to bring in revenue, allowing low-quality paid content to flood its streams, accelerating its own demise. While this process is seen over and over again with platforms operating as Connected Communities, the lesson is applicable to any brand that tries to serve Incompatible Segments through the same offerings.

Of course, serving Incompatible Segments is not always the result of missteps or greed by the brand. There are also times when customers themselves drive conflict with other customer segments. LinkedIn started as a platform used strictly for professional networking and for posting job- or industry-related content. But as Twitter and Facebook have become less attractive social media sites, some users have migrated to LinkedIn as a space for sharing personal posts. A recent *Washington Post* article summarized this shift: "Workers have become comfortable getting personal on LinkedIn, sharing engagement announcements, their fertility journeys, cancer diagnoses, relationship statuses, funny pet moments, even what they cooked for dinner."[6] Specific examples highlighted in the story included a CEO who announced his divorce, the VP of an e-learning company who posted about her struggles with self-harm and binge drinking following an assault, and a chief marketing officer who shared an update about her fertility struggles, complete with a tear-streaked selfie.[7]

This shift in content created conflict between those users who want LinkedIn to become a new space for personal sharing and seeking emotional support, and those users who want to protect the sterile professionalism of LinkedIn as a job-focused networking site. The change in user behavior was not driven by anything LinkedIn did. It arose spontaneously, as users with incompatible preferences started using the platform in divergent ways, generating tension. LinkedIn was just left to figure out how to manage the conflict. As part of its effort to course-correct and return the platform to its professional function, the site's algorithm was tweaked to prioritize professionally relevant content over personal posts on users' feeds.[8]

Conflict created by drifts in how consumers use a product or service, or which consumers use it, is not unique to the digital world. In the 2020s, makeup retailer Sephora also faced Incompatible Segment conflict when kids and tweens started flocking to Sephora stores like moths to a heavily perfumed flame. They were there to buy expensive skin care products—including anti-aging creams containing retinol. (Because if you don't start using anti-aging treatments when you are ten, before you know it, you'll have the skin of a twelve-year-old.) Sephora traditionally served adult consumers, who shopped its stores to sample products, consult with beauty advisers, and attend community events with other beauty enthusiasts. But their desire for a sophisticated and relaxing beauty experience did not jibe with the new segment of tween customers. Sephora kids were boisterous and disruptive and took the attention of beauty advisers away from adult customers. In some cases, these young customers were rude to employees and destroyed products and makeup displays. The presence of Sephora kids in the store made the shopping experience clearly worse for its adult customers.

Adult customers decried the invasion and called on Sephora to do something about it. Some posted on Sephora's Beauty Insider Community, suggesting the retailer put an age restriction on stores or set up a separate area of the store for kids. It is not yet clear how Sephora will handle the burgeoning conflict between these Incompatible Segments. For both Sephora and LinkedIn, it was the behavior of consumers they neither invited nor wanted that led to Incompatible Segments. It is not enough for a brand to be cognizant of how its decisions can create clashes between Incompatible Segments. It must also stay vigilant over the behavior of its current customers—or the arrival of new customers—which can easily stir up conflict.

Pros and Cons of Incompatible Segments

The other three quadrants of the Segment Compatibility Matrix all include substantial strategic trade-offs. There are pros and cons to cultivating each type of segment relationship. Here, with Incompatible Segments, there are vanishingly few pros. This quadrant, which we affectionately refer to as the "conflict zone," is not generally where brands strategically choose to be (with some *very* narrow exceptions, which we will discuss in chapter 9). The potential cons of Incompatible Segments are straightforward: abandonment of the brand, reduced sales and revenue, negative press, and the tarnishing of the brand's image. Given the risks of conflict, whenever a brand finds itself with two segments in conflict, the best move is usually to resolve the tension as quickly as possible. Even better is to act with foresight, to anticipate and avoid conflict in the first place. The next few chapters will explain in detail how to do just that.

PART TWO
THE CONFLICT ZONE

6

How and Why Customers Clash

Customer segments clash when the presence of one segment impedes another segment's ability to get what it wants or needs from the brand. This is the central predicament of the growth dilemma. When brands serve Incompatible Segments, they provide divergent sources of value for different segments, and in doing so, it limits at least one segment's ability to get the full value it seeks from the brand. As a result, customers are left feeling alienated or underserved, causing them to look for other ways to meet their needs, and in the process of winning new business, the changes brands make cause them to lose old business. Subsequent chapters will address how to anticipate, avoid, and escape the conflict zone. But first, we will define conflict between customer segments, the different sources of conflict, and the ways it can take shape.

The story of the quick and astronomical growth of Starbucks offers examples of several different types of conflict. Howard Schultz's original vision for Starbucks, inspired by his experiences at Italian cafés in the early 1980s, was to create a "third place," a space between work and home where people could congregate, relax, and slow down the day. Schultz was already working for a small coffee retailer at the time, one that specialized in selling whole arabica beans to coffee connoisseurs, but he dreamed of transforming Starbucks into something more communal—a distinctly American take on Milan's coffeehouses. Schultz was given the chance to bring his idea to life when the founders agreed to sell Schultz the company in 1987.

Starbucks quickly became the dominant brand for people who wanted the full specialty coffee experience. Employees reinforced the brand's warm image by providing personalized and friendly service and engaging in conversations with customers as they took orders and handcrafted their drinks. The authentic appeal of the coffeehouse chain was further legitimized by the two customer segments it attracted in its early days, primarily, the "coffee sophisticates," customers looking for the specialty beans and handcrafted drinks available almost exclusively at Starbucks at the time, and "third placers," people who used Starbucks for lounging, lingering, working, and socializing.

Starbucks's early growth was astounding. But no brand can grow infinitely with just one or two segments. To grow, Starbucks expanded its retail presence, eventually occupying nearly every strip mall, office lobby, and airport terminal in the country. These new locations included variants on the traditional faux-European lounge design, including kiosks and shops with much smaller footprints (and fewer places to sit). Starbucks coffee shops became so ubiquitous that it's seemingly never-ending expansion became a punchline. One headline from the satirical news source *The Onion* read, "New Starbucks Opens in Rest Room of Existing Starbucks."[1] The brand also expanded its menu, adding new food and drink products. The strategy was successful in attracting additional segments beyond the coffee sophisticates and third placers. New menu items, expanded geographic presence, and additional distribution channels attracted younger consumers who increasingly started to make daily specialty coffees a part of their lives, and commuters looking for a quick pick-me-up on the way to work.

We will refer to the new, younger customers as "Starbies," an affectionate nickname many members of this segment started using for the brand. The members of this segment treated the to-go cups with the Starbucks siren logo as a status badge, carrying around their Starbucks drinks as a fashion accessory. Celebrity Starbies were frequently photographed with the iconic cup in hand. And that branded cup they carried around is almost certainly not filled with flat white, but with some overly sugared, sometimes-not-even-coffee Frankenstein of a latte. Starbies started using ornate, bespoke specialty coffees as a means of self-expression, developing signature beverages unique to them. Starbucks lattes in the early 2000s were akin to Erewhon smoothies in the 2020s. This segment appreciated the brand's "Just Say Yes" policy for baristas, who were policy-bound to just grit their teeth and smile as customers rattled off alchemical lists of half a pump of this and a quarter pump of that topped with whipped cream and cocoa powder. You can easily identify Starbies on Instagram, where they post photos of themselves candidly sipping pumpkin spice lattes at pick-your-own apple farms to celebrate the arrival of fall. #blessed

Another large segment of new customers that started frequenting the coffeehouses during this early phase of growth was the "on-the-go" segment. This group valued Starbucks primarily as a place to pick up their coffee in a hurry, as part of their daily routine. They loved the fact that Starbucks were everywhere, convenient to anywhere they were leaving from or headed to. They were seeking a fast, predictable, and ubiquitous coffee option for their commute.

Each of these customer segments—the original coffee sophisticates and third placers, as well as the new Starbie and on-the-go segments—wanted divergent value from Starbucks. The differences between the wants of the coffee sophisticates and the wants of the third placers were compatible enough that their coexistence didn't cause problems. We would characterize that relationship, in Starbucks's early days, as one of Separate Communities. Both segments got what they wanted out of Starbucks without stepping on each other's toes. But as more customer segments were added, and as they ballooned in size, this increased the friction between groups of customers.[2]

Unlike third placers, the on-the-go segment cared primarily about getting its coffee order quickly and efficiently. The problem was that the on-the-go customers' frenetic pursuit of caffeine on a schedule eroded the relaxed neighborhood coffee bar atmosphere so valued by third placers. But it wasn't just the mere presence of harried commuters that risked making Starbucks less appealing to the third placers. Starbucks also made changes to better serve the on-the-go segment. The brand introduced preground coffee beans, automated machines that could create drinks without a barista, and food items such as breakfast sandwiches that made the once romantic coffeehouse atmosphere start to feel—and smell— like a fast-food restaurant.[3]

The Starbies were causing their own conflicts with their penchant for complicated orders. In theory, one customer's drink preferences should not affect other customers, but the lengthy and excruciatingly specific orders that facilitated self-expression through coffee slowed down the line. This affected both the on-the-go crowd who wanted their coffee fast, and the third placers who were trying to enjoy a quiet and uncongested atmosphere. Pleasing the Starbies also risked making Starbucks less appealing to coffee sophisticates. If Starbucks made itself a place to get sugary concoctions of syrups, drizzles, and whipped cream, this might degrade the perception of the brand as a purveyor of authentic, high-quality coffee. It was unclear whether Starbucks could please both its original customer segments and newer customer segments in the same coffee shop environment. There were inherent trade-offs for Starbucks in choosing to serve each of the customer segments over the others. Because of this, Starbucks found itself at a crossroads in the early 2000s: Should the brand continue to make changes to serve its newer, faster-growing customer segments, or should it continue focusing on serving its original customer segments that drove the brand's authentic coffeehouse image?

As it turns out, this wasn't an either-or choice for Starbucks. Instead of abandoning one set of customers in favor of another, Starbucks took several strategic steps to effectively reduce the conflicts between its customer segments. But we will save that part of the story for chapter 12. First, it is useful to consider the different sources of conflict that emerged between Starbucks customers as the brand added new segments to its customer base.

One source of conflict for Starbucks was that different customers wanted to use the Starbucks brand in different ways that were incompatible with each other. It is exceedingly difficult to create a physical retail space that is both high-volume, assembly-line efficient, as well as relaxed, warm, and friendly. Another source of conflict was rooted in the different meanings various customer segments attach to the brand. Was Starbucks a place to get authentic artisanal coffees? Or a place to get coffee-scented liquid candy bars? It's hard to maintain a brand credibly known for the former if you mostly serve the latter. Finally, there was potential conflict stemming from how customers use the Starbucks brand as an identity signal. Do coffee sophisticates and third placers want to be associated, through the Starbucks brand, with the white-chocolate-mocha-drinking middle schoolers and aspiring social media influencers who make up the Starbies segment? Or did the presence of these customers make the coffeehouse feel less authentic and sophisticated? And if Starbucks was to be consumed by the masses and wasn't the most expensive coffee on the block anymore, was the green mermaid still a status symbol?

These are the types of questions brand managers should be asking—but often fail to ask—before they make the decision to target new customer segments. Starbucks illustrates some of the different sources of friction between customers, and the extent to which they relate to the brand's offerings, to the meaning customers attach to the brand, to the identities of users, or to the values and beliefs associated with customers. We divide potential conflict between customer segments into four types along these lines:

1. **Functional conflict.** When customer segments seek different practical benefits from a brand's offerings or use a brand's product or services in a way that conflicts with another segment's ability to use the brand's offerings.

2. **Brand image conflict.** When one customer segment threatens the meaning, authenticity, credibility, or purpose of a brand or its offerings to another segment.

3. **User identity conflict.** When one segment erodes the identity-signaling value of the brand for another customer segment.

4. **Ideological conflict.** When the values and beliefs of one customer segment clash with those of another segment.

Before digging into the specifics of the four types of conflict, keep in mind that the focus of this book is on the relationships *between* customer segments. Therefore, in terms of conflict, we are referring to conflict that is generally caused by the divergent needs, preferences, or values of multiple customer segments being served by the same brand. There are other types of conflict, of course. A service failure can cause conflict between a brand and its customers. A brand using unethical manufacturing practices can create friction between the brand and its customers. But that's not what we are talking about here. We are focused on conflicts between customer segments. Also note that each of the different types of conflict can originate from a decision made by a brand *or* from the independent behaviors of customers. Brands can stir up conflict between customer segments when they do things like modify offerings, (re-)affirm an ideological stance, or target a new customer segment. But customers can also stir up conflict among themselves when they do things like co-opt the brand for identity-signaling or ideological purposes or use a brand's offerings in a way that makes it harder for other segments to get the practical benefits they seek.

The next four chapters will explore each of these four sources of conflict in detail.

7

Functional Conflict

Drunk Adults at Disney Want
a Hug from Mickey, Too

Sometimes, a brand can provide different practical benefits to different customer segments without causing problems. Pedialyte simultaneously serves its segment of parents who need to hydrate sick kids with the flu and its segment of adults who can't handle drinking as much alcohol as they used to. Both segments get their hydration needs met without impinging on the other segment's ability to meet its needs.[1] Other times, creating value for one customer segment erodes functional value for another. When Apple released Final Cut Pro X in 2011, it changed and removed certain features to cater to the video specialists segment. In doing so, it created functional conflict for the established and aspiring filmmaker segments. Functional conflict can also emerge as a result of customer behaviors. Starbucks's on-the-go segment wanted to use the brand as a place to grab a coffee in a rush, which negatively affected the experience for third placers, who used the coffeehouses as a refuge. When some users started posting personal and emotional content to LinkedIn in the 2020s, it made the platform less useful and enjoyable to those who wanted to use it strictly for professional net-working. Functional conflict can arise from many sources. But the two most common are:

- The behaviors of one segment—often a new segment, courted for growth—impinge on the functional value other segments had previously been getting from the brand. Star-bucks's on-the-goers ruining the atmosphere for third placers is a good example of this, as is LinkedIn's users posting more personal and less professional content on the platform.

- A brand changes its offering in some way to appeal to one segment (again, often a new segment) and, in the process, makes its offerings less appealing to current segments.

Let's explore some examples of these causes of functional conflict.

The behaviors of one set of customers reduces the value of the offering for other customers: Disney adults getting hammered

Disney Parks and Entertainment recently found itself managing a functional conflict between customers seeking different sources of enjoyment from its theme parks. The "happiest and most magical places on Earth" (Disney's words, not ours) have for many years been dominated by families with young children: parents who want to give their kids a memorable family trip in an immersive and whimsical environment where they can meet their favor-ite characters. Accordingly, these customers want rides the whole family can enjoy—nothing too scary or stomach churning—fun snacks and souvenirs, and PG entertainment. This all worked fine until a new segment showed up: child-free adults, who started vis-iting the parks in droves in the 2010s and grew steadily from there. The start of the adult segment was serendipitous for Disney, with childless adults seeking the nostalgia of their youths and having the discretionary income to spend on magical trips.

By 2023, one former executive estimated that on any given day, 40 to 50 percent of the visitors at Disney World were child-free "Disney Adults."[2] This set the scene for functional conflict between segments: yes, the new segment wanted the same wholesome, family-friendly fun they remembered from their childhood. But they also wanted more adult-friendly diversions. They preferred more exciting rides, the kind that tend to come with height restrictions. They wanted high-quality dining. And they wanted booze.[3] Disney, never one to pass up an opportunity to grow, got behind this segment and pushed. This included creating offerings exclusively for adults, such as Disney weddings and honeymoon packages, and adult-exclusive "Adventures by Disney" travel.[4] Disney also introduced more sophisticated (and expensive) dining experiences, more high-tech rides, more areas themed for an older, childless audience, and started selling alcohol more widely throughout its parks.[5] Alcohol was not part of Walt Disney's original vision for Disneyland and Disney World. He told the *Saturday Evening Post* in 1956, "No liquor, no beer, nothing. Because that brings in a rowdy element. That brings people we don't want, and I feel they don't need it." But over decades, alcohol became more accessible across Disney parks.

It should be the case that Disney adults and Disney families can all get a hug from Mickey and joyfully coexist in the parks. But the reality is that these segments are increasingly demanding more and more divergent value from Disney, and acting in ways that degrade the Disney experience for the other segment. A former member of Disney's theme park engineering team characterized it as a "tug of war" between adults and families.[6]

Complaints about drunken Disney adults became a problem in the 2020s. Frustrated family-oriented park goers reported seeing adults vomiting in bushes. EPCOT, a theme park at Disney World that purportedly caters to all ages, became known as a "festival of drunks."[7] EPCOT features a "world showcase," a series of eleven food and beverage pavilions encircling a pond. Each pavilion rep-resents the culture, cuisine, and beverages native to its country. "Drinking around the world"—in which Disney adults would stop for a drink at each "country" all the way around the pond—became excursions in and of themselves. An online search generates dozens of helpful guides facilitating this international-themed Disney pub crawl.[8] Booze wasn't the only conflict, though. Both park goers and character actors complained about adults without kids adding to long lines to meet iconic characters.

For Disney, the dilemma goes to the core of its business. Child-free Disney adults are lucrative. And this segment is dominating at a time when sky-high ticket prices, inflated food and drink costs, accommodations, and pricey add-ons have made Disney vacations unaffordable or unjustifiable for many families. Lots of brands are going after the wallets of the DINKS: dual income, no kids. But it's obviously unwise for Disney to reorient parks to only serve adult park goers and alienate the segment of families with young children. After all, it is those kids who will become the next generation of Disney adult vacationers, if they can cultivate fond childhood memories now. Disney also probably doesn't want its parks overrun with adults to the extent that it becomes the theme park version of Dave & Buster's adult arcades. But how can Disney serve both without alienating either?

As of this writing, the tug of war continues, unresolved. In 2023, Disney announced it would be dedicating $60 billion to its theme park division.[9] But it's unclear how much of this investment will go toward resolving the conflict between these segments, and/or toward creating more value for either segment over the other. Like Starbucks, Disney grew beyond its initial target cus-tomers in a way that allowed for conflict to emerge. It remains to be seen whether it will find a way, like Starbucks, to successfully resolve these tensions before they cause greater problems. But at this point, it seems clear that the conflict will only grow unless it is addressed.

Rebranding for a new customer segment:
JCPenney tries to become "affordable luxury"

Ron Johnson is often blamed for singlehandedly causing the implosion of the iconic retailer JCPenney. Johnson was appointed CEO of JCPenney in 2011 after a string of retail successes. He was part of the team that turned Target into *Tarzhay*, a winking term marking Target's evolution from a thrifty box store to a hip, fun, and accessible lifestyle brand. From there, he went to Apple, where he pioneered its wildly successful retail stores. He is credited with the introduction of the Genius Bar to Apple stores. JCPenney jumped at the chance to turn its struggling brand over to Johnson, hoping he could revitalize the store's image and attract new customers.[10] Six months into his new job, Johnson laid out his plan to revolutionize the shopping experience at JCPenney during a highly anticipated investor presentation.

Johnson told investors that, historically, JCPenney relied heavily on a high-low pricing strategy: frequent promotions, sale prices, and deep discounts reinforced the feeling that customers were getting a bargain on their cookware or bedding or sweaters. But Johnson argued for ditching this approach. Gone would be inflated shelf prices paired with continuous discounts and promotions—more than five hundred promotions per year by Johnson's count—on nearly every item in stock. In its place, Johnson wanted "Fair and Square" pricing: whole-dollar prices (no $.99 endings) and predictable price discounts that rotate every month.[11]

Branding and merchandising would change, too. JCPenney would partner with more upscale brands and create a stores-within-a-store marketplace atmosphere. JCPenney wanted to become a brand known for "affordable luxury," a notoriously difficult positioning to nail. "We want to be the favorite store for everyone, for all Americans, rich and poor, young and old."[12]

Core to the new JCPenney strategy was a two-part targeting goal: first, triple the frequency of visits by current customers from four to twelve visits a year. And second, attract new customers who would be lured in by its new brand positioning. Given its 3 percent market share (for every one hundred shoppers, three were coming to JCPenney), Johnson saw this as a huge growth engine. "That means if you can keep those three and get one more customer, you can grow 33 percent," Johnson told the crowd. "If you get three more, you can double your business!" Johnson drew parallels between the JCPenney he was inheriting and what he'd inherited at both Target and Apple. The vision was compelling. The stock price jumped by almost 25 percent after the investor presentation.

Then the turnaround plan abjectly failed to attract new customers. The most immediate short-term effect of the big changes made by JCPenney was that it drove away current customers because it took away what they valued most in the JCPenney shopping experience: the delight in finding a great deal.

What was left unexamined in Johnson's presentation, and later within JCPenney's front office during this transition, was the functional conflict it might create between the new and old segments. The two segments were fundamentally different, and they wanted fundamentally different things from a department store. The values they sought were incompatible.

Existing JCPenney customers skewed toward middle-age, were mostly women, and mostly from lower- and middle-income households. They went to Penney's mostly for clothing and housewares. They valued steep discounts, indicators that they were getting a good deal on quality products. It also made them feel savvy, as though they had outsmarted the retailer when they found high-priced items being sold for a fraction of the list price. Frequent sales and coupons kept them coming back, lest they miss out on a good deal.

In contrast, the new customers that JCPenney wanted to start coming to stores were younger, more affluent, and *cooler*. More fashionable. They pursued trends, not discounts. The new brand partners Johnson was courting might entice them to stop in and pick up sleek appliances and high-end cosmetics, along with towels and kids' clothes. Simple, no-gimmicks pricing would reinforce the affordable luxury positioning. Reducing the emphasis on sales and discounts would keep items affordable while making the brand, and any customers who shopped there, feel less deal-oriented, less cheap.

It's not hard to see how deeply in conflict these two segments are once you lay it out this way, rather than how Johnson did in the investor call. Removing price discounts removed one of the things JCPenney's current customers valued most about shopping there. Reports indicated that, on average, customers were paying about the same or less under the new pricing strategy, but that didn't matter, because those customers did not perceive it that way. They were there for the deal, and the feeling of getting that deal, not the absolute price they paid for their goods. So, they stopped coming in as much because they weren't going to get the rush that comes from finding a spectacularly deep discount on a particular item.[13] As CNN put it, "Without testing shoppers' reactions first, Penney changed its advertisements, its logo, its store designs and its pricing model, all attempts to make the retailer more palatable to wealthier shoppers."[14]

But the wealthier shoppers never showed up. The stores were not located in areas that would naturally attract the desired segment. Everyday low pricing wasn't sufficiently different enough from its cheap brand image, thus failing to entice those looking for affordable luxury. The affordable part of the message got through, but the luxury part had to fight against a hundred years of brand history. Adding more prominent brand partners further weakened JCPenney's own brand identity, offering little appeal for new customers—why go to Penney's to get Carter's when you could just go to Carter's? And if you do go to JCPenney, are you paying attention to the JCPenney brand at all, or just concerned with shopping the Carter's brand? This functional conflict resulted in around $4 billion in sales lost *in the first year* of Johnson's turnaround plan, and annual revenue slid to its lowest in a quarter century.[15]

As the *New Yorker*'s James Surowiecki put it, rather than becoming America's favorite store, as Johnson had promised, JCPenney has instead become "America's favorite cautionary tale."[16] Among the lessons to be learned from Penney's mistakes, we suggest the most fundamental—and most widely applicable—is the failure to anticipate and grapple with the potential functional conflict between customer segments that can happen when a company grows. Management didn't recognize the incompatibility between the two segments it wanted—it needed—to grow. Instead, in trying to make a space for both, it created a space that appealed to neither.

In 2008, Frito-Lay introduced a new, compostable bag for its SunChips, in an effort to appeal to environmentalist snack-chip consumers. But the trade-off was that in order to make the bag biodegrade properly, it was now louder when it crinkled. A *lot* louder. Like louder than a lawn mower or the inside of a fighter jet. In exchange for a mild and somewhat esoteric benefit that few would appreciate, SunChips imposed a rather large, deafening inconvenience, and functional conflict, onto everyone else who wanted to eat chips without waking the neighborhood. This may sound trite, but the bag malfunction and related bad press (people reported little kids were scared of the sound) resulted in a more than 11 percent sales decline over a year. Frito-Lay discontinued the bags in 2010.[17]

We saw a similar instance of functional conflict when Starbucks introduced automated coffee-making machines to appeal to the on-the-go crowd. These new barista-less automations allowed people in a hurry to get their coffee faster. But for the coffee sophisticates who appreciated the ritual of an inefficient, multistep process performed by an expert, the change made their experience worse. In both cases, the brands changed their offerings to cater to a segment it wanted to grow or attract, but it made the experience of using the offering worse for another segment in the process.

8

Brand Image Conflict

Chads and Brads Wear Patagonia

A brand's image includes the values, emotions, personality, and associations that consumers attach to a brand. The brand meaning of Airbnb is centered around belonging, community, and unique experiences. Airbnb has cultivated this meaning in the minds of consumers by associating itself with these values through its marketing messaging and products. Airbnb's slogan is "belong anywhere," and it often encourages hosts and guests to interact and share stories, experiences, and recommendations.[1] Much of Airbnb's messaging relates to the concept of finding connection no matter where you are in the world, as was clear in its "live there" campaign, in which it encouraged consumers to not just see or visit a place but to have a more authentic experience and live like a local by staying in an Airbnb. Unique stays are also prominent in the brand's communications and website, including the chance to stay in treehouses, yurts, castles, lighthouses, and igloos.[2] Airbnb ran the "Night At" campaign that gave consumers the opportunity to spend the night at iconic destinations such as the Louvre Museum and at Dracula's Castle in Transylvania.[3] Creating a clear and cohesive brand image requires a clear vision by management, and then ruthlessly focused messaging to continuously reinforce the message over time.

But consistency by the brand is not enough. A brand's image is also a function of the customers who are associated with it. Airbnb's carefully crafted brand includes widely reported stories of hosts who charge rapacious cleaning fees running into the hundreds of dollars and *also* still require guests to complete extensive cleaning checklists upon checkout.[4] The brand's image may also include experiences with obnoxious guests who use the service to rent houses in quiet neighborhoods to hold raging parties until the wee hours on school nights. Not that that has ever happened to one of your authors. Multiple times. That example is purely hypothetical.

The different customer segments using a brand can easily affect what the brand starts to mean to each segment—and to potential customer segments. When that effect is negative, it can create brand image conflict. Brand image conflict arises primarily from three sources:

- When brands try to *vertically* expand their customer bases by attracting higher- or lower-status customers

- When brands try to *horizontally* expand their customer bases by capturing new segments in the same or different product categories

- When new customer segments organically associate themselves with the brand in such a way that it threatens the meaning of the brand's image, purpose, or function

Let's take each in turn.

Vertical expansion: Teenage girls get Tiffany heart necklaces

Luxury brands often try to expand their customer bases by creating a few affordable offerings to complement their more expensive product line. This can be an effective strategy for growing the number of customers and adding new revenue streams. It explains why luxury car brands are willing to put their logo on everything from hats and jackets to cologne, watches, and wallets.[5] But this strategy also runs the risk of alienating wealthy customer segments by removing the sense of exclusivity and specialness if the brand becomes too accessible to or overly associated with less wealthy customers.

Tiffany dipped its diamond toes into brand image conflict in the late 1990s when its silver jewelry became popular among younger and less affluent customer segments. When Tiffany started selling lower-priced silver jewelry, such as its $110 charm bracelet, teenagers showed up in droves to buy the baubles as fashion pieces or to profess their love to high school sweethearts. Investors were pleased with the highly profitable development, but Tiffany executives worried. Then-CEO Michael Kowalski told the *Wall Street Journal* in 2007, "The large number of silver customers did represent a fundamental threat—not just to the business but to the core franchise of our brand."[6]

To address this concern, Tiffany pulled the plug on its cash cow by raising prices on silver jewelry—especially on the pieces most popular with teenage girls—and introduced more expensive silver collections created by famous designers and artists to lure back its older, wealthier customers. The jeweler also renovated stores so that they would better showcase coveted gems and designs, while redirecting lower-tier jewelry shoppers away from the main showrooms. In fact, some stores featured side entrances for "transactional" customers, which guided shoppers directly to the Tiffany's silver jewelry counter.[7] Even with its relatively quick response, it took a few years for Tiffany silver mania to die down and for Tiffany to begin to rehabilitate its luxury image and signaling power for wealthy customers.

Nevertheless, Tiffany found itself back in brand image conflict in 2021 when the brand introduced its "Not Your Mother's Tiffany" campaign featuring edgy-looking models next to that tagline in ads lacking the brand's signature blue color and traditional font.

But longtime customers felt disrespected. The "mothers" were not amused. Instead, they (reasonably) felt cast aside in the brand's attempt to appeal to younger customers.[8]

As part of its attempt to appeal to youth, Tiffany also collaborated with brands such as Nike, Supreme, and Pokémon—because what Gen Zer doesn't want a $29,000 Pikachu necklace encased in a Tiffany-blue Poké Ball![9] Yes, that is a real product, one that is an especially embarrassing choice for the brand, given that Audrey Hepburn clearly seems like she would have been more of a Dragon Ball Z kind of woman. Trying to attract a new generation of customers makes sense for the brand—it needs to make sure there is a new base of customers ready to fill the shoes of its aging customer base. But Tiffany probably could have implemented this growth strategy without stirring up generational division or creating collaborations that cheapened the brand.[10] At the very least, it didn't have to plaster the Not Your Mother's Tiffany posters all over major cities and in plain view of those mothers.

Luxury brands, in particular, regularly cycle through this type of brand image conflict. This happens because they try to capture revenue by extending down-market, then become overexposed or start to lose a grip on their core upmarket customers. So, they retreat and refocus on the smaller, wealthier segment. Louis Vuitton, Coach, Gucci, and Prada have gone through this cycle. In reference to Tiffany's success selling more affordable jewelry, *Wall Street Journal* reporter Ellen Byron said, "Like a growing number of publicly traded luxury-good makers, Tiffany is attempting to walk a razor-thin line: broadening offerings to the upper-middle-classes while pitching privilege to the truly rich. The dilemma is particularly common these days, as investors clamor for sales growth on one side and fickle luxury buyers demand exclusivity on the other."[11]

Although it is less common, image conflict can also occur when a brand tries to move up the social ladder and targets a more upscale market segment. In contrast to Tiffany, Pandora jewelry grappled with image conflict after it attempted to target wealthier customer segments with higher-end offerings. While some loyal customers appreciated the expansion, many felt uncertain or resistant. There was a sense of confusion and concern among existing customers, who had initially been attracted to Pandora for its accessible, customizable jewelry. The attempt to cater to a wealthier demographic created a disconnect for some existing customers, casting doubt on the brand's image.

This kind of meaning conflict is not limited to segments separated by wealth. Status isn't always based on economic considerations. Athletic brands such as Under Armour and ASICS have both faced moments when athletes questioned the performance quality of the brands—whether they were sufficiently committed to the athletic excellence their brands promised—after they attempted to broaden their customer bases through product and line extensions. Puma has gone through several cycles of leveraging its athletics credentials to extend into fashion spaces, only to pull back from fashion to reestablish itself as an athletic brand. One such retrenchment happened in 2014, when Puma refocused away from its fashion offerings and partnered with athletes like Usain Bolt in a performance-focused campaign it called "Forever Faster."[12] Less than a decade later, athletics credibility apparently restored, Puma announced its triumphal reentry into the fashion space.[13]

This dynamic occurs in places where (perceived) intellect is the source of status too. Such was the case with TED. Founded in 1984, TED (technology, entertainment, design) gained global recognition for its elite conferences and TED Talks, which featured experts and thought leaders sharing innovative ideas in short, engaging presentations. TED Talks were first posted online for public access in 2006 and were positioned as providing a global audience "free access to some of the world's greatest thinkers, leaders, and teachers." TED Talks became a viral sensation. For better and worse, TED also gained a reputation as an elitist intellectual brand, a forum for thought leaders to bloviate on a red-carpeted soapbox. In fact, on a page of TED's website called "Debunking TED myths," the first "myth" listed is the question: "Is TED elitist?" Pro tip: if you need to explain to people that your brand isn't elitist, it's definitely elitist.

Regardless of what TED was, the sense of elitism clearly worked for the brand. The consumers of TED's content, both at the elite-but-not-elitist in-person conferences and by the millions via streaming video, *liked* the perceived elitism. People who watched TED Talks felt like they were part of an exclusive club, getting the inside scoop from people in the know. They would eagerly spark up an erudite discussion at cocktail parties about TED Talks they recently watched. It felt to fans as if they were getting access to ideas normally reserved for closed-door events like the Davos World Economic Forum or the Aspen Ideas Festival. But TED Talks were available to anyone willing to put in the time to seek them out and watch them. It was an everyman's elitism.

And because TED is a two-sided market, that perceived elitism worked to attract top-notch speakers as well. Being selected to give a TED Talk was a badge of honor and a signal that a person was important and had something important to say.

Then, the nonprofit opened up its technology and brand platform for licensing, via TEDx events. TEDx allowed independent event organizers to host and manage TED-affiliated speaking events and submit the talks to be posted on the TED website. TEDx stages looked like TED stages. And the talks were structured mostly like TED Talks. Financially and operationally, TEDx events were great for TED. The decentralized community made it possible for the organization to offer a lot more content at a fraction of the cost of classic TED events.

However, the authentic intellectual image of TED as a curator of content by the world's experts and top speakers quickly eroded under the weight of TEDx Talks, thousands and thousands of them. Worse, TEDx Talks were notably less curated than TED Talks. TEDx videos surfaced featuring pseudoscientific ideas, nonsensical theses, patently false claims. Topics ranged from vortex-based mathematics to Egyptian psychoaromatherapy. (Yes, those are real TEDx Talk topics.)

Because many customers did not know the difference between invited TED Talks and locally organized and independently vetted TEDx Talks, TED's prestigious brand image dimmed. Many TEDx speakers also do not try to clarify this confusion, crowing about their "TED Talk," which really was a TEDx Talk, eroding the power of the brand as status symbol. TED benefited from the additional content provided through TEDx Talks, but the brand was tarnished by this downward extension.[14]

More recently, the company has made changes, but at this point, it is unclear if it will be able to rehabilitate the brand. Some of the changes appear to risk further erosion of its meaning as an elite, intellectual brand. For example, TED has promoted a new format, "TED in 3 minutes," which is short snippets of (already fairly short) TED Talks. It has also developed TED-Ed animations that compress complex ideas or histories into five-minute animated explainers.[15] Effectively, TED is trying to TEDx-ify its original TED content. But that may very well deepen the brand image conflict for genuine experts who once valued the exclusiveness of an invitation to give a TED Talk or users who turned to TED because its "ideas worth spreading" were . . . genuinely ideas worth spreading. Experts and earnest learners may come to view the brand as less authentically serious and intellectual. Cartoons and commercial-length edits of complex phenomena are not what they wanted TED for.

Horizontal expansion: Weight Watchers sells wellness solutions

For years, WW (formerly Weight Watchers) dominated the weight loss market with its proprietary points system, in-person meetings, coaching services, consumable products, and a fiercely loyal community. The brand also earned the support of the most iconic TV personality of all time, Oprah Winfrey, when she became a brand ambassador in 2015.

However, Weight Watchers executives felt uneasy in the 2010s. Consumer interest in dieting and weight loss was slowly being replaced with an emphasis on wellness and behavior change. Body positivity was also becoming more popular, as were free or low-cost digital health and wellness apps. And Weight Watchers' customer base was aging—in 2018, the average customer was fifty-five. Oprah's influence alone did not feel like a viable long-term solution.

To attract a new segment of younger consumers, Weight Watchers rebranded in 2018. It changed its name from Weight Watchers to WW, a name that is shorter but somehow contains more syllables. The organization's original mission, "Be the leading provider of diet and weight loss services," was refashioned to "Inspire healthy habits for everyone, and create a world where wellness is accessible to all." To support this new mission, WW changed the logo, packaging, and advertisements for the brand. WW also introduced a new vocabulary to describe its services—"Weigh-Ins" became "Wellness Check-Ins," and "Meeting Leaders" were renamed "Wellness Guides and Coaches." It expanded digital offerings, added mindfulness programs, and updated the points system. It redesigned some products to inspire behavioral change and not just weight loss; changed the nutritional content of its packaged foods; launched a meal prep product called WW Healthy Kitchen; released branded recipes, cookbooks, and cooking classes; and acquired a youth-friendly mobile health app for kids called Kurbo. In short, WW upended decades of brand building in an effort to transform itself to be more appealing to new customers and did it all in *just three years*.[16]

Almost immediately, intersegment conflict reared its head. WW's existing customers were passionate about Weight Watchers as a *weight loss* solution. Rebranding as a wellness solution was not only ambiguous, but it threatened the authenticity of the brand for core customers. Was WW even a weight loss partner anymore? There was also functional conflict, as digital-only plans attracted more attention from new customers, undercutting the brand's signature group meetings. Entering the youth market also angered many customers who felt it could be harmful to kids, posing an ideological conflict between segments.[17] WW's stock value declined sharply, and subscribers abandoned the brand.[18]

WW was forced to make a strategic retreat. Management publicly admitted the rebrand should have been more weight-loss focused, and that the link between Weight Watchers and WW should have been clearer. Like X, formerly called Twitter, it's unclear whether people will ever refer to WW as "WW" without appending "formerly called Weight Watchers." The brand started adding references back to its former identity, including adding "Weight Watchers Reimagined" to the new WW logo. It also attempted to reinvigorate interest by making its partnership with Oprah more visible again through her "Campaign for Wellness" tour. The tour was emblematic of WW's problematic re-rebranding, backtracking toward making the brand about weight loss, but still clinging to its vague new focus on wellness, while relying on celebrity power unlikely to draw in younger customers.[19]

In 2022, CEO Mindy Grossman, who oversaw the rebrand, was replaced by Sima Sistani, who pledged to reorient the brand around weight loss through a more contemporary lens.[20] While there were many factors that contributed to WW's lackluster rebrand, much of its failing can be attributed to the brand image conflict it created by going too far, too fast in pursuit of growth.

But turning the brand around was not so easy for Sistani. WW did refocus on weight loss, but in a new way that invited its own controversy and conflict between customer segments. Under Sistani's leadership, WW moved away from the will-power-and-self-restraint approach to weight loss that the brand had championed for decades. Instead, WW became more open to other weight loss tactics, including pharmaceuticals. In 2023, the brand went so far as to acquire a subscription telehealth platform that allows users to get weight loss medications like Ozempic and Wegovy. While this move is clearly more in line with the brand's core image as a weight loss partner than its previous move into general wellness, it again generated brand image conflict among core customers. Many long-time members recalled that Weight Watchers was originally introduced as an alternative to crash diets and weight loss pills. After decades of messaging on willpower, portion control, points-tracking, community, and self-mastery, a sudden openness to weight loss medicines was a jarring pivot. Many loyal customers felt the brand had abandoned its core values in pursuit of the semaglutide market.[21] WW struggled to compete with semaglutide solutions and simultaneously failed to retain or win back its core customers. In 2024, Oprah gave up her board position and donated her stock to the National Museum of African American History and Culture. A few months later, Sistani stepped down as CEO, less than three years after taking the job. Between January and October 2024, WW's market value fell from $700 million to $65 million.[22]

Organic growth: Chad and Brad wear Patagonia

Perhaps the most challenging brand image conflict for companies is the one that's least under their control, such as when a segment organically attaches itself to the brand without any direct intervention from the company. What do you do when new customer segments start using your brand in a way that conflicts with the brand image your existing customer segments value?

Patagonia faced this problem. Founded in 1973, the preeminent purpose-driven brand in the outdoor recreation space reflected its founders' passion for protecting and restoring the environment. As early as 1985, Patagonia pledged to donate 10 percent of company profits to conservation groups.[23] In 2001 it upped that to 1 percent of total *sales*, whether profitable or not.[24] In the 2010s, Patagonia garnered significant attention with its Black Friday "Don't buy this jacket" ad that encouraged consumers to reduce, repair, reuse, and recycle their Patagonia clothing rather than purchase new.[25] Patagonia lists "protecting our home planet" as a core value on its website and notes that it aims to build high-quality, long-lasting, and re-pairable products. Its core values statement says, "Our ideal is to make products that give back to the Earth as much as they take," and for years, its mission statement included the goal to use business to inspire and implement solutions to the environmental crisis.[26] In 2022, Patagonia founder, Yvon Chouinard, and his family gave up ownership of the company—valued at about $3 billion at the time—and transferred the company's voting stock to a specially designed trust, donating the remaining 98 percent to a nonprofit organization called Holdfast Collective to combat climate change and protect undeveloped land around the globe.[27]

It's no surprise, then, that Patagonia's core customer segments have long included outdoor enthusiasts and environmentalists—people who value Patagonia's image as a company that prizes sus-tainability and environmental care. But in the late 2010s, the authentic, nature-oriented image of the brand was threatened when new seg-ments of customers started sporting Patagonia fleeces in masse: tech and finance bros. For more than a decade, investment firms and technology companies had worked with Patagonia to create fleeces embroidered with their corporate logos. Brokerage houses and trading platforms gave away truckloads of these cobranded zipper vests and collared pullovers to employees and clients. Soon, Patagonia fleece vests, as well as the Nano Puff, became the unofficial uni-forms of Wall Street and Silicon Valley—signifiers of status, exclu-sivity, and yuppie membership. The association between tech and finance bros and the Patagonia fleece became so entrenched in cul-ture that television shows such as *Silicon Valley* and a popular Insta-gram account called "Midtown Uniform" mocked the vest's ubiquity among "Chads" and "Brads"—derisive terms for affluent profession-als who are also usually white men.[28]

Ultimately, the more the Patagonia brand became associated with tech and finance bros, the more that association threatened the brand's image as warm and environmentally oriented for its outdoor enthusiasts. The droves of urbanites commuting between

Manhattan skyscrapers and San Jose office parks donning Patagonia vests started to erode what the brand said it stood for. The optics were terrible. The finance and tech bros segments represented the very companies Patagonia often positioned itself *against*, namely, those focused on profit over people or planet. How could the brand sustain its authentic image as an exemplar of sustainable business and also serve this new segment in such large numbers?

Patagonia adeptly steered the brand away from this conflict by changing its policies on corporate merchandising. To start, the brand stopped partnering with firms that did not share its commitment to social and environmental causes. This immediately eliminated large financial and technology companies. One finance firm reached out to Patagonia to create cobranded products and received the following response: "Patagonia has nothing against your client or the finance industry, it's just not an area where they are currently marketing through our co-brand division." At one point, Patagonia entirely shuttered its corporate branding program, citing waste concerns if people are less willing to pass on or wear their corporate fleeces after changing jobs or in nonprofessional environments.[29] Ultimately, Patagonia reverted to allowing for corporate branding, but on an application-only, case-by-case basis, and only after finding a partner who could remove embroidered logos from used garments.[30] It is also working to make sure that corporate wear is eligible for its Worn Wear program, which repurposes and resells old gear that would otherwise be condemned to a closet or tossed in a landfill.[31]

9

User Identity Conflict

Supreme: From Skaters to Sellouts

Consumers use brands for social reasons as much as they do for practical reasons. Brands are badges that help us communicate who we are and what we like. Brands can also serve as signals of one's identity or membership within a certain community or subculture. Just as important, brands can signal that you are *not* a member of certain groups, a preemptive move to avoid being misjudged as a person. You see this defensive brand identity in classic binary discussions around brand preferences. There are some Android people who would rather starve in the desert than use a friend's iPhone to call for help. And for your own safety, never offer a Dunkin' person a Starbucks coffee.

While the value of a brand as an identity badge can be crucial for cultivating brand adoption and loyalty, it can also pose a barrier to growth, allowing brands to only attract segments with compatible identities. When new consumers adopt a brand, it can create problems if the new users undermine the brand's signaling power for the original group.

Researchers from Stanford vividly demonstrated the importance of membership signaling in adopting and rejecting a brand based on its use by other segments of customers. In 2004, cancer survivor Lance Armstrong created the Livestrong Foundation, which raised money for cancer research by selling yellow silicone bracelets. Eighty million bracelets were sold in the decade after their launch, and for a few years, the rubbery yellow bangles were a genuine fad and a signal for people who wore them of a somewhat active and mildly philanthropic lifestyle.

During this time when Livestrong bracelets were starting to get trendy, researchers from Stanford went door-to-door in an on-campus dorm, selling the bracelets on behalf of the charity. Many students bought them and started wearing them. One week later, the researchers went door-to-door in the neighboring academic dorm and made the same pitch to those residents. It may surprise readers to learn that there are more- and less-nerdy dorms at Stanford. The academic dorm, in this case, was the nerdier dorm. When the kids from the cool dorm saw that their nerdier neighbors had also started wearing the yellow bracelets, many of them stopped. In a survey conducted one week after the nerds donned the bracelets, more than a third of the residents of the standard dorm who had initially worn their bracelets had stopped wearing them. By contrast, at a control dorm across campus, where no nerds-next-door had also adopted the trend, only 6 percent had stopped wearing theirs over a similar time frame.[1]

Signaling which groups we belong to, and which we don't, is a major driver of brand adoption and avoidance. And when a brand that is used as an identity badge no longer serves as an indication of group membership, it can lead customers to abandon that brand due to user identity conflict or confusion. We know this sounds similar to brand image conflict, but they are not the same. Brand image conflict is tension over what the brand stands for, its mission, its purpose, or its personality. User identity conflict relates specifically to whom the brand represents, or what club consumers signal they are a part of when they use the brand.

When Harley-Davidson started selling electric motorcycles in 2019, it created brand image conflict for some Harley Owners Group (HOG) members who thought electric bikes departed from the Harley tradition of producing motorcycles with loud and powerful V-twin engines. There was concern that the move to engine-less, electric-motor-powered bikes signaled that the brand would soon no longer have the same meanings it had historically. This redefining of the brand to appeal to more eco-friendly customers created brand image conflict for HOG traditionalists, who liked Harley just the way it was. But even though the introduction of electric motorcycles generated brand image conflict, we suspect it did not, by itself, create user identity conflict. Unless and until electric Harleys are adopted in large numbers by decidedly non-Harley people, there is little risk people will start to associate the HOG customers with another customer segment through the brand.

A bigger risk of user identify conflict for Harley-Davidson would present itself if some group of nontraditional customers started adopting the brand. Imagine, for example, that the classic Harley-logo-embroidered leather jackets, vests, or HOG membership patches became a popular, ironic fashion trend among preppy high schoolers. This might not cause brand image conflict if the brand remained wholly committed to its motorcycles and continued to promote its traditional image. But the adoption of the brand by a very different group of customers would likely create user identity conflict for HOGs, who might no longer be able to accurately signal their affiliation—and toughness—via the Harley brand.

To be fair, brand image conflict and identity conflict often co-occur or feed into one another. But there is nuance in the sources and expressions of conflict, which make it worthwhile to define them individually. As the saying goes, "The [conflict] devil is in the details." Identity conflict most commonly occurs when:

- Brands pursue new customer segments whose identities do not align with those of existing customers.

- The brand's offerings are adopted by, or become associated with, a segment of customers whose identities conflict with those of existing customers.

Pursuing customers with conflicting identities: Does this Supreme shirt make me look like I know how to skateboard?

Born in the streets of downtown Manhattan in 1994, Supreme leveraged the legends of skateboarding culture to become a cult streetwear brand. Its partnerships with influential skate icons and artists, and its limited drops of streetwear clothing, accessories, and skateboards, solidified its status as must-have gear, revered by skateboarders. To reinforce its authentic image, Supreme's stores were designed as much to be hangouts as retail shops. They blared loud music, played skate videos on loop, and employed skaters—some even had indoor skate bowls. For much of the late 1990s and into the early 2000s, Supreme, and its iconic red box logo, served as an identity badge signaling one's membership in the skateboarding community.

But its allure eventually spread far beyond that rather narrow segment. Using similar tactics it used with skaters—limited-edition product drops, strategic brand collaborations, and celebrity endorsements—Supreme propelled itself from a niche skate shop to "the coolest streetwear brand in the world right now," as described by GQ in 2017. Supreme departed from its origins by producing notably high-priced luxury products like a $54,000 Louis Vuitton glass cube and $5,000 co-branded Rimowa luggage, as well as perplexing brand extensions, such as co-branded Oreos, dog bowls, fire extinguishers, and branded bricks. Yes, literal bricks, which retailed for $30 a pop. Despite the ridiculousness, or more likely because of it, Supreme drew in customers and fans from all areas of fashion and counterculture. In 2020, the apparel and footwear company VF Corporation bought Supreme for $2.1 billion.[2]

Consumers in the new luxury-fashion segment, most of whom could not tell an ollie from a goofy-foot frontside air, lined up outside Supreme stores to buy the latest goods. Secondary markets teemed with the products, often selling for many times the retail prices. Fashion influencers and resale investors became dominant customer segments for the brand. Meanwhile, price hikes, increased store traffic, and limited product availability made the brand less accessible to its original skateboarding segment. Predictably, Supreme was criticized for being a skating culture sellout.

Supreme's ambitious pursuit of growth was partly a function of the brand's interest in increasing its influence and presence in popular culture, and partly a function of the fact that half of the company was acquired by the private equity firm in 2017. The PE firm playbook for brands tends to focus less on nuances like customer segment conflict and more on growing a brand quickly and profitably over a short time horizon. And that worked—to a point. Eventually, Supreme's meteoric growth became a liability for the brand that built itself around scarcity and authenticity. Supreme's red box logo lost its power as an identity signal. By the 2020s, it wasn't clear if someone buying the Supreme brand was a real skateboarder, a true streetwear enthusiast, a resale investor, or just a trend follower trying to look like the cool kids.

This is a classic example of what happens in a Leader-Follower market when the brand becomes too associated with the Follower segments (fashion influencers, etc.). Consequently, the Leaders (skaters, in this case) mostly abandoned the brand in favor of what felt like more authentic skating brands, like Santa Cruz, Element, and Quartersnacks. The hype around Supreme has shifted from subcultural appeal to mainstream mass appeal. When we tell the story of Supreme in class, many student-skateboarders note that

the brand is unquestionably uncool, and wearing Supreme today
makes a skater look like a "try hard." The author of an op-ed in the
UC Santa Barbara student newspaper put it bluntly: "Supreme is
not a skate brand. Supreme will never again be a skate brand. Supreme has turned into the very thing it once was against: mainstream, and any attempt to deny or obfuscate it is nothing more
than a marketing ploy."[3] Ouch. Supreme reported declining revenue in the fiscal year ending March 2023, almost $40 million off
from the previous year.[4]

Identity conflict can also occur for brands that do not originate
as or consider themselves identity-based brands. Power tools seems
like a category for which objective performance, not signaling one's
group affiliation, should be the major driver of purchase. Torque,
power, battery life—these are the attributes that should dominate
the choice of a power tool. No one is buying a particular belt sander
or circular saw because of its aesthetics, right? This should be
especially true of professional tradesmen. People like electricians,
carpenters, and roofers, who rely on their tools to make their living,
should be investing in tools that perform well, are reliable, and last
a long time, not ones that come in a particularly fetching shade
of teal.

In the early 1990s, when pitted against the competition in both
controlled laboratory tests and uncontrolled, real-usage, on-site
field tests, Black & Decker's tools were as good or better than its
competitors' on performance, reliability, and durability. Objectively, it made high-quality tools. But its sales were abysmal. Black
& Decker tools were popular with nonprofessional do-it-yourselfers
(DIYers), capturing 45 percent of that category, but it grabbed only
9 percent of the professional tradesmen market. The professionals
preferred the Japanese tool brand Makita, which ruled with a
50 percent market share.

The problem wasn't functional; it was rooted in identity. At the
time, Black & Decker was the only company that served both the
mass market consumer segment and the professional tradesman seg-

ment under the same brand. It sought to leverage nearly a hundred years of accumulated brand equity by selling both the black-and-charcoal-gray consumer-grade tools, and its charcoal gray-and-black professional-grade cousins under versions of the same Black & Decker logo.

But professional members of the trades had their own brand image to maintain, and they wanted it to be distinct. Tradespeople found it professionally threatening to be associated with tools that amateurs used. Contractors might reasonably worry that if they showed up with tools that could be mistaken for the same ones the homeowner used to hang Christmas lights, it might make them seem less credible. The fact that the same Black & Decker logo could also be found on popular home appliances like popcorn poppers, waffle makers, and portable vacuums didn't help. As one tradesman put it, "On the job, people notice what you're working with. If I came out here with one of those Black & Decker gray things, I'd be laughed at."[5]

To resolve this identity conflict, Black & Decker had to create barriers between its product lines. Given the strength of the brand among the nonprofessionals, management decided to keep the Black & Decker brand on the consumer-grade products and completely rebrand its professional line. It chose to elevate a neglected brand from its portfolio: DeWalt, a well-respected maker of large stationary woodworking equipment that Black & Decker had acquired three decades before. That brand had atrophied as the company focused on smaller tools and equipment. But internal research revealed that despite the neglect, the DeWalt name still carried value among professionals. Black & Decker Professional was dead. DeWalt was resurrected.

It changed more than just the name. It redesigned the tools to look more rugged. Charcoal gray was gone, and bright yellow was in, a color deliberately chosen to invoke the yellow ubiquitous on construction sites, from Caterpillar earthmovers to hard hats and safety vests. The yellow even had the benefit of easily showing scrapes, dirt, and wear. Well-used equipment can be one sign of an experienced professional.

As soon as Black & Decker broke the branding connection between the professional tradesperson and the amateur consumer, sales skyrocketed and DeWalt captured 40 percent of the professional market in just two years. Note that these were fundamentally the same products as before, just with a new logo and color scheme. But sales increased by more than four times when the identity conflict between the two customer segments was resolved.

The wrong influencers flex your brand:
"The Situation" wears Abercrombie & Fitch

MTV's reality series *Jersey Shore* showcased the antics, relationships, and party life of a group of housemates spending their summer on the bustling shores of Seaside Heights, New Jersey. Through its blend of drama, humor, and larger-than-life characters, the series became a pop culture sensation. The show popularized the catchphrase "Gym, Tan, Laundry," often abbreviated as GTL, which encapsulated the lifestyle priorities of the show's stars. Cast members were known for their bold and distinct fashion choices, which included tight-fitting graphic tees and tank tops, heavily gelled hair, and many, many animal prints. Fans eagerly tuned in each week to see what DJ Pauly D, Nicole "Snooki" Polizzi, JWoww, and Mike "The Situation" Sorrentino would do and say next.

But the cast members themselves reflected a very particular consumer identity that might not jibe with the identities of people who watched them each week, or the identities of those who liked the brands that popped up in the show. As a result, brands went to sometimes hilarious lengths to try to dissociate themselves from cast members lest they spark identity conflict with their customers.

Continuous free product placement on one of the most popular shows on TV might normally be considered a stroke of enormous good fortune for a brand, but Abercrombie & Fitch wasn't celebrating when it showed up on *Jersey Shore*. One cast member in particular, "The Situation," seemed to adore the brand, sporting the large A&F logo on his pants, hats, the exposed elastic band of his underwear, and on the rare occasions when he would wear one, his shirts. Abercrombie, by its own estimation, was a status symbol among preppy suburban teens, and the brand did not want to become an identity symbol for raucous Jersey Shore partiers. This would almost certainly create user identity conflict for Abercrombie fans, potentially driving them away. Even among fans of the show: those who loved watching the cast didn't necessarily want to *be* the cast.

Anticipating identity conflict, Abercrombie engaged in defensive dissociation from the customer segment, a strategy sometimes referred to as "unbranding." It released a statement trying to create some distance: "We are deeply concerned that Mr. Sorrentino's association with our brand could cause significant damage to our image. We have therefore offered a substantial payment to Michael 'The Situation' Sorrentino and the producers of MTV's *Jersey Shore* to have the character wear an alternate brand. We have also extended this offer to other members of the cast and are urgently waiting a response." Abercrombie very publicly offered The Situation an anti-endorsement deal.

Rumor had it that Abercrombie was not the only brand that took active measures to unbrand itself from *Jersey Shore* stars. A story circulated that Louis Vuitton sent Snooki handbags from its rival Gucci after noting her affection for luxury handbags—effectively trying to poison the enemy army's water supply.[6] Sun Tzu would have approved. As Louis Vuitton saw it, its traditional customer base does not typically GTL before clubbing on the boardwalk. For what it is worth, Snooki denies that anyone ever sent her free luxury handbags of any brand.[7]

So as not to sell the cast of *Jersey Shore* short, there are brands that *do* want to associate with the customer segments they represent. In 2023, the convenience store and gas station chain Wawa released a television ad and social media images featuring cast members in front of its stores along the Jersey Shore as part of its "Wawa has pizza" campaign.[8] Wawa has a large presence in New Jersey and the surrounding area. Wawa is also a popular late-night food destination, including among summertime Jersey Shore partygoers. Wawa fans' love for the brand is real, but these fans also tend to mock and exaggerate their own fervor for the brand, realizing the ridiculousness of their love for gas station food. The brand is also known for its ironic, humorous, and sometimes self-deprecating advertising. It makes sense that Wawa would want to partner with *Jersey Shore* cast members—who also seemed to be in on the joke. They reflect the customer identity of some portion of Wawa customers and do not risk alienating the other Wawa lovers, even if they don't see themselves as similar to The Situation or DJ Pauly D.

10

Ideological Conflict

Elmo Gets His Covid Shot

Brands often serve customers with diverse ideological views without a problem. Apple sells iPhones to Democrats and Republicans; to Christians, Jews, Muslims, and Hindus; to Hatfields and McCoys; to fans of Manchester United and Liverpool F.C. And importantly, these diverse groups of customers, with their conflicting ideological views, are all happy to buy from Apple, despite knowing their ideological counterparts also use an iPhone.

Clearly, ideology does not factor into every purchase people make. But occasionally, and increasingly, customers seek out brands that explicitly reflect their values and reject brands that don't. And when a brand hasn't voiced an opinion on certain issues? Well, sometimes customers will choose to infer a brand's point of view based on who else is buying, or to whom the brand is making overtures in its marketing. Ideological conflict occurs when a brand becomes associated with the values or beliefs of one segment of customers, and customers who fundamentally disagree with those values tend to react negatively, either by abandoning the brand or by demanding the brand change its position and reaffirm their preferred values instead.

There are two basic situations that can land a brand in the midst of an ideological conflict between segments:

- A brand takes a stance, affirming or reaffirming its alignment with the values and beliefs of a particular customer group.

- A segment of customers hijacks or co-opts the brand for its own purposes, redefining the brand's image as consistent with its ideological beliefs and values.

Brands takes a stance: YETI (sort of) cuts ties with the National Rifle Association

YETI is a premium outdoor lifestyle brand known for its high-quality coolers, drinkware, and camping gear. YETI's coolers, which are famous for their ability to keep contents cold or hot for days, sell for between $250 and $1,300, depending on the size, and tumblers go for between $30 and $40. YETI's primary customers include fishers, campers, hunters, and outdoor sport enthusiasts. In 2018, YETI notified the National Rifle Association (NRA) that it was ending a seven-year-long discount program with the organization. Former NRA president Marion Hammer didn't take the news lightly. Hammer wrote a letter saying YETI had decided to stop doing business with the NRA and "they no longer wish to be an NRA vendor."

Ideological conflict ensued. NRA members swiftly took to social media to express their displeasure:

> *Are you nuts or something #Yeti, Your [sic] cutting ties with the very type of people that buy your products #Liberals don't hunt, fish or go Boating.*[1]

> *I own several expensive Yeti products and planned on purchasing more, however, NOT NOW.*[2]

But why limit one's expressions of discontent to words or boycotting, when one has the option of violent destruction? NRA members posted videos of themselves blowing up YETI coolers and using YETI products for target practice. One video that made the rounds on social media and in news coverage featured a man shooting at a Tannerite-filled YETI cooler with an AR-15, which, predictably, blew it to pieces. And this wasn't an isolated display of protest. NRA members created the #YetiCoolerChallenge, encouraging others to post videos of themselves using guns to destroy YETI products. Adherents followed suit, and some also posted images of their YETI products with bullet holes in them or being crushed in a vise.[3]

But then things took a turn for the confusing. YETI spoke out a few days after the fury broke, explaining that it was *not* cutting ties with the NRA. According to the brand, the removal of the discount program was part of a larger organizational change that ended a particular type of discount for a number of organizations. The brand further clarified in a statement on its Facebook page, "YETI is unwavering in our belief in and commitment to the Constitution of the United States and its Second Amendment." YETI also noted it had included the NRA in the offer of an alternative customization program. It appeared consumers had . . . jumped the gun! (We refuse to apologize for that joke. We regret nothing.) According to YETI, it hadn't taken an explicit stance in opposition to the NRA; the former president just *thought* it had. Not everyone bought this story. Some felt YETI tried to get away with distancing from the NRA and then backtracked after the vociferous response. And regardless, the damage resulting from the (real or perceived) ideological conflict had already been done.

The YETI backlash was particularly hostile because many NRA members felt that YETI was turning its back on a group that considered itself the core customers of the brand. According to one Twitter user: "Everyone in my friend group that owns a YETI is a Conservative. Their demographic is Conservative Middle Class

Americans. . . . [T]hey just shot themselves in the foot (no pun intended)."[4] And another user tweeted directly at the company: "Do you not understand who your base is? Will never buy or use any of your products again and we had a bunch."[5]

YETI's apparent distancing from the NRA came at a time when the topic of gun control was a particularly hot-button issue—it was shortly after the school shooting at Marjory Stoneman Douglas High School in Parkland, Florida, which engendered widespread advocacy for stricter gun control legislation. In response to this event, a number of brands explicitly ended their support for or special treatment of NRA members too. Outdoor retailer REI paused orders of products whose brands were associated with the NRA. Delta and United Airlines ended their NRA discount programs, as did MetLife insurance. Dick's Sporting Goods, Walmart, and L.L. Bean all announced they would stop selling firearms in their stores.[6] These announcements sparked their own respective backlashes. These companies were trying to align with the values of the large segments of the market who were demanding stricter gun control. But by drawing closer to gun control advocates, these brands were moving away from gun rights advocates, who were feeling the pressure of so many brands pulling back on the various sources of value they provided to them in the past. By the time the news broke about YETI, the context was overripe for conflict.

Although it did not spur quite the same frenzied response as YETI ending its NRA discount, a similar instance of ideological conflict occurred when the *Sesame Street* characters Big Bird and Elmo announced they had been vaccinated against Covid-19. Big Bird, the eight-foot-two feathered yellow puppet, tweeted in 2021: "I got the Covid-19 vaccine today! My wing is feeling a little sore, but it'll give my body an extra protective boost that keeps me and others healthy." Some Democratic politicians, including President Joe Biden, commented on their support for Big Bird, while some conservative politicians and influencers condemned the fictional Muppet. Senator Ted Cruz tweeted, "Government propaganda . . .

for your 5-year-old!"[7] One Fox News pundit described Big Bird's messaging as "brainwashing children" and "twisted."[8] *Sesame Street*, which receives federal funding, waded deeper into controversy when it posted a video in partnership with the Centers for Disease Control and Prevention and the Ad Council as part of an ongoing campaign in which Elmo talks about getting his Covid-19 vaccine. The public service announcement featured Elmo and his dad, Louie, talking about why he decided to get Elmo vaccinated after talking to his pediatrician.[9] (If you're curious, the reason for the staggered rollout was that Big Bird's character is canonically six years old and Elmo is officially three years old, so the vaccine was made available to them at different times.)

This isn't the first time Muppets waded into the culture wars. While *Sesame Street* has been beloved by parents and children of all political leanings for over half a century, factions of conservative audience members have turned away from the show as it has hewn more closely to the values of its more liberal viewers. In 2020, the show featured Billy Porter, an openly gay actor and singer, who wore his famous black tuxedo dress for the occasion. A petition to have the episode pulled made the rounds.[10] That same year, Fox News host Tucker Carlson (who will return to our narrative shortly for his take on another fictional character's behavior) ranted against Elmo when *Sesame Street* aired a segment showing Elmo and his father discussing racism.[11] In all of these instances, *Sesame Street* made a calculated decision to weigh in on politically charged issues in ways that aligned with its brand mission. While the decisions sparked conflict for viewers—or more likely, viewers' parents— who held ideologically opposed beliefs, the brand decided that the loss of some viewers was worth the upside of speaking out in each of these instances. In many cases, brands make their values clear despite knowing it will likely result in conflict or controversy because it is a calculated business decision designed to attract or serve certain customer segments, because they believe it is their moral obligation, or both.

International brands are increasingly in danger of stepping into ideological conflict rooted in nationalist sentiments. In 2019, protests consumed Hong Kong after the government introduced some restrictive bills pushed by the Chinese government. Feeling sympathy for the protestors, Daryl Morey, the general manager of the Houston Rockets basketball team, tweeted out an image with the phrase "Fight for Freedom. Stand with Hong Kong" in support. His ideological support for a protest movement in Hong Kong enraged many Chinese NBA fans, of which the league estimates there are about half a billion.[12] The NBA tried to distance itself from Morey's comments, and so did individual players, who found themselves suddenly asked in interviews about the political crisis in Hong Kong. Most prominent among these was LeBron James, who claimed that Morey "wasn't educated" on the situation in China and that his tweet was "misinformed."[13] This response produced a reaction that was just as enraged from residents of Hong Kong and their allies in America and elsewhere.

Ideological conflict doesn't necessarily need to be related to politics. It can also be rooted in discordant ethical beliefs or values of segments more generally. Pricing schemes that charge one group of customers more than the other, known as price discrimination, regularly trigger ideological conflict. In 2021, Disney Parks and Entertainment created Lightning Lane, a paid version of its now-retired FastPass program.[14] Park goers can use Lightning Lane to reserve spots in line for popular rides and attractions, giving them the ability to skip the line at the time of their reservation. But this perk costs an additional $7–$20 per person, *per ride*, depending on the park, the ride, and when you are visiting. Lightning Lane adds hundreds of dollars a day for families traveling to Disney parks. This generates ideological conflict between customer segments who disagree over whether providing people with the option to pay to skip the line is fair or ethical. When the ski resort Snowbird created a similar program allowing visitors to pay more to use expedited lines for chairlifts, thirteen thousand people signed a petition in protest.

Note that price discrimination tends to trigger functional conflict along with ideological conflict. It interferes with customers' experiences of goods or services when customers have to spend more time waiting in line because others paid to skip ahead of them (which can also mean less time on rides or fewer runs down the mountain), or when they can't access goods or services because they're bought up by VIP customers. While Lightning Lane customers at Disney World can scoot right on the Slinky Dog Dash roller coaster, regular customers wait an average of eighty-eight minutes (*eighty-eight minutes!*) for the same ride. This may partially explain why people are drinking more alcohol at Disney parks.[15]

A customer segment claims or rejects the brand based on ideological motives: New Balance becomes the preferred sneaker brand for extremist groups

In some cases, brands make a deliberate decision to align with ideological customer segments, as seen in the preceding examples; in other cases, they are dragged into culture wars completely against their will. After Donald Trump became president-elect of the United States in 2016, a representative from the footwear brand New Balance told the *Wall Street Journal* that he felt "things are going to move in the right direction" for its business because of Trump's trade positions. As the only leading athletic shoe manufacturer to still make shoes in the United States, New Balance was opposed to the Trans-Pacific Partnership, a free trade agreement the Obama administration had been pushing in the years leading up to the election. When New Balance had warned of the damages to American businesses, it said, Obama had "turned a deaf ear" to its complaints.[16]

The company was not trying to make a statement about its principles, beliefs, or values, except perhaps the rather banal belief that "Made in America" is something that should be encouraged and protected. The New Balance statement was intended to apply narrowly to the proposed free trade agreement, something the company later clarified in a statement to the *Guardian*, saying that the spokesperson's comments were "correct only in the context of the topic of trade, and nothing else."[17] In other words, the company was not endorsing Trump, nor his other policies, nor his various inflammatory statements . . . just trade. Nothing else.

Unfortunately, the clarifying statement was the equivalent of closing the barn door after the barn had burned to the ground. First came the reaction from enraged liberals, who took the statement to mean that New Balance was indeed aligning itself with the values and beliefs of the newly elected Donald Trump. People complained online, called for boycotts, and posted videos of themselves burning their New Balance sneakers in protest.[18] (And thus, we discover one thing conservatives and progressives agree on: immolating things that one has already paid full price for and then posting the results on social media is a viable form of political speech.)

In reaction to the wave of protests from liberals came a counter-wave of conservatives embracing the brand. One agitator in particular seized on the nascent controversy by trying to redefine the brand and align it with his ideology. An editor at the neo-Nazi website the *Daily Stormer* wrote, "It's time to get on-board with New Balance now. Their brave act has just made them the official brand of the Trump Revolution." He said that the company's statement endorsing Trump's trade policy was actually "a gesture to support White people and to support US manufacturing." He proposed that New Balance become the "uniform" of those with white supremacist beliefs: "We will be able to recognize one another by our sportswear."[19] Cue panic at New Balance headquarters.

The ideological conflict that started with an inartful interview quote from a single employee blew straight past boycott hashtags and spun deliriously into New Balance's unwillingly alignment with neo-Nazis. A *Washington Post* headline summed it up well: "We live in crazy times: Neo-Nazis have declared New Balance the 'Official Shoes of White People.'"[20] Crazy. But increasingly, not unusual.

For what it's worth, if you're looking down at your New Balance sneakers wondering if you can ever wear them out in public again, New Balance has since wrested the brand back from the clenched fists of extremists who tried to claim it as their own. This controversy occurred before New Balance reemerged as a legitimate running sneaker and preferred casual sneaker by both dads and runway models in the 2020s, which increased the brand's popularity sufficiently and widely enough to fully dissociate from white nationalist groups.

You may be inclined to assume that the example of New Balance is uniquely bizarre and unlikely. However, particularly in the United States, as every issue risks becoming politicized and people are increasingly polarized in their politics, it is more common for customer segments or influential figures to try to force brands into alignment with the ideologies of a particular party or group. There is a trend toward wanting to know where brands stand on social and political issues, and to try to infer a brand's position based on weak evidence or irrelevant brand actions. Worse, influencers, pundits, and political figures try to grab onto brand statements or actions as opportunities to vilify the other side and stoke the flame of an us–versus–them mentality.

In 2022, M&M's engaged in the typically anodyne task of updating its brand characters. There will always be neophobes who complain about any attempts to freshen up the look of Tony the Tiger, the Keebler Elves, or The Most Interesting Man in the World. But people don't usually care and, more often, don't even notice. The updated cartoon M&M's mostly just had updated footwear. The brown M&M now had a shorter, blocky heel, the blue M&M wore a type of Ugg, and the green M&M traded in her signature go-go boots for a pair of practical, casual sneakers. According to the CEO, the changes were intended to be more "representative of our consumer."[21] We're not entirely sure how cartoon chocolate candies' footwear can be more representative of consumers, or why consumers would care, but the changes were, most emphatically, not intended to endorse a set of fundamental brand values or provoke a larger discussion of hot-button topics.

But influencers across the political spectrum weighed in and used the change as an opportunity to turn the M&M's brand into an ideological strawman they could knock down. The loudest voices came from the political right. One Fox News pundit called the new go-go-boot-less green M&M "opportunistic" and "evil." Tucker Carlson, then also of Fox News, and freshly off his take-down of Elmo, said, "M&M's will not be satisfied until every last cartoon character is deeply unappealing and totally androgynous. Until the moment you wouldn't want to have a drink with any one of them. That's the goal. When you're totally turned off, we've achieved equity."[22] Ultimately, M&M's ended up dropping its animated "spokescandies" altogether and replacing them (for a while) with actor Maya Rudolph.[23]

While the preceding examples might make it seem as though ideological conflict rooted in political disagreement or culture wars is mostly a conservative or even more specifically a Fox News issue, that's not true. Yes, Fox News hosts seem to be particularly quotable when one is writing a section on the ideological positioning of brands, but liberal pundits and media outlets also inspire or enflame conflict by trying to wedge brands into ideological boxes. In the 2010s, liberal consumers called for a boycott of the arts and crafts store Hobby Lobby, in response to its policy against providing access to contraceptives as part of its health-care insurance coverage for employees, and called for boycotts of Chick-fil-A when its then-president Dan Cathy spoke out against the legalization of same-sex marriage.[24] Progressive customers also rallied against Equinox and SoulCycle after their owner hosted a lavish fundraiser for Donald Trump.[25] Even the M&M's spokescandies redesign drew ire from some commentators on the left, who complained that the focus on gendered clothing in the redesign was antifeminist.[26] In fact, some evidence suggests liberal Americans are more likely to stop buying a product or service based on a company's political stance than are conservative Americans.[27]

Categorizing Conflict

The four categories of conflict are not mutually exclusive. It is possible for two segments to be in conflict for multiple reasons. It is possible that Starbucks third placers and Starbies could be in conflict that is both functional, rooted in how the two groups want to use the space within the store, and brand image–based, rooted in differences over what each segment thinks makes Starbucks authentic. We argued that the conflict Patagonia faced was based on brand image, but the conflict between environmentalists and finance bros could also come partially from customer identity. Those in the core environmentalist segment might have started to harbor the concern that their fleece could accidentally mark them as a Brad. And the New Balance customers who don't identify as neo-Nazis may be in both ideological and user identity conflict with those who do. WW (formerly Weight Watchers) may have conjured up brand image conflict with its semaglutide drug investments, but this also stirred ideological conflict for customers who are opposed to the use of pharmaceuticals for weight loss or think of weight loss drugs as "cheating."

. . .

Understanding the different sources of customer conflict and the nuances between them is crucial for determining the optimal solution for mitigating conflict, as we will see in the next chapter. Table 10-1 is a brief review of the four types of conflict, with the examples discussed so far.

TABLE 10-1

Sources of intersegment customer conflict and corresponding examples

Functional conflict: Conflict rooted in the practical benefits that customer segments want from the product or service

Cause	Examples
Attracting and serving new customer segments	– Starbucks: Coffee on the go vs. third placers – Disney: Families vs. childless adults – SunChips: Environmentalists vs. people who want to eat chips without earplugs
Rebranding for a new customer segment	– JCPenney: Traditional bargain hunters vs. consumers seeking affordable luxury

Brand image conflict: Conflict rooted in the image or meaning of the brand

Cause	Examples
Vertical expansion	– Tiffany: Wealthy people seeking class, status, and history vs. teens seeking baubles – TED: Talks by renowned experts vs. TEDx Talks from decidedly less renowned "experts"
Horizontal expansion	– WW: Weight loss vs. wellness
Organic growth outside the brand's base	– Patagonia: Environmentalists vs. finance Chads and tech Brads

User identity conflict: Conflict rooted in different customer segments' self-image, including how they define in-groups and out-groups

Cause	Examples
Pursuing segments with conflicting identities	– Supreme: Legit skateboarders vs. poseur fashionistas and small-time investors – Black & Decker: Professional tradespeople vs. casual DIYers
The wrong influencers flex your brand	– Abercrombie & Fitch: Preppies vs. *Jersey Shore* – Gucci: Luxury elite vs. *Jersey Shore*

Ideological conflict: Conflict rooted in the values or beliefs of different customer segments

Cause	Examples
The brand makes its values clear	– Bud Light: Partnering with Dylan Mulvaney – YETI: Supposedly ending discount programs for NRA members – *Sesame Street*: Elmo gets the Covid-19 vaccine – Disney parks: People who pay to skip the line vs. people who resent those who pay to skip the line
An ideological customer segment claims or rejects the brand	– New Balance: Customers looking for dadcore running shoes vs. neo-Nazis – M&M's: Green M&M gets new kicks

11

Assessing the Risks of Conflict

Subaru Understood the Assignment

The risk of any two customer segments falling into conflict and the severity of the consequences of that conflict vary considerably based on the particulars. When serving multiple customer segments, it is worth considering whether you are running the slight risk of a minor irritation or are dancing on a powder keg juggling fireworks. It is also worth considering: Is there a way to tell which is more likely, aside from just waiting to see if things blow up? Accurately assessing the risks of conflict between customer segments requires understanding the pieces of the conflict puzzle, namely, what different customer segments want and expect from the brand, what the brand means to those customers, the extent to which that meaning can be stretched to include new customers, and the competitive and cultural forces at play in the marketplace. Absent this information, it is nearly impossible to predict which seemingly innocent marketing moves will turn catastrophic. In contrast, when a brand has a thorough understanding of its customers, brand, and marketplace, decisions that seem bound to invite controversy may be managed to successfully sidestep conflict entirely and instead ignite growth. Let's start with two examples of brands that tried to grow via similar target customers with wildly different levels of success.

Bud Light Partners with Dylan Mulvaney

According to a letter Bud Light sent to its wholesalers, one of the costliest marketing errors ever made—one with massive financial and brand reputation repercussions—really came down to "one single can, given to one social media influencer."[1]

The can in question was a custom version of the classic blue Bud Light tallboy, with the smiling face of transgender influencer Dylan Mulvaney superimposed over the logo. This was a common promotional tactic for Bud Light: "From time to time we produce unique commemorative cans for fans and for brand influencers," an Anheuser-Busch representative later said in an interview. The occasional customized beer can gave some of Bud Light's "hundreds of influencers" something to show off in social media posts. It is only "one of the many ways [we] authentically connect with audiences across various demographics."[2]

Mulvaney posted a one-minute video thanking Bud Light for the customized can, which was a congratulatory gift celebrating one year since her transition. Conservative activists latched onto the promotion, reposting the video as evidence of the brand's "woke" agenda. Politicians, commentators, and celebrities called for a boycott. Some customers posted videos of themselves in gleeful acts of violent destruction: stacking up cases of beer and then shooting them with assault rifles, lighting cases of beer on fire, smashing them with bats, and running over them with trucks. Bud Light distribution warehouses received bomb threats.[3] Unlike the vast majority of brand boycotts, which tend to blow over with no lasting damage, the backlash against Bud Light was devastating. This single customized can, and Mulvaney's accompanying video, caused a 20 percent year-over-year decline in sales for Bud Light, a twenty-point decline in its share price, and the dislodging of the brand from its twenty-year perch as the number-one bestselling beer in America.[4]

Experts were quick to diagnose the source of Bud Light's error. The former chief creative officer of Anheuser-Busch, Robert Lachky, blamed the (once proudly American) company's acquisition by Belgian conglomerate InBev a few years prior. He implied that the European cultural values of the parent company alienated the brand from the concerns of ordinary Americans. He claimed that the marketing executives were out of touch with Bud Light's customers and hostile to their values. "None of these marketing folks has ever been to a NASCAR race, none has been to a football game or a rodeo," he said. "That's insanity. That's marketing incompetence."[5] Others blamed management's lax oversight of its creative partners, with Bud Light later claiming that an unnamed third-party ad agency had run the Mulvaney promotion without seeking prior approval from corporate.[6]

In hindsight, it seems obvious that the brand's decision to work with Mulvaney would launch a firestorm among some of its customers. Why didn't it see that freight train barreling toward it?

Much of the criticism of Bud Light focused narrowly on the decision to partner with Mulvaney in the first place, and the clumsy and unsatisfying way the brand handled the backlash from that decision—a too-little-too-late statement crammed with watery corporate speak. Bud Light's response neither tried to win back its core audience nor stood its ground in support for Mulvaney and the customers she represented. But the Bud Light controversy is best understood by taking a step back. It is worth considering the years-long strategy that led Bud Light to the tactical decision of sending out that single customized aluminum can in the first place.

Bud Light had the same goal that most brands do: it wanted to grow. But growth can be difficult, especially for big brands that have fewer new prospective customers out there that fit their target customer profile. In a podcast interview recorded mere months before the fateful Mulvaney promotion, Alissa Heinerscheid, vice president of marketing at the time, was blunt: "This brand is in decline. It has been in decline for a really long time. And if we do not attract young drinkers to come and drink this brand, there will be no future for Bud Light."[7] Part of the plan to attract young drinkers involved making some changes to the brand, evolving it into something more inviting, and elevating its current image in the eyes of potential new customers. She continued, "What does 'evolve and elevate' mean? It means inclusivity. It means shifting the tone. It means having a campaign that's truly inclusive and feels lighter and brighter and different and appeals to women and to men."[8]

A part of the Bud Light story that many casual observers missed was that the decision to partner with a trans influencer did not come entirely out of nowhere. Bud Light didn't suddenly "go woke" in the spring of 2023. That one small promotion was part of a much larger, long-running growth strategy of outreach to new, mostly younger customer segments. Most notable among these target customers was the LGBTQ+ community. At the time of the boycott, Bud Light had already been advertising to the gay community and sponsoring Pride parades for *decades*. CEO Brendan Whitworth reminded critics of that in an interview after the Mulvaney backlash, pointing out that Bud Light had been openly supporting the LGBTQ+ community for more than twenty-five years at that point.[9]

It was in this context—of a brand looking to grow by adding new segments to its customer portfolio, of seeking younger segments to offset the eventual declines in its current core segments, of more inclusive branding, and of more than twenty-five years of LGBTQ+ outreach—that Bud Light made the decision to give a customized promotional can to a trans activist. From this perspective, it's not hard to understand how the managers at Bud Light might have seen the partnership with Mulvaney as another small, incremental step in a long, slow process that had been in motion for decades. And by viewing the partnership through that lens, it is easier to understand how Bud Light's leadership might have been caught completely off guard by the astonishing reaction.

From another perspective, of course—one that became clear after it happened—the backlash seemed inevitable. Bud Light was pursuing new segments of customers that had very different values and wanted very different things than its current core segments. The new target customers appreciated the brand's trajectory toward inclusivity. Factions of existing customers viewed that shift as a threat. In pursuing such different segments simultaneously, Bud Light was increasing the risk that these customer groups would eventually come into conflict with one another.

There were signs that these customer segments were incompatible years before the Mulvaney promotion, signs Bud Light apparently ignored. In 2016, Bud Light launched a campaign that featured comedians Seth Rogen and Amy Schumer pitching Americans on the "Bud Light Party." This mock political movement was about bringing people together by emphasizing the things Americans agree on. ("Like Paul Rudd. Everybody loves Paul Rudd!")[10] They claimed that the Bud Light Party was for everyone: "Men! Women! People of all genders!" To which Amy Schumer added as a quick aside, "But, you know gender identity, it's really a spectrum."

Some consumers were happy with the Schumer-Rogen ads: perceptions of the brand improved among millennial and Hispanic consumers during the campaign.[11] But others were angry: the hostility coming from some customers was enough to force Bud Light to disable YouTube comments and ratings on videos of the ads, and the brand ended the campaign early amid declining sales.[12]

While the campaign did not generate any serious controversy, the divided response to the Schumer-Rogen campaign portended a larger clash. Had the brand fully appreciated the signs of incompatibility from past campaigns, or considered the larger cultural and political context, it may have foreseen the coming conflict. Had Bud Light been more attentive to the relationships between the different customers it wanted to serve and viewed its marketing decisions more holistically—at the level of the entire customer eco-system versus at the level of the individual segment it was intended to attract—it may have avoided catastrophe.

Subaru Becomes the Car for Lesbians

Contrast Bud Light's unwitting stumble into conflict to Subaru's courting of a similar segment years earlier. Faced with slumping sales, Subaru executives in the 1990s were desperate to reinvigorate the car brand. Rather than target the same mainstream demographic segments all the other car manufacturers were also pursuing, Sub-aru sought growth opportunities in the underserved niches. To do this, it looked to current Subaru owners to identify hidden subseg-ments within its customer base that it could target in future mar-keting campaigns. (Note: this is a really smart and underutilized marketing strategy. The natural tendency of brand managers is to look outward for growth opportunities and subsequently spend a lot of time and money trying to convince uninterested groups to buy their products. Instead, it is often more productive to first see whether there are customer segments that are *already* buying the brand and then go out and find more of them.[13]) Unsurprisingly, Subaru consumers tended toward outdoorsy lifestyles. People who drove Subarus valued the sturdiness and all-terrain capabilities of the cars. As Subaru dug deeper into this flannel-wearing customer base though, it discovered several subsegments with the potential for further growth, including medical professionals, teachers, and a more extreme wilderness-oriented group of customers, which it referred to as "rugged individualists."

But one subsegment of customers looked especially promising to Subaru marketers. Through research, Subaru realized it was selling a lot of cars to unmarried female heads of households, which subse-quent research revealed to be mostly lesbians.[14] These customers held many of the same core values as every other Subaru customer: they liked the reliable utility and unflashy design of the vehicles, which fit their active, low-key lifestyle.[15] But this segment also had some unique needs, for which Subaru could provide additional value. As an underserved and often ostracized segment, lesbians might be especially appreciative of the simple recognition of and support for their community—a value few, if any, other brands offered to them at the time.

At first the acknowledgment was understated. The brand created advertisements that included subtle messaging intended to speak to lesbian consumers, like showing Subarus sporting a small rainbow flag bumper sticker. In one ad, the car had a license plate that read, "XENA LVR," a reference to the nineties fantasy-action show *Xena: Warrior Princess*, a mainstay in lesbian culture. Over time, the ads got less subtle. One set of ads featured headlines stating, "It's Not a Choice. It's the Way We're Built," and "Entirely Comfortable with Its Orientation," which were ostensibly statements about the car and its features. Lesbians began looking out for the winks and nods toward the community, many of which went unnoticed by non-lesbian consumers.

Although it started with Easter eggs in its advertising, Subaru's support for the LGBTQ+ community rapidly got more overt: the brand sponsored Gay Pride parades and gay film festivals. It was one of three charter sponsors of Logo, the first cable TV channel explicitly created to serve the gay community. It partnered with the Rainbow Card, which donated to LGBTQ+ organizations.[16] Subaru hired lesbian tennis superstar Martina Navratilova as a spokesperson. Then, in an *Inception*-level twist, it replicated this sponsorship within the Lesbian Cinematic Universe by hiring a fictional lesbian tennis star, Dana Fairbanks, as its fictional spokesperson within the Showtime drama *The L Word*.

Subaru's overt embrace of the lesbian community produced enormous brand image, user identity, and ideological-alignment value for this segment. The cars provided the same functional value (rugged, outdoorsy, all-wheel drive, roomy storage) that this group had always preferred. But the additional sources of value cemented the relationship. Subaru didn't just rainbow-wash its messaging. Rather, it provided genuine support for and recognition of the LGBTQ+ community at a time when few brands were willing to do so. And it worked. In the early 2000s, NPR's *Car Talk* ran a survey asking listeners to vote on the Ultimate Gay and Lesbian Cars of All Time. The top vote-getter was the Subaru Outback. The Subaru Forester came in second.[17] Subarus resonated so strongly with lesbians that at one point, they were four times (!) more likely to buy a Subaru than the average customer.[18] LGBTQ+ consumers became one of Subaru's largest customer segments. And in part because of its "Lesbaru" strategy (no, we did not make that term up), Subaru became the second-fastest-growing carmaker in the 2010s.[19]

With the perspective of years, Subaru's strategy is widely praised as groundbreaking. But it is important to remember the enormous potential for intersegment conflict that a strategy targeting the lesbian segment *could* have generated, especially at that time. Remember, this marketing strategy was executed in the 1990s, decades before brands started seeing LGBTQ+ customers as a marketing opportunity and well before it became common for brands to rainbow-ify their logos and social media for the month of June. This was the era of "Don't Ask, Don't Tell" and the Defense of Marriage Act. Ellen DeGeneres starred in her own sitcom in 1997. When the character she played came out as gay, major companies—including car brands—pulled their advertising from the show.[20] There was real risk of backlash.

So how was Subaru able to pull off an outreach strategy without significant blowback, decades before a seemingly similar strategy blew up so spectacularly for Bud Light? It wasn't just good luck. Before embarking on this strategy, executives assessed the potential for intersegment conflict. They concluded that the other Subaru customer segments they served (all those outdoorsy doctors, teachers, and rugged individualists) were not likely to be offended if the brand overtly marketed to lesbians. Yes, they anticipated that some people would react negatively—and they did—but they realized that those threatening a boycott were not Subaru customers and probably never would have been anyway. In fact, according to later reporting, some of the angry letters admonishing Subaru for its LGBTQ+ marketing efforts had spelled the brand's name wrong.[21] Actual Subaru customers were simply unfazed by the brand's inclusive marketing. They were just as unbothered by driving the same Outbacks and Foresters that lesbians liked, as they were sharing the same hiking trails and dog parks with them.

Subaru's lesbian-oriented marketing worked for two reasons that link explicitly back to the Segment Compatibility Matrix. First, the Subaru customer base happened to be one that was pro- (or at least not anti-) LGBTQ+ rights. In other words, their orientation toward the lesbian customer segment was somewhere between positive and indifferent. This reduced the risk of user identity and ideological conflict. Second, in catering to lesbian customers, Subaru didn't change anything about its cars or take away the value that other customer segments derived from its vehicles. The different Subaru customer segments derived the same functional value from the vehicles, and the additional value Subaru provided lesbians was independent of that functional value. This reduced the risk of functional conflict and brand image conflict. Subaru understood its customer segments, what each of them valued, and what additional value it could offer each group of customers without ruffling the feathers of other segments. As a result, Subaru was able to successfully grow the brand within the Separate Communities quadrant of the matrix. By knowing its customers so well, and what value each derived from the brand, Subaru made a well-informed bet that the strategy was not going to cause conflict, even if it might have looked like a big gamble from the outside.

Brands can anticipate and evaluate the risks of conflict like Subaru did by focusing on three prerequisites for devising effective growth strategies. We feel so strongly about the three imperatives for anticipating conflict that we have phrased them as King James–style commandments:

- **Know thy customer.** To effectively serve multiple segments, a brand must understand each customer segment, what is important to it, and how each segment's values are likely to interact with those of the other segments.

- **Know thy brand.** A brand must understand its history and meaning—from the perspectives of its customers (i.e., not the history and meaning from the perspective of the brand's managers).

- **Know thy marketplace.** Risk of conflict will always be a function of the various competitive, economic, and technological forces that shape how a brand competes with its rivals. Understanding the context is thus an imperative for assessing the risks of conflict.

Know Thy Customer

We cannot overstate how crucial it is to understand both the value customers derive from the brand, and the orientation they are likely to have toward the brand's other customer segments. These two pieces of information are the backbone of the Segment Compatibility Matrix. Achieving this kind of thorough understanding of customer segments is not easy. But two simple steps can help:

1. Define customer segments based on the value they derive from the brand's offerings.

2. Give segments names that intuitively communicate that source of value.

Brand managers can use the four sources of intersegment conflict as a guide for evaluating the different value customers derive from a brand's product or services. Specifically:

Functional. What functional value does this customer segment get from the brand's products and services, if any?

Brand image. What value does this customer segment derive from the brand's meaning or image, such as emotional or psychological value, if any?

User identity. What identity-signaling value does this customer segment get from the brand, if any?

Ideological. What ideological value does this customer segment have that might intersect with the brand, if any?

Answering these questions for current and prospective customer segments can help a brand begin the process of assessing the risks of conflict between segments. Of course, this process requires having already defined customer segments in such a way that it is easy to determine the key benefits they derive or reasons they use the product or service. Too often, we see brands characterize their customer segments demographically, claiming to target "new parents," "college-aged women," or "Gen Z." Don't do this. Demographics-based segmentation is almost always a terrible idea because demographics almost never correlate well with what people want. For almost any type of product or service, most demographic segments have a diversity of preferences.

We all intuitively understand this principle—at least we do when we are not being marketers. To illustrate the point, consider any high school. High schools are generally demographically circumscribed: small range of ages, tiny geography, often a relatively narrow socioeconomic span. But if John Hughes movies like *The Breakfast Club*, *Ferris Bueller's Day Off*, and *Sixteen Candles* have taught us anything, it's that within this homogenous demography, there is a diverse ecosystem of jocks, cheerleaders, motorheads, geeks, and stoners. Think of your own high school experience. Did everyone at your high school listen to the same music? Have the same hobbies? Wear the same brands of clothes? If someone wouldn't be able to accurately predict your preferences by knowing which high school you attended, how much less accurate will our predictions be with more general demographic descriptors, like "young men, aged fifteen to twenty"?

It's even worse when marketers try to target entire generations. Gen Z, as a group, doesn't have a consistent set of preferences. Millennials, statistically, don't have coherent needs. And Alphas are not a singular consumer segment. Each of these groups is staggeringly diverse. And how could they not be? There is nothing useful that can be said about *everyone* born within a fifteen-year time span. You might as well try to target an astrological sign.

Seeing customers through a demographics-only lens can leave brands far less capable of anticipating conflict. Imagine a brand manager selling a line of fashionable watches who has defined the brand's target customer as "twenty-five-to-forty-year-old working professionals who make over $100,000 a year." The watches have sold well to this demographic, and the company is looking to expand. So, the brand manager suggests expanding to a new demographic: "eighteen-to-twenty-one-year-old college students." Because she's smart, and has read through the first several chapters of this book, this brand manager considers whether targeting this new segment might create any type of conflict with the existing customers and concludes . . . probably not?

She should have read through this chapter, too. Young professionals and college students are not natural enemies. There is no reason to worry about conflict based on these demographic descriptors alone. It is not until our smart brand manager can articulate the values, preferences, and beliefs that each segment holds that she is able to assess the risk of conflict. It is only after she understands the problems each segment is trying to solve that she can identify potential functional conflicts; only after she understands the identity benefits (if any) that these segments gain from the offering that she can assess the risk of identity conflict; only after she understands the segments' deep cultural, moral, political, and religious values that she can anticipate ideological conflict. None of that is clear from the demographics.

If our brand manager had dug in, she might have discovered that the core segment of young professionals valued the watch as a status symbol, signaling a transition to independence and establishing oneself as a working adult. If that were the major source of value, then selling the same brand in large numbers to college students could very well lead to user identity conflict (professionals may not want to be associated with younger students) or brand image conflict (they may come to see the brand as less sophisticated and adult if it comes to be associated with frat parties and weekend tailgating). On the other hand, if both segments mostly liked the watch for its functional value (sleek design, reasonable price, etc.), then the risk of potential conflict goes way down. Again, demographics alone are seldom enough to diagnose the potential for conflict.

So, you need to be more specific in your segmentation. But there is a risk of getting too specific, even with value-based segmentation. If you try to convey an entire personality or set of preferences, you can end up with something needlessly granular. Creating customer segmentations based on very detailed personas or archetypes makes more work for marketers without offering additional useful or actionable insights. Without calling out any specific companies, in our work, we have encountered brands that have used segment descriptions, sometimes called personas, very similar to the following: "Patrick: a middle-aged working dad who lives in the suburbs and enjoys spending time with his family. He is an accountant with a dog and a cat and loves to play video games after he puts the kids down for the night." Or "Felix: a work-hard/play-hard, high-income-but-not-yet-rich professional with no kids and an active lifestyle. He is active in politics, which skew conservative, and loves golf." While more multidimensional than demographics alone, the personas that brands create still often fail to communicate the most important piece of information: *why* the customer would choose or not choose your brand! Based on the description of the consumers in the Patrick segment, what type of messaging would be most likely to convince them? If someone were to redesign a product or service for the consumers in the Felix segment, what changes would most improve their customer experience? Without knowing what motivates their decision-making or what specific benefits they're looking for, personas are just a creative-writing exercise for marketers who secretly wish they were working on screenplays instead of segmentation schemes.

Archetypal and persona-based segmentation descriptors can be particularly pernicious because they provide an illusion of insight and depth for marketing teams. The ease with which employees can visualize the general customer type makes it feel like they have a deep understanding of the customer. But they don't. Or at least, not an understanding that is useful for assessing the risks of conflict between customer segments. Even just pushing slightly harder to pin down exactly what value the customer type wants from the brand causes this type of segmentation to break down, revealing the lack of insight it provides for product and service management.

We are not arguing that demographics have no place in segmentation and targeting. Far from it. Knowing your customers' demographic and psychographic profiles is vital for selecting the right media and retail channels for reaching them. It can also be useful for creating resonant messaging and other marketing tactics, such as Subaru did with its lesbian customer base. Further, some needs only exist within certain demographic groups. It was probably mostly the male demographic that was interested in the "more masculine" diet soda craze of the late 2000s that led to the launch of options like Coke Zero, Pepsi Maxx, and Dr. Pepper TEN.

But recognizing that it is overwhelmingly men whose masculinity is threatened by a Diet Coke is *not* the same thing as defining a segment as "men" in strictly demographic terms. A need may exist primarily within a demographic group. But your target is people with that need, not the entire demographic. So, the better, more efficient way to group potential customers is according to what they *want*. A good rule of thumb is that when a description of a segment includes demographic information, it should also always include a relative pronoun: "who" or "that" or "which." The target segment for Coke Zero wasn't all men, but instead might have been described as men who want a diet soda but are too insecure to drink a Diet Coke.

Segments also need to be labeled intuitively, in a way that clearly communicates the value they seek. Recall the way we labeled Starbucks's customer segments: "third placers," "on-the-goers," and "Starbies." We chose those names to succinctly describe what each customer segment values in Starbucks. Those labels clearly indicate the user type, the benefits sought, and/or the use occasion for each segment, all of which link up to the value each customer segment seeks from Starbucks. These labels make it easier to intuit whether there are risks of conflict, or how segments might interact with or influence one another. Likewise, if we were to ask someone to try to improve Starbucks coffeehouses or products to better serve one of these segments, or what changes to the offerings might erode value for these customer groups, based on the descriptions of the segments, it should be fairly easy for that person to quickly generate ideas.

Some organizations make things needlessly difficult for the marketing team by picking entirely uninformative labels such as colors, animals, or simply the names of products they consume. This would be like McDonald's defining the target customers for its various offerings as "Big Mac customers" and "McNugget customers." (Note: as far as we know, McDonald's doesn't actually label segments this way.) Labels like these are terribly confusing for the people in marketing and branding who have to reinterpret segment meanings each time they try to apply them. The additional logical leaps required in moving from unintuitive segmentation labels to what a segment values invite endless assumptions and miscommunications, creating a game of telephone within the organization. And making it hard to intuit whether there is a risk of intersegment conflict.

Maybe frequently digging through old PowerPoint decks to remind yourself of the difference between a "Patrick" and a "Felix" or a "red" versus a "blue" customer is your idea of fun. If it isn't, defining customers based on the value they seek, and labeling them accordingly, can save time and headaches. The labels don't have to be long or complex, but they should describe customers' needs and preferences. (See table 11-1.)

TABLE 11-1

Segment descriptions

Brand	Bad segment description	Better segment description	Useful segment label
Coke Zero	Men, aged 18–28	Men aged 18–28 who are too insecure to drink a diet soda because they think diet sodas are for girls	Insecure men
Starbucks	Young urban professionals	Young urban professionals who are looking for a place outside the house and office to work, socialize, or relax	Third placers
Starbucks	Young urban professionals	Young, urban professionals who want fast, convenient, and reliable coffee	On-the-goers
Crocs	Boaters, gardeners, health-care workers, kids	People who value comfort and practical utility over fashion	Feel goods
Subaru	Lesbians	Lesbians who want a car that fits their love for an active, outdoorsy lifestyle	Outdoorsy lesbians
LEGO	Adults	Adults who are looking to recapture the fun and challenge of building LEGO models that reflect their current interests	Adult fans of LEGO (AFOL)

After segments are defined and labels are assigned based on customer value (i.e., based on how they are making decisions), brands
can more easily evaluate risks of conflict between segments. For
example, Starbucks can look at the third placers and on-the-goers
and better intuit the Venn diagram of what segments want from
their local coffeehouse, and where incompatibilities may arise. (See
figure 11-1.) Subaru can determine the compatibility of creating
more value for outdoorsy lesbians versus rugged individualists. And

FIGURE 11-1

Customer segment values Venn diagrams

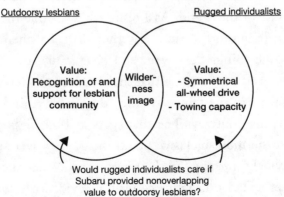

Starbucks third placers versus on-the-goers

Third placers — Low-risk place to add value — On-the-goers

Value: Quaint coffeehouse atmosphere

Value: High-quality coffee

Value: Fast and efficient service

Would satisfying either of these conflict with the other?

Subaru outdoorsy lesbians versus rugged individualists

Outdoorsy lesbians — Rugged individualists

Value: Recognition of and support for lesbian community

Wilderness image

Value:
- Symmetrical all-wheel drive
- Towing capacity

Would rugged individualists care if Subaru provided nonoverlapping value to outdoorsy lesbians?

Crocs can more readily anticipate that feel goods and explorers are likely to be indifferent to one another.

Where there are open questions about whether brands might risk conflict, value-based labels also make it easier for brands to know where to dig in or which customers to talk to in order to learn more, and when to use good old-fashioned market research. When Subaru was considering whether to provide more ideological and identity value to its segment of lesbian customers by actively supporting the LGBTQ+ community, it knew it had to check its other wilderness-oriented segments for potential user identity and ideological conflict. Sometimes, risks of conflict can be easily intuited—such as with serving third placers and on-the-goers at Starbucks—but other times, it requires research. Sometimes, you need to ask segments how they would feel if the brand was more explicitly aligned with the values of a particular segment, or if it catered to a certain segment's preferences. Bud Light's managers were very open about their strategy for moving the brand in a more inclusive, pro-LGBTQ+ direction. What they apparently never bothered to do was go out and ask their large, loyal customer base how *they* felt about that move. Doing so might have saved them a lot of regret.

One explanation for why these missteps are so common is that brand managers often project their own beliefs onto customers. They fall into the trap of what's called "naive realism," or the tendency for individuals to believe their perception of the world is the objective state of the world. As a result, they assume their customers see their brand in the same way they do. That their customers want the same things they want and have values that align with their values. And they assume that their customers view other customer segments in the same way they do. Naive realism can resist evidence to the contrary. The managers at Bud Light seemed to believe that the more inclusive brand image they were promoting would be widely appealing to their customers. When the Schumer-Rogen ads provided some rather compelling evidence to the contrary, they seemed to have largely ignored that message. Ultimately, what

DO YOU KNOW YOUR CUSTOMER?

1. Have you identified the key value(s) that customers derive from your brands? Have you created segments around those distinct values?

2. Do the labels you use for your customer segments intuitively convey the specific sources of value each segment finds in your brand?

3. How actively do you seek feedback from customers to get an accurate sense of the value they receive from your brand? Are there established channels for ongoing communication to ensure your understanding of their preferences remains current?

4. Does providing value to one or more customer segments negatively affect the ability for any other segments to get the functional, brand image, identity, or ideological value they want from the brand?

the folks at corporate think the brand stands for, or who they think would be OK with including or not including in the brand community, is irrelevant. It is the *customer's* perspective of the brand, and who *they* think it should serve and not serve that matters.

Know Thy Brand

Knowing your brand in the context of anticipating conflict requires:

- Understanding what your brand means to customers at the segment level

- Determining the "stretchability" of your brand's meaning to include new customer segments and their values, preferences, and—in some cases—ideologies

First, brand managers must do the legwork (i.e., the market research) required to understand what their brand means to customers, both current and prospective. It's not enough for brands to establish a clear understanding of their positioning, meaning, or purpose internally. They also need to determine whether that understanding of the brand is shared externally by their customers. The most useful way to think of a brand is as a memory structure that exists in the minds of consumers. Whatever it is that people think and feel when they think of your brand, *that* is the brand.

Consumers don't make purchasing decisions based on how a brand perceives itself. They don't care how sexy, innovative, or joyful the brand's marketers think the brand is. The opinions of the people who work for the brand are irrelevant. Consumers make decisions based on *their* perceptions of the brand. They sense conflict based on how *they* use and perceive the brand—and how *they* see other people using the brand. Because of this, understanding what the brand means to different customer segments, and what they perceive to be as consonant or dissonant with that meaning, is a prerequisite for anticipating conflict between customer segments. This requires going out and talking to customers, conducting sentiment analyses on social media, using surveys and instruments to track perception over time, and so on.

Next, it's important to assess the brand's ability to stretch its meaning to include new customer segments and all that is associated with them. Sometimes, the meaning of a brand can be construed such that it naturally makes new customer segments compatible with existing segments, thereby reducing the risk of alienating current customers. Brands can increase their stretchiness when they construct a more abstract, less concrete brand image. When the North Face extended from outdoor apparel to streetwear, it ran the risk of disaffecting its core group of outdoor adventurers in pursuit of a segment more focused on looking good when walking around a city. The North Face tried to reduce the likelihood of these segments having to fight over the meaning of the brand by repositioning the brand around a value both segments could hopefully get behind: "exploration."

In reference to its campaign aiming to attract urban-dwelling artist customer segments, the brand stated, "Whether you're a mountaineer or a musician, what connects us all as explorers is a shared mindset of curiosity paired with the courage to try something new. This campaign will work to expand that spirit of exploration through different cultural touch points in music and art as well as our traditional mountain sports."[22] The North Face reflected on its core values—the brand has used "Never Stop Exploring" as a tagline since 1988—and rearticulated them to include new customer segments, specifically urban explorers.[23] Linking customer segments through shared value creates a feeling of compatibility between customer segments by reducing the perceived divergence in what they value in the brand, allowing brands to grow to new audiences and launch new types of products without necessarily alienating existing customers or threatening the brand's authenticity or identity-signaling value.

However, there are limits to how far a brand can be believably stretched. When consumers receive new information about a brand, they compare that information with their existing beliefs about or attitudes toward the brand. In doing so, people essentially have a range or spectrum that consists of three zones—acceptance, neutrality, or rejection—that reflects the extent to which consumers see information as consistent with the brand image and thereby their likelihood of accepting it as part of the brand's image or meaning. When the North Face expanded the brand's meaning from "wilderness exploration" to "exploration" more broadly, the customer response indicates this move fell within the zone of acceptance. But we can imagine lots of ways the North Face could have pushed its brand's meaning that consumers would probably have been less willing to accept. If the North Face tried to expand the brand's meaning around something like performance and then created running shoes or a sports car, that would be confusing, at best. Or if it tried to stretch the concept of exploration to include the exploration of different social strata and so started selling a line of formal wear—tuxedos, formal gowns, tiaras—this would likely fall into the zone of rejection for both current and prospective customers.

Knowing the boundaries of a brand's meaning, and what claims or positioning would likely fall into the zone of rejection for consumers, can help marketers anticipate conflict that might arise from trying to fit a new customer segment under the brand umbrella. A brand's stretchiness is a function of its original positioning and purpose as well as everything it has done since. Ideally, brands can seek feedback from existing customers to assess the extent to which new brand meanings feel natural and authentic, or fit with existing understandings of the brand before introducing them to the market. (Pro tip: founders can do themselves a favor by considering stretchability when creating new brands. Brands should be like spandex: they should fit tightly around your initial customer base but also be conceptually stretchy enough to accommodate future growth.)

Some indicators of the stretchability of a brand include the extent to which a brand is positioned as inclusive versus exclusive, the abstractness versus concreteness of a brand's meaning or positioning, the variety of the brand's current portfolio of goods and services, and the versatility of a brand's offerings for different use occasions. Brands that are positioned as more inclusive tend to be more stretchable than those that are positioned as exclusive. Consider Crocs, which is marketed as explicitly inclusive. Everybody should feel comfortable in their own shoes, according to Crocs. The inclusivity of the brand is a key buffer against intersegment conflict. There are few new customer segments that could create conflict for current Crocs wearers. It's hard to imagine one Crocs wearer scoffing at another Crocs wearer as not being a *real* Crocs fan. Of course, inclusive brands come with their own risks: sometimes a brand for everyone can feel like a brand for no one. This is part of the trade-off. Exclusive brands have the advantage of cultivating a stronger connection with specific segments but usually have an increased risk of intersegment conflict as the brand tries to grow. Luxury brands must constantly balance the benefits of being exclusive (i.e., charging a price premium) with the downsides of being exclusive (i.e., limited ability to grow without creating conflict).

Brands that are defined more abstractly also tend to be stretchier than brands defined concretely. If the North Face defined itself as a brand that "sells outdoors apparel," it would be difficult to convincingly stretch the brand to the streetwear space. By having a more abstract positioning around exploration, the brand evokes a broader concept that can more flexibly extend to new categories. Similarly, Uber could very concretely define itself as a "taxi service," as it did early on, but this would make it difficult for the brand to convince consumers it can play in other realms of transportation and delivery. But by broadening its positioning to be a "delivery service for people and things," and eventually as a "technology and logistics company," it made it easier for Uber to grow through new categories with extensions such as Uber Eats, Uber Connect, and Uber Freight.[24] The benefit of a very concretely defined brand is that it is typically tightly connected with a specific product or service, which makes it easier for customers to understand the offering. Consumers know what to expect from Tesla if the brand defines itself as one that "sells electric vehicles." But the benefit of a more abstractly defined brand is the ability to grow through new customer segments or into new categories while avoiding intersegment conflict or brand confusion. Tesla can grow in other categories more easily if it redefines itself as an "innovative clean energy company."

Finally, variety and versatility of offerings are additional indicators of the ability to stretch a brand without creating conflict. (See figure 11-2.) By adding new products and services over time (music retail, air travel, mobile phone service, casinos, wines, and commercial space flight), Virgin has expanded the meaning of its brand

FIGURE 11-2

How stretchy is your brand?

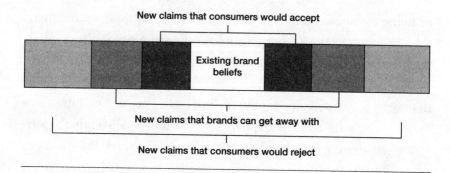

to the point where it could accommodate nearly anything. Under Armour initially built its brand around a specialty athletic fabric designed to be worn under football pads—hence the name. But this material, specially designed to wick sweat, feel light, and keep players cool on the field, had category-spanning potential. Once the T-shirts caught on in the football category, other athletes and coaches wanted the HeatGear to stay cool during their training and performing. The versatility of the materials—and UA's broadly defined purpose of empowering athletes—made it easy for the

DO YOU KNOW YOUR BRAND?

1. What is the meaning of your brand to customers?

2. Are there ways you can make the meaning or purpose of your brand more abstract, general, or encompassing to serve new customer segments?

3. Is your brand positioned as inclusive or exclusive? How does that influence which new customer segments you can reasonably attract without generating conflict?

brand to stretch (literally and figuratively) into new categories without creating brand image or identity conflict. Now, UA also sells ColdGear and AllSeasonGear for helping athletes stay comfortable in cold and moderate conditions, further expanding the meaning of the brand.

Know Thy Marketplace

Assessing the risks of conflict also requires awareness of relevant societal, political, cultural, environmental, and competitive forces that might influence intersegment relationships. Conflict, like most things, is contextual. Knowing the prevailing winds is vital for anticipating intersegment conflict. The backlash Bud Light faced for supporting the transgender community in 2023 was, in our opinion, at least partly the result of timing. The political and cultural zeitgeist of that moment made the T part of LGBTQ+ a political lightning rod. It is possible that similar marketing initiatives, had they come several years earlier or later, might have generated less conflict.

But the risks of conflict aren't just a matter of what topics are trending in political discourse. Risk also depends on other marketplace factors, too, such as the presence or absence of competition. The strength of direct competitors within a market segment determines how substitutable a brand's offering is for customers, which is a vital predictor of the risks and consequences of intersegment conflict. Brands that provide nonsubstitutable offerings generally run a lower risk of driving customers away when conflict occurs between customer segments. For example, brands like the NFL can risk more conflict between its customer segments because there are no real substitutes for their product in the market. NFL fans who are agitated by conflict with other segments could abandon the brand. But would they? Are they really going to stop supporting their beloved Cowboys or Patriots and switch to watching the Canadian

Football League instead? Probably not. The enormous market power of the NFL gives it far more freedom than most brands to court conflict in the service of reinforcing its brand image or appealing to new segments. We will dive deeper into how the NFL has done just this in a future chapter.

When intersegment conflict occurs in a highly competitive market, on the other hand, consumers have a wide range of alternative brands they can buy instead. The conflict between old and new Starbucks customers became increasingly problematic as competitors tried to siphon off segments that were suddenly less happy. For many years, Starbucks was essentially the only game in town for coffee fancier than drip brewed. During that time, the risks of conflict were low. After all, where might those customers experiencing conflict go? But then shops like Dunkin' and McDonald's McCafé upgraded and expanded their coffee and non-coffee-drink menus to pull in the on-the-goers and Starbies. And brands like Peet's and Caribou Coffee created specialized atmospheres to better serve third placers and coffee sophisticates. As a result of changes in the competitive marketplace, the need to resolve conflicts became more pressing for Starbucks as substitutes became more available for each customer segment.

But substitutability alone is not enough to predict the risks of conflict. Brands also must consider switching costs or how costly it is—in terms of time, money, or effort—for customers to switch to an available substitute. For example, in the case of Subaru, yes, cars are highly substitutable, but there are also high switching costs, especially over a short time horizon. (We could find no examples of people setting their own cars on fire in protest.) Even if lesbian-focused marketing had created intersegment conflict, its immediate impact would be lessened by the high switching costs of getting rid of a car and buying a new one.

On the other hand, beer is highly substitutable, and the switching costs required for buying a new brand of beer are negligible. Sure, many people, through loyalty or habit, tend to stick to the same brand. But there are lots of other options out there if a beer brand ever does something a customer doesn't like. In fact, researchers have found, repeatedly, that beer drinkers who are loyal to a particular brand of beer cannot identify that beer in a blind taste test.[25] So Bud Light drinkers obviously valued Bud Light's *brand*, since they—empirically—were not drinking it for the taste. Thus, when Bud Light waded into conflict by hiring Dylan Mulvaney as a brand ambassador, it was easy for dissenting customers to just pour out their Bud Lights and switch to something else. Did these unhappy customers have to react performatively on social media? No. Did they have to destroy cases of beer in violent ways to demonstrate their disagreement? Also no. But the point is that it was easy for unhappy customers to ditch the brand and find another go-to beer. The more substitutable a product or service and the lower the switching costs, the larger the risk of driving customers away because of intersegment conflict.

Substitutability and switching costs also partly explain why boycotts typically don't result in deleterious long-term outcomes for brands. The effectiveness of boycotts usually lies in generating negative buzz around the brand, not typically in sales over time.[26] Most

DO YOU KNOW YOUR MARKETPLACE?

1. To what extent are hot-button political, social, or cultural topics relevant and important to the segments you serve or want to serve? Are any of your segments, or potential segments, on opposite sides of these topics? How relevant are they to your brand or messaging?

2. How substitutable is your offering?

3. To what extent are the switching costs for consuming an alternative to your offering low or high?

boycotts work as PR stunts but tend not to work as actual boycotts that affect long-term sales. Part of this is because if it makes consumers' lives harder or more inconvenient to shop for a different brand, or if they can't find the value the brand offers elsewhere, then consumers will usually come back at some point, if they leave at all. Bud Light was a rare example of an effective boycott, which resulted in sales declines of 25 percent to 30 percent each month for several months after the initial blowup.[27] But, beer is a uniquely high-volume, frequently purchased, low-switching-cost, near-commodity product. The consequences of conflict were bound to be greater.

12

Avoiding and Escaping Conflict

Why Scandinavian Couples Sleep Better

In 2003, a group of young men referring to themselves as "The Burberry Boys" rioted at an English soccer game, attacking a bus full of Turkish fans while wearing Burberry hats, shoes, and jackets. The following year, at least two pubs in Leicester told their staff to turn away anyone wearing the iconic check pattern.[1] The ban was not limited to rowdy-looking young men in baggy Burberry tracksuits. Young women were turned away for the sin of carrying handbags or umbrellas festooned with the "chav check."[2] The "chav" is a variety of soccer hooligan, typically young and less affluent, with preferences for hanging out at small-town shopping centers, smoking cigarettes, and intimidating people, and at least in the early 2000s, with a strong preference for wearing as much Burberry as they could layer on.

A brand's meaning is not dictated by the company that owns it. Instead, it's the result of an ongoing negotiation between the company and the public. Burberry could poshly insist that its brand symbolized timeless elegance and high-class sophistication. But its widespread adoption by a group more inclined toward fistfights and vandalism than high tea and foxhunting suggested otherwise.

As if an association with chav culture was not enough of a headache for the brand, Burberry was also simultaneously becoming strongly associated with another set of customers that were nearly as problematic: old, boring people. Burberry's traditional customers were aging, making the brand feel stodgy and out of touch—at least to customer segments not busy throwing bricks at rival soccer fans' buses. Burberry had built its brand by associating its trademark trench coats with the British royal family, the British military, and movie stars like Humphrey Bogart, Lauren Bacall, and Audrey Hepburn. But anyone who still valued those decades-old associations did not belong to the cool, hip, and wealthy customer base Burberry would need to attract to maintain itself as a high-fashion brand.

Burberry had also spent years boosting its profits through broad international licensing deals. This led to high variability in price, design, and quality of goods sold under the Burberry logo. Lax oversight also contributed to many counterfeit products flooding the market. Burberry's reputation for high-quality goods was challenged due to cheap, internationally licensed products being purchased by segments with significantly lower willingness to pay for what was intended to be a luxury brand. Moreover, its image as a quintessentially British brand was diluted as it became more popular internationally, particularly among Asian consumers.

Once renowned for quality craftsmanship, timeless elegance, and an authentic British appeal, Burberry became associated with, in no particular order, soccer hooliganism, stodginess, and Asian tourists. It was a hearty stew of identity and brand image conflict.

Burberry desperately needed to find a path forward that would grow the brand—via both large and promising international markets, and young consumers who would be its next loyal customer base—without losing control of the brand or alienating current customers. Somewhat miraculously, Burberry clawed its way out of this conundrum, but it required making a few bold strategic moves.

First, Burberry moved to reduce both user identity and brand image conflict by creating sub-brands that focused on different styles and price levels. Sub-brands created observable and psychological boundaries between different customer segments that might not be interested in sharing the brand with each other. A new, premium line was created called Burberry Prorsum (named after the Latin word for "forward," which is written on the pennant waving above the knight in Burberry's iconic 1901 logo). This label included hand-tailored, innovative pieces intended for runway shows and very limited distribution. Burberry also launched Burberry Bespoke to try to lure back wealthier customers. Bespoke gave patrons the ability to customize garments, beginning with trench coats. Customers could choose different cuts, fabrics, colors, and embellishments for their coat, which could range from about $1,800 to nearly $9,000 depending on the combination of elements a customer put together.[3]

Below these lines was Burberry Brit, which included the brand's classic line of trench coats, accessories, and other fashion staples. The most casual and least expensive rung on the brand ladder (relatively speaking) was Burberry London. Burberry's sub-brand strategy allowed the brand to create vertical differentiation among customers. The Prorsum and Bespoke lines catered to wealthy, high-status, highly fashionable customers who might become a Leader segment that less wealthy London and Brit customers would want to follow and emulate. Even just the existence of the Prorsum and Bespoke labels, regardless of how many customers bought them, created the perception of a Leader segment in the brand, making the less expensive Brit or London labels more attractive to Follower customer segments.

Burberry also created lower-priced labels such as Thomas Burberry, Burberry Blue, and Burberry Black specifically for international markets. These brands offered more localized collections, giving

Burberry the ability to capitalize on its international popularity without posing a threat to the perceived Britishness of the flagship brand. For example, Blue and Black were exclusive to Japan and offered designs that were more modern and mixed traditional and urban elements. These sub-brands were part of the new brand hierarchy at Burberry and helped the brand create separation between its British and international customers.

Most dramatically, and painfully, Burberry addressed user identity conflict by firing customer segments. A lot of the strain on the brand was due to current and potential customers not wanting to be associated with some groups that had started wearing lots of Burberry (while starting bar fights, in some cases). So, Burberry started pruning its customer base. It discontinued several of its most popular offerings, including its line of check baseball caps, due to their particularly strong association with raucous soccer fans. The brand took greater control of licensing and distribution to ensure more consistency within the brand and to restore its authentic luxury image. In effect, the brand broke up with some of its most enthusiastic buyers. By restricting supply, Burberry told the chavs and some international customers that it did not want to be their brand anymore. Of course, firing these customer segments meant forgoing the money these segments were spending on the brand. This is often why brands hesitate to fire customer segments. But had Burberry not taken such severe action, it could have lost even more money from customers defecting from the brand or the brand losing its relevancy with luxury and British consumers.

Burberry sought to further limit user identity conflict by changing the design strategy of the brand from "broadcasting" to "narrowcasting." Specifically, Burberry reduced the number of items featuring the check print from 20 percent of its portfolio to 5 percent, and it implemented a "check under cover" strategy that retained the iconic design in more subtle ways, making it more valuable by making it less visible.[4] Researchers have documented that as a brand's offerings get more expensive, the branding tends to get more subtle.[5] Burberry deliberately made its offerings less useful to those who wanted to broadcast their association with the brand, shifting to more subtle branding that would only be appreciated by customers who wanted to signal to other "in the know" fashionable sophisticates.

If we zoom out, we see that Burberry used three core strategies to escape conflict:

- Cultivating Separate Communities within its customer base

- Defining Leaders and Followers more clearly

- Firing customer segments that were creating conflict with the segments it wanted to keep

Before we expand on these and other strategies for pulling a brand out of intersegment conflict, it is worth noting our lack of distinction between avoiding conflict and escaping conflict, from a tactical perspective. A brand can avoid conflict by identifying the risks and taking action to diffuse conflict before it arrives. That's great. Alternatively, a brand could, like Burberry, find itself waist-deep in conflict and need a way out of the morass. But the actions a brand would take in either instance are likely to be the same. Had Burberry seen problems coming, it might have reasonably headed off conflict by creating sub-brands to establish boundaries between segments, letting go of product lines and distribution channels favored by potential customers it wanted to avoid, and so on. As you go through this chapter, you will see many examples of brands that, like Burberry, dug their way out of conflict. There are fewer examples of brands that avoided conflict before it came, simply because those counterfactuals are harder to identify: conflict avoided is usually invisible to people outside the company. The *Wall Street Journal* doesn't publish many articles about how smoothly everything is going for a brand because of the conflict it avoided between customer segments. But the tactics outlined in this chapter should work for conflict prophylaxis as well as for conflict treatment.

Strategy 1: Cultivate Separate Communities

The most straightforward strategy for avoiding or escaping conflict between Incompatible Segments is to create distance or separation between them within the brand. (See figure 12-1.) In some cases, keeping otherwise incompatible customer segments apart from each other can help create a more indifferent relationship between them, allowing them to exist as Separate Communities. For example, consider a married couple, sleeping soundly except for the moments when they tug the blankets back and forth between them. Each time one person pulls the covers toward them to grab more warmth, it leaves the other shivering in the cold. Incompatible blanket segments. The couple *could* just keep fighting the blanket battle each night, inching their way closer to divorce with every night's lack of REM sleep. *Or* they could borrow a page from the Scandinavian sleep method and use two individual duvets rather than sharing one. Now, Separate (cozy) Communities. Relationship restored; marriage saved. (No wonder Scandinavian countries regularly top the list for happiest countries on earth.) Anyway, back to brands.

FIGURE 12-1

Segment Compatibility Matrix: Moving from Incompatible Segments to Separate Communities

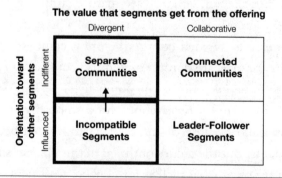

Tactics for creating separation between customer segments include talking to customer segments in different ways via different communications channels, creating different distribution channels for different types of customers, offering different products or services designed to fit the needs of different customer segments, or developing sub-brands to allow for symbolically different offerings. Ideally, brand managers can deploy more than one of these distancing tactics simultaneously to maximize the separation between conflict-prone customer segments.

Separate messaging

Creating distinct messages for channels geared toward a particular customer segment is probably the most common and least costly way to create separation between customer segments. This tactic was much easier to implement before the internet. Marketers in the pre-historicinternet age could craft messages for different channels—print media, radio, and television—that they knew would primarily reach only one segment or another. Messaging for older customer segments could run during *Matlock* reruns, and ads intended to attract tech-savvy customers could be placed in *Wired*, without fear that other segments might see the communications and get riled up or confused by the messaging.

A particularly memorable example of avoiding conflict by using siloed communications channels is BMW Films. In 2001, marketers at BMW green-lit a series of short films to showcase the cars in an entertaining way that would reinforce its "ultimate driving machine" image and inspire the next generation of BMW drivers. Each film featured a high-profile director and A-list actors. Each was a stand-alone story that varied in intensity, suspense, and storytelling. The films were a cinematic feat that pioneered a new kind of branding: *advertainment*.

The campaign also ran a real risk of producing user identity and brand image conflict. Some of the films featured BMW cars being driven recklessly, getting smashed, and taking gunfire. One was a short film directed by Alejandro González Iñárritu, the Mexican filmmaker who would later go on to win the Academy Award for Best Director for both *Birdman* and *The Revenant*. In the tense and graphically violent *Powder Keg*, a driver, played by Clive Owen, desperately drives a critically wounded reporter, played by Stellan Skarsgård, across the countryside of an unnamed South American country, trying to escape the army of a corrupt political regime. In his history of BMW, author David Kiley describes the visual effect of the film, noting that the blood is "almost black in the sharply contrasted production, [as it] pools all over the X5's interior."

BMW's management rightly worried that some of its older, more conservative core customers could be offended or turned off by the edgy shorts. It was therefore crucial that the brand avoid intersegment conflict with its core of more affluent, conservative customers, as they tended to be the most profitable segment that purchased the most luxurious and profitable vehicles in the BMW fleet.

So, BMW released the films only online. That may not sound too clever, but this was in 2001. At the time, watching films online required a newer computer with a media viewer, and a broadband connection. In other words, it required technological know-how, time, and high internet bandwidth. All three of those prerequisites were uncommon at that time with the segment of older traditionalists that BMW wanted to avoid conflict with. They were far more likely to be found among young, potential BMW customers.

Among this audience, the films were a smashing success. Many viewers passed the films on, showing them to friends and coworkers, and almost 90 percent of visitors to the website requested additional films. Some have credited the campaign with sleeper-effect success years later, as those young people who patiently downloaded the films aspired to one day own a BMW when they could afford one. Importantly, BMW's target audience for the films also tended to be technologically oriented and valued BMW's focus on technology. Using the internet as a communication channel was thus not just a way to silo communications toward younger consumers but also reinforced a key positioning point for the brand. Meanwhile, most of BMW's older customer segments did not see the films; many did not even know they existed.[6]

Internet availability is no longer a viable way to screen customer segments, of course. For most consumers, the internet is ubiquitous, so this lightning-in-a-bottle ad campaign would be difficult to recreate. However, there are still some spaces that are more or less populated by some types of consumers than others. In the 2020s, luxury brands have used the metaverse (RIP) and TikTok in a similar way as BMW used the internet. Brands like Gucci, Louis Vuitton, and Prada have created metaverse experiences and TikTok content geared toward making the brand aspirational for young consumers in ways that would likely not resonate—and perhaps even create conflict with—their older, wealthier, more profitable segments.[7] These brands reasonably assumed that many of their older customers wouldn't know how to access the metaverse even if they wanted to.

That said, it is true that it is more difficult today to narrowly target communications to one customer segment without significant risk of those communications also reaching other customer segments. Paradoxically, there are ever more channels for targeting niche audiences—think of all the obscure websites and oddly specific Reddit groups out there—while at the same time, there are fewer and fewer channels through which brands can target their messaging without being exposed to audiences beyond that niche. Many brands have multiple social media accounts or handles for different types of audiences or special interest groups. But any general user can still see a brand's other handles. Following one of a brand's accounts will likely encourage the algorithms to serve up content from the others. This can be problematic if there is a risk of identity, ideological, or brand image conflict. And it only takes one person posting a screen grab or picture of a brand's messaging to make a brand's narrowly targeted content visible to a much wider audience.

That neatly sums up much of what drove conflict for Bud Light in 2023. For nearly two decades prior, Bud Light had sponsored Pride events in the United States and Canada and partnered with LGBTQ+ advocacy organizations like GLAAD. Bud Light created a campaign in 1998 supporting LGBTQ+ consumers called "Be Yourself" and ran print ads in national gay magazines. For the most part, these efforts went unseen, unnoticed, and unremarked upon by conservative or anti-LGBTQ+ Bud Light drinkers. Dissenters likely didn't attend the Pride Parades to witness Bud Light's participation. But in 2023, conservative consumers and media outlets shared and reposted influencer Dylan Mulvaney's Bud Light Instagram post. The siloed communication became mass communication, leading to intense vitriol toward Bud Light. Brands must face the reality that siloed communications, especially those that might generate conflict, can no longer be assumed.

Historically, when communications did stir up controversy, it was also difficult to mobilize groups or galvanize support for each side before the age of social media. In fact, religious leader Jerry Falwell did try to call for a boycott in response to the 1998 Bud Light ads, but his ability to stimulate widespread support was limited.[8] And Bud Light set up hotlines for people to call in to express their agreement or disagreement with the brand's LGBTQ+ advertising in response to Falwell's call for boycotts. But it was impossible to observe how many people were calling in on either side, and what they were saying.[9] So, conflict sputtered out quickly. Information—and outrage—could not be spread as efficiently or transparently then. Brand managers must be cognizant of this. No longer is it reasonable to assume a brand can get away with conveying one set of brand values to one consumer segment and another to a different consumer segment without the potential for cross-visibility.

To be clear, separate messaging and communications channels can still be part of a strategy to create space between segments. The risks come when the strategy relies on strict quarantining of messages from certain segments. But often segments are not turned off or angered when they discover messages directed at other segments; they just appreciate when they also receive separate communications directed at them and their needs. One interesting example of nonproblematic separate communications comes from Pedialyte. This electrolyte drink was developed to quickly and easily rehydrate children suffering from dehydration due to flu and stomach bugs. But the brand gained an underground following among adults as a hangover treatment.[10] Pedialyte saw this secondary segment as a market with real growth potential and so worked to embrace both segments but used separate messaging and communication channels to reach them. It continued to run ads directed at the parents of young children, which touted its number-one pediatrician recommendation. But it also started running ads showing bleary-eyed adults pouring themselves some Pedialyte in what was clearly the morning after a good time. These ads included taglines like "Save the day" and "The Secret to a Good Morning." There is no evidence that the parents segment was offended by the ads' winking references to hangovers—they may have even taken them as a signal of the effectiveness of Pedialyte for helping their sick kids. Even so, the separate communications undoubtedly helped define and create space between these two segments.

Separate distribution

Starbucks used a separate distribution strategy to diffuse functional conflict between segments. It introduced new store formats that catered to the distinct needs of different segments. The original "third place" cafés, with the oversize padded chairs and cozy dark wood paneling, continue to serve the third placers segment as places to leisurely work and socialize. But to reduce conflict, Starbucks invested in drive-through and small-format coffee shops in high-traffic areas, which are distinctly *not* third places for chilling out. These stores cater to the on-the-goers and the Starbies. Different store formats allow these segments to self-segregate, so they do not have to disrupt each other's experiences.

Starbucks also tried to win back the coffee sophisticates segment that helped launch the brand in the 1980s but that had more recently started defecting to other, more highbrow or "authentic" coffee-houses. To do this, Starbucks developed its Reserve line of premium coffee, and it created unique distribution points for sophisticates in new, separate spaces: Starbucks Reserve Stores, Reserve Bars, and Roasteries. Many locations feel different from the cookie-cutter third space stores. They're upscale with exclusive coffee options, be-spoke brewing techniques, fancier food offerings, and in some spots, even alcohol service. The atmospheres are carefully crafted with unique interior designs. Coffee preparation is front and center, with fully visible specialty equipment and baristas trained to describe the coffee blends with oenological-like sophistication: not with pumps of vanilla or hazelnut syrups, but specialty coffees with "floral aromas and lemon-pepper notes."[11] One reporter claimed that a Reserve Bar they visited felt more like an art gallery than a coffee shop. Another described the Reserve Bars as taking customers "on the entire coffee journey, from on-site roasting to specialty beverage menus, adventurous coffee flights, and learning how to create coffee concoctions from Certified Coffee Masters. From curated hammered copper fixtures to coffee-book libraries and mixologists splashing up coffee cocktails, it's java nirvana."[12] The existence of these locations also reinforces a premium brand image for Starbucks and cultivates a Leader customer segment with an aspirational air. Even the to-go coffee cups at Roastery bars have a different design and logo from those at a standard Starbucks.

Separate sub-brands

Just as Burberry did with its different clothing lines, and Starbucks did with its Roastery line, many brands create separate sub-brands to avoid or escape conflict between customer segments. A unique example of this strategy comes from Dow Corning, an industrial silicone producer.

Silicone is one of those basic additives that can be found in everything. Like, *everything*. It protects delicate electronics in computers and cell phones; it goes into paints, cables, medical implants, and waterproof fabrics. It is used as a sealant in construction, a lubricant for syringe needles, and it helps laundry detergents make whites whiter. It can be found in cosmetics and food. Apparently, it can be used to defoam flavor concentrates. We don't know what that means exactly, but silicone does it.

Industrial silicone is a good business to be in, and Dow Corning was the single largest provider.[13] But, as happens in most mature markets, lower-priced rivals edged in and started to put pressure on Dow Corning's margins. Across the markets it served, from automotive and aerospace, to health-care and household products, to food and beverage, customers were pushing back on Dow Corning's prices, threatening to go elsewhere to get a better deal. By 2001, it was losing money, despite its massive market share.

Dow Corning was in a bind. The brand was built around a high-touch, high-service model, providing its clients with testing, training, custom reformulations, specialized packaging, and consulting on new product development. This white-glove service came at a premium price. Lots of expensive overhead, including all those PhDs in chemistry and materials science, and the equipment to support them; lots of specialized manufacturing, packaging, and shipping apparatus, were part of the business model. Historically, customers had been happy to pay. But there were some customers who just didn't need the bells and whistles, and they didn't want to pay for them anymore. These customers wanted standard materials in standard sizes without any additional services. Just the silicone, please. Increasingly, competitors could provide that level of (non-)service at a much lower price.

Dow Corning needed to escape functional conflict between customer segments. But its current business model would not allow it to serve both groups well simultaneously. If it stuck with the expensive high level of service, it would continue to lose customers. Competing on price would alienate most of its high-touch customers who spent a lot with the company. It would also require a wholesale reconfiguration of the company into a no-frills commodity supplier to operate on those lower margins. That would also demand a massive change of culture. All those employees who had, for years, defined their success in terms of close customer relationships and solving customer problems would now need to redefine their roles in terms of pushing volume and minimal cost.

To escape the conflict, Dow first re-segmented its market around customer needs. It identified four main segments, each rooted in a different type of value that they were seeking from the company:

- **Innovative solutions seekers.** These customers integrated Dow Corning into their R&D, jointly developing new products. They often invited Dow to be a part of their customer research, leveraging its expertise in assessing customer needs and spotting trends.

- **Proven solutions seekers.** These customers could be characterized more as fast followers than first movers. They used Dow Corning for consulting, guiding them toward established products and processes that would keep them competitive.

- **Cost-effective solutions seekers.** These customers still leaned on Dow Corning for advice but wanted advice specifically focused on cost savings and efficiency, rather than market innovation. The premium prices they paid for their materials from Dow Corning were worth it to realize cost saving on the back end.

- **Price seekers.** These customers wanted the lowest price they could get on silicone. They were uninterested in the extra services Dow Corning could provide.

Dow Corning also sized these groups. Combined, the three solutions seekers segments made up 65 to 75 percent of the market. Price seekers made up the remaining 25 to 35 percent.

Note that these four values-based segments spanned the industrial verticals that Dow Corning served (e.g., automotive, aerospace, etc.). We want to pause here and acknowledge the very, *very* good decision Dow Corning made by re-segmenting around what its customers valued, rather than categorizing them just according to the industry they belonged to. Looking across industry verticals, a reasonable manager might conclude that because there were cries coming from all quarters demanding lower prices, the company simply had to start competing more aggressively on price. But this would have been the wrong decision.

When the market was segmented properly—based on what was driving customers' decision-making—managers got a clearer vision of what was going on. Yes, there was pressure to lower prices coming from customers. But not all customers. *Most* of Dow Corning's customers still valued their current level of high service and were still willing to pay a premium for it. So instead of racing to cut costs and lower prices or, worse, transforming the company into a commodity provider, it pursued a separation strategy.

The company spun up a new division for price seekers, thereby freeing up the rest of the company to continue doing what it did so well. The new division was built from the ground up, like a separate business. Its product lineup was limited to only the most popular silicone compounds. It sold only large volumes. No special orders, and no tailored packaging solutions. Orders were made only through a website, with no sales or support personnel involved (a completely novel process for Dow Corning—and most of the chemicals industry—in the early 2000s). Prices were aggressive and updated frequently, and they were consistently 10 to 15 percent lower than the prices Dow Corning would charge for the same thing under its parent brand.[14]

Crucially, this venture was given its own identity via a sub-brand: *Xiameter from Dow Corning.* From the perspective of separating conflicting segments, a sub-brand allows a clearer demarcation in the minds of customers than would be possible if the company were to try selling the same products with two very different levels of pricing, service, and support under a single brand. Customers were now able to self-select the brand that best fit their needs. The price seekers would decide they were now Xiameter customers, while the three solutions-oriented segments would continue to self-identify as Dow Corning customers.

Sub-branding can also serve as a buffer against cannibalization. If Dow Corning had sold identical silicone compounds at different prices, with the different levels of service being the factor in the higher-priced version, there was a risk that customers might start claiming the lower price but then feel confused, frustrated, or angry when they discovered that they were denied some of the services Dow Corning had always provided. A sub-brand helps make the division of benefits clearer to customers. *You get that consult with Dow Corning, not with Xiameter.*

The final benefit of sub-branding was internal. The culture, focus, and success metrics of Xiameter employees would necessarily be different. By creating a new identity for that division, Dow Corning was also able to create separation in the minds of its employees. If ever employees were to switch divisions, for example, they would have a new psychological anchor with which to reorient themselves to their new jobs. While they might be slinging the same silicone, someone working for Xiameter should expect to do their job in a fundamentally different way than when working in the rest of Dow Corning.

In the four years after the launch of Xiameter, Dow Corning's overall sales grew by almost 60 percent. The company went from losing money when trying to simultaneously serve conflicting segments, to a net income of more than half-a-billion dollars after separating the segments via a new sub-brand. Reducing the customer segment conflict also reportedly improved morale within the company.[15] An article in *Harvard Business Review* noted that Dow Corning paid back the initial investment in IT infrastructure and operations changes to get Xiameter off the ground in just three months.[16]

Strategy 2: Clearly Define Leaders and Followers

Status-based and prestige brands often fall into brand image and user identity conflict when lower-status consumers claim the brand as their own, thereby alienating traditional users. (See figure 12-2.) Researchers Silvia Bellezza of Columbia University and Anat Keinan of Boston University called this "brand immigration."[17] Think of someone who considers themselves a Harley-Davidson person because they wear a lot of Harley-Davidson–branded apparel— jackets, T-shirts, bandannas—but who doesn't actually own or ride a Harley-Davidson motorcycle. Or imagine someone who considers themselves a "Deadhead" despite never having attended a Grateful Dead concert and only rarely listening to their music—but they proudly wear the T-shirts. Or picture someone who never ran

FIGURE 12-2

Segment Compatibility Matrix: Moving from Incompatible Segments to Leader-Follower Segments

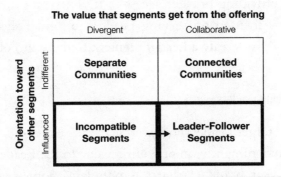

the Boston Marathon constantly showing up at the gym wearing the shirt given only to those who complete the race, which they found at a thrift shop. You can imagine how some of each of these brands' core customers might respond to encountering such an interloper.

Brand immigrants instigate conflicts when the core users are territorial about membership. For example, many Harvard students bristle when people who attend short-term, nondegree programs at Harvard place the university seal on their LinkedIn profiles or claim to have "gone to Harvard." Tyra Banks ruffled a few Ivy League feathers when she claimed to have graduated from Harvard Business School in 2012 after she attended a nine-week executive program.[18] No one had any issue with Banks attending the intensive session—on its own, a quite admirable endeavor—but the fact that Banks claimed membership in the Harvard alumni community without really being admitted into, let alone graduating from, the school bothered some graduates. MBA alumni might reasonably feel that expanding the HBS community to include people who took far less exclusive short courses might reduce the status of their accomplishments (user identity conflict). It might also cause people to wonder how committed HBS is to its historically high educational standards if it starts allowing far more people to access its facilities, faculty, and content (brand image conflict). In these cases, it can be useful to try to reestablish hierarchy among core brand users and aspirational Followers to protect the brand while still providing broader access to it. There are three ways to do this: stay focused on serving Leaders, unlink Followers from Leaders, and (re-)create a Leader segment to draw in Followers.

Focus on serving Leaders

Brands that target Leader-Follower Segments can avoid conflict by focusing predominantly on providing value to the Leader segment. The workwear brand Carhartt is popular among two primary customer segments: workers and style mavens. Workers value Carhartt's durable, functional, weather-resistant, and comfortable workwear. Style mavens primarily value the fact that workers value Carhartt. In an inversion of many Leader-Follower relationships, where Leaders are those with more wealth, status, and power, workers are the Leader segment, providing blue-collar authenticity that the style maven Followers crave.

In 2019, the Carhartt brand generated over $1 billion in annual revenue.[19] Part of Carhartt's staying power is owed to its steadfast loyalty to the workers customer segment. Tony Ambroza, a senior vice president of marketing for Carhartt, told *Esquire*, "We stand for hard work. We've stood for that since 1889 when [Hamilton Carhartt] was focused on making a better product for workers that didn't get a better product. . . . Times will come and go, times will change, but we've consistently stood with the working class."[20] For Carhartt, functionality always comes before fashion. The brand also values consistency over novelty. Many of Carhartt's more popular products have stayed the same for decades, including its chore jacket, beanies, pocket tees, and bib overalls.

Even as Carhartt gained popularity with style mavens, the brand has resisted the urge to cater to them at the expense of workers. If Carhartt wanted to, it could respond to the whims of style mavens—maybe Carhartt Crocs?—but this would have come with a risk of brand image conflict, potentially driving away the workers who are the brand's lifeblood. Carhartt avoids conflict between customer segments by remaining consistently focused on serving its Leader segment above anyone else.[21]

This doesn't mean that Carhartt has completely neglected the style segment, of course. In 1994, the sub-brand "Carhartt Work in Progress (WIP)" was established to distribute fashion-focused clothing collections based on the original Carhartt workwear. WIP was initially predominantly focused on serving European markets—putting a European fashion twist on the rugged American brand. Today, WIP is available in both markets. But while WIP clothing features more modern cuts and colors for style mavens, the more avant garde designs do not come at the expense of durability and functionality. The vice president of creative at Carhartt, Brian Bennett, told *Esquire*, "When you have such a loyal passionate base, you want to make sure that's something you consider and you respect. And what we focus on are the commonalities." Sounds like he would appreciate the Venn diagrams in chapter 11.

Through WIP, Carhartt can provide unique value to the Followers, the style mavens, without alienating its Leaders, the workers, who shop the original Carhartt brand. And across both lines, Carhartt reinforces its focus on quality and durability for manual work, even if the brand knows that Glenn Close—who sported a Carhartt outfit at the Golden Globes in 2021—is unlikely to be working on an oil rig on her way home from working the red carpet.[22] But by staying true to its workwear aesthetic and function, if she had chosen to, her outfit would have been up for it.

Unlink Followers from Leaders

One risk of Leader–Follower strategies is that the mere presence of too many brand immigrant Followers can drive away Leaders. This is an especially acute risk when part of the value that the Leader segment is seeking is exclusivity. In cases like these, it may be necessary to buffer Leaders from Followers to avoid or escape conflict. Luxury brands, such as Coach, Michael Kors, Dolce & Gabbana, Fendi, Tory Burch, and many others, frequently create separation between Leaders and Followers through the introduction of "diffusion lines" or "secondary lines." This is a unique flavor of the subbranding strategy designed to reduce conflict between Leaders and Followers. Diffusion lines are made to be sold through separate retail channels, often department or outlet stores. They give brands leeway to target new customer segments or grow the brand to more mainstream audiences while reducing the risk of conflict between hierarchical customer segments.

Diffusion lines are typically manufactured with different materials, designs, or quality standards compared to their mainline products and are thus unlikely to be mistaken for full-priced or flagship items—especially among the high-status customers in Leader segments. Even though purses in the MICHAEL by Michael Kors line and those in the Michael Kors line have the same logo on them, the Leaders know which products are high end and which are not. They know which items are *really* Michael Kors, so they are not negatively influenced by large numbers of Followers carrying around MICHAEL by Michael Kors bags. Meanwhile, Followers still feel like they are getting a genuine piece of the brand because it still says Michael Kors on the bag. It still counts as a Michael Kors bag even if I bought it at an outlet, right? Right?? This is crucial to successful diffusion lines: that Leaders can discern signature line products from the diffusion line products—reducing the risk of user identity and brand image conflict—but Followers still feel part of the brand community when they purchase the latter.

Many brands use diffusion lines, which are usually separated by distribution channels, to create hierarchical separation between Leader and Follower segments. Levi Strauss & Co. sells the Signature by Levi Strauss & Co. sub-brand via Walmart and the Denizen from Levi's sub-brand via Target. Marc Jacobs sells Marc by Marc Jacobs through lower-priced channels, and Alexander McQueen sells less expensive items under the McQ brand. Similarly, we saw how Burberry introduced many price-quality tiers within its brand to create new hierarchical delineations.

Sub-branding as a way of reducing conflict in Leader-Follower relationships is not unique to fashion and beauty. Goldman Sachs used a similar strategy when it launched Marcus by Goldman Sachs in 2016. This retail bank provided services such as personal loans, savings accounts, and certificates of deposit to mainstream bank customers. Marcus's everyman's offerings were a contrast to Goldman Sachs's traditional fare of investment banking, institutional trading, and asset management for high-net-worth individuals and institutional clients. Goldman Sachs—or just "Goldman," for those who pronounce it "*fin*-ance" and not "*fine*-ance"—is associated with global elites. Marcus, on the other hand, is like Goldman's casual cousin for a customer segment with different needs and preferences. While Main Street banking customers (Followers) might love to use the exact same bank as the Wall Street multimillionaires and titans of business (Leaders), Goldman's traditional core customers would probably react negatively if their formerly highly exclusive financial partner were to start serving everyone under the same brand. It also could have created confusion around Goldman's image or the services it offers.

Typically, Leader segments consume the more expensive, formal, or professional-grade products—which most often stay under the main brand name—while Follower segments purchase less expensive, more casual, or lower-grade products under a sub-brand. This gives the brand the ability to grow to new segments and broaden its appeal to larger markets, while minimizing the risk of intersegment conflict. This is also why sub-brands often keep parent brands somewhere in the name (e.g., Marc by Marc Jacobs, Xiameter from Dow Corning, Carhartt WIP, Signature by Levi Strauss & Co.). It gives brands the ability to leverage the brand equity they have built as a parent brand to attract customers but also separates them from the parent line, particularly in the eyes of the Leader segment, to diminish the risk of conjuring conflict between old and new customer segments.

In Carhartt's case, WIP garments tend to be more expensive. A Carhartt chore jacket can be found for about $120, while the WIP chore jacket goes for close to $210. But Carhartt is a somewhat unique case in which the Followers segment is uncharacteristically less price sensitive than the Leaders. Typically, Leaders—because they are often wealthier, more professional, or more expert—tend to be the less price-sensitive segment.

Brands can also unlink Leaders and Followers through tiered offerings or different product lines under the same brand. For example,

Tough Mudder—the facilitator of thirteen-mile obstacle-course mud runs—creates hierarchy by selling a line of "finisher only" merchandise exclusively available to participants who complete a Tough Mudder race. Spectators or aspiring Tough Mudder runners can still purchase branded merch but cannot access items reserved for finishers. Credit card companies create different cards to delineate between tiers of customers. Loyalty programs with customer tiers can serve a similar purpose.

(Re-)Construct a Leader segment

In some cases, rather than creating a hierarchy by extending a ladder downward (e.g., Michael Kors, Levis, Goldman Sachs), brands push the ladder up. When Burberry created its runway line, Burberry Prorsum, it suggested the presence of a new Leader segment of elite, trend-setting customers to enhance the attractiveness of the traditional Burberry London line. Prorsum signaled that, as an entity, Burberry still stood for luxury and high fashion, so to be like those who value luxury and high fashion, consumers should buy Burberry.

Luxottica used a similar strategy to create a new Leader segment for Ray-Ban in the early 2000s. Ray-Ban emerged as a symbol of American cool from the 1940s to the 1980s primarily because of its Aviator and Wayfarer models that were sported by pilots in the US military and in films like *Rebel Without a Cause*. Audrey Hepburn wore Wayfarers in *Breakfast at Tiffany's*, and Michael Jackson sported Aviators at the 1984 Grammy Awards show. But by the 1990s, Ray-Ban had all but lost its social cachet, partly because the brand's owners, Bausch & Lomb, tried to turn it into a mass-market brand. The brand produced massive quantities of poor-quality glasses that could be bought for around $20 at convenience stores (#brandimageconflict). Once worn by James Dean, Ray-Ban was seen as more cheap than cool. After buying the brand from Bausch & Lomb in 1999, Luxottica set out to resuscitate Ray-Ban's cool.

First, Luxottica cut off supplies to over 13,000 low-market outlets and switched to selling Ray-Ban in high-end stores such as Saks Fifth Avenue and Neiman Marcus instead. It simultaneously improved the quality of Ray-Ban glasses through new materials and technology.[23]

In 2007, the brand then launched the "Never Hide" campaign, which was designed to convey rebellion and individuality, and associate Ray-Bans with a segment of consumers who looked cool and upscale.[24] Ads featured a mix of actors, musicians, and models such as Chloë Sevigny, Iggy Pop, Slash from Guns N' Roses, and Agyness Deyn—but also everyday people appearing confident and doing things like bungee jumping, getting tattoos, or crowd surfing at a concert.[25] Luxottica targeted a Leader segment that we will call the "rebel cools" and created the feeling that this segment was representative of its core consumer in its ads. This, of course, piqued the attention of a much larger Follower segment, whom we will call the "wanna feel cools."

Luxottica also changed its pricing to reflect its updated image. By 2009, the entry price for Ray-Bans was $129. Today, some models retail closer to $500—and one model of 18 karat gold aviators goes for $3,800—but many can be bought for around a $100 price point. Ray-Bans are premium sunglasses made for rebel cools, but they are accessibly priced for the wanna feel cools.

The strategy worked. Ray-Ban sales increased from about $260 million to over $2.20 *billion* for Luxottica between 2000 and 2014. And Ray-Bans have remained a cultural mainstay, thanks largely to the brand's ability to attract a Leader segment back to the brand.[26] A 2024 GQ article put it this way: "Ray-Bans . . . make *you* feel like the superstar. The brand spent nearly 90 years cooking up sunglasses that somehow give everyday Joes (and Janes) the same swagger as a *Risky Business*-era Tom Cruise and the same animal magnetism of Lenny Kravitz."[27] Ray-Ban navigated its way out of brand image conflict by distancing itself from its cheap perception and re-courting a Leader segment to revive its rebellious, cool, upscale image. We saw a similar strategy deployed when Crocs captured the explorers segment to make plastic clogs the object of fashion influencers' envy and pull in the fashion followers (see chapter 1).

Strategy 3: Eschew and Fire Customer Segments

A primary point of this book is to help managers think about how to grow a brand and what *new* customer segments to target. However, conflict is sometimes best avoided through the surgical removal of current customer segments. Of course, the necessity of firing a segment will be greatly reduced if a brand is able to create an initial customer base that is compatible with subsequent segments. Founders often focus on the most obvious customer segments for gaining early market traction, while failing to consider how initial customer segments might affect the ability to grow later. But when, through bad luck or bad planning, new segments and old segments fall into conflict, it may be that one of them has to go (see figure 12-3). The path to long-term growth sometimes leads

FIGURE 12-3

Segment Compatibility Matrix: Moving out of Incompatible Segments by firing a customer segment

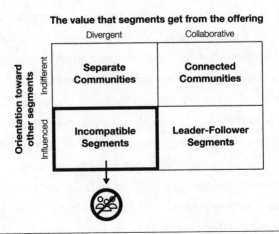

through a short-term reduction in the number of customer segments the brand is serving.

Avoid (or casually fail to mention) customer segments

When Bill Shufelt cofounded Athletic Brewing Company with John Walker in 2017, he said he wanted to take nonalcoholic (NA) beer options "out of the penalty box." Shufelt wanted to enjoy the professional and athletic performance benefits of abstaining from alcohol without the social stigma or feeling of compromise that often comes with choosing NA options at social gatherings. Accordingly, Shufelt made two crucial strategic decisions with Athletic: first, he would only release truly high-quality nonalcoholic craft beer that could compete head-to-head on taste with alcoholic beer options; and second, Athletic would not be explicitly marketed to people recovering from alcohol abuse disorder or to people seeking sobriety due to problematic relationships with alcohol.[28]

Recovering addicts might be an obvious target customer segment for Athletic. But Shufelt intuited that if the brand explicitly targeted this segment—or became too closely associated with it—Athletic could introduce a long-standing user identity conflict with people who are enjoying an NA beer at the party for reasons other than addiction recovery. Customers looking for a drink that would leave them able to wake up early the next morning to train for a marathon or to parent small children might be turned off by a brand associated with a historically stigmatized group. NA brands that had become overly associated with recovering addicts, such as O'Douls, tended to repel other customer segments that did not want to be mistaken for addicts themselves. So Athletic focused on three primary customer segments: weekend warriors (think: that annoying friend or spouse who has already run five miles, hit up the grocery store, and reorganized the hall closet before you've gotten out of bed), young parents, and serious athletes. Sure, people with alcohol abuse disorder might also be consumers of Athletic—it's not like the brand was actively discouraging them from drinking its beer. They were just not explicitly targeted by the brand. Consumers in the brand's ads and social media were mostly highly active, high-achieving people who wanted to socialize and drink beer without compromising on other pursuits. And as Athletic grew, this is the audience that was drawn to the brand. About 80 percent of Athletic's customer base reports they sometimes drink alcohol in addition to NA beer.[29]

By 2023, Athletic had become a top nonalcoholic beer brand, driving a significant proportion of category growth. In 2023, the brand made more than $90 million in sales.[30] By 2024, it was valued at roughly $800 million.[31] Had Athletic come out of the gate explicitly targeting recovering addicts, it likely would have made it much harder for the brand to capture other, broader customer segments like the weekend warriors and athletes. Athletic avoided conflict between customer segments by carefully choosing its customer segments at launch.

Fire customer segments

While it may seem counterintuitive to push customers away from a brand looking to grow (more revenue is more revenue, right?), doing so can sometimes be effective, or even necessary. Firing customers allows a brand to escape the conflict zone by simply eliminating one of the segments involved in the conflict. When Patagonia chose to discontinue corporate merchandising, the brand was effectively firing the finance and tech bros from the brand. In doing so, Patagonia left a lot of money on the table but preserved and reaffirmed its authentic environmentally friendly image. Patagonia was able to invite back parts of the corporate customer segment when it found ways to make the value it sought more compatible with its environmentally oriented customers—such as by making corporate embroidery more ecofriendly and by being more deliberate about which organizations it accepted orders from.

Brands can dial up or down the "loudness" with which they fire customer segments. Loud firing involves making the dissociation public, sometimes including an official pronouncement of the brand's desire to be rid of the segment, as when New Balance needed to demonstrate that it did not intend to embrace neo-Nazi consumer groups. Loud firing can also be the result of a brand explicitly "hiring" a customer segment that is clearly incompatible with the one being fired. As we will discuss in more detail in the next chapter, when Nike chose to ally itself very publicly with Colin Kaepernick—a well-known advocate of social justice issues— the brand's loud stance implied its willingness to fire customers who disagreed with the decision.

But sometimes brands don't need to broadcast their intentions on the evening news. Instead, they "quiet fire" by ceasing to sell certain products or making offerings less attractive to the customer segment(s) they'd like to move on from their brand. Tiffany did this when it eliminated the cheap silver jewelry to distance itself from teenagers. Burberry took a similar path by discontinuing its baseball caps, rather than explicitly announcing it no longer wished to be the brand of choice for hooligans. In the case of Burberry, loud firing would have likely drawn more attention to the problem, something the brand wanted to avoid. And the message was received either way.

Increasing prices is another way for brands to quietly nudge some customers out the door. The amusement park company Six Flags sharply raised its ticket prices in 2022 and eliminated most discount ticket programs. Predictably, attendance dropped—by a staggering 26 percent in fact—costing Six Flags significant revenue right at the point that many of its competitors were starting to finally recover from the pandemic era.[32] In online forums, customers, employees, and investors called for CEO Selim Bassoul to step down. Although the drop was steeper than anticipated, it was what Bassoul expected and wanted: he wanted to fire some customers. In an earnings call explaining the price hike to investors, Bassoul argued that some Six Flags customers brought in little revenue. These segments often bought discounted tickets to get into the park and then spent practically nothing on high-margin food, drink, and collectible items once inside. Further, in accommodating so many of those customers, Six Flags was creating a less enjoyable experience for everyone else, as these extra customer segments caused functional conflict: overcrowding, longer wait times, and increased incidents of violence and theft within the parks. Bassoul argued that Six Flags had become "a cheap day care center for teenagers during breaks and the summers."[33] The price increase was designed to discourage the rowdy teens and provide a better experience for families willing to spend more. Bassoul's vindication came in 2023; less than a year after the price hikes, Six Flag's attendance was down but revenue had reached record highs. Its stock price soared by 20 percent as investors warmed to the strategy.[34] The brand escaped functional conflict to retain and win back a more profitable crowd.

Escape Conflict Bonus Strategy: Build a New Brand

OK, we cheated a little. We told you there were three ways to avoid or escape conflict. But there is a fourth strategy worth considering: building a new, separate, and unique brand. Or acquire one. We left this strategy out of the original discussion because it's usually very costly, and it disallows brands from leveraging the equity or awareness they have created with their main brand. For these reasons, it should be reserved for rare and special cases. Also, as a solution, it falls outside of our Segment Compatibility Matrix because it doesn't change the relationship between customer segments within the same brand; it leads to an entirely new matrix of possible segment relationships for the new brand.

Still, building a new brand is sometimes the optimal route for avoiding conflict and capturing new markets. Take the Match Group, which owns about a dozen of the most well-known and

most-used dating apps. Why would a company need to own so
many brands doing essentially the same thing? Because people have
different preferences, especially when searching for love (or something love-adjacent), and trying to serve all of them under the same
brand would cause all kinds of conflict. The Match Group owns
Tinder, an app that is best known for facilitating casual hookups.
But it also owns Hinge, an app designed to serve people serious about
getting into long-term relationships. Hinge's tagline is "the dating
app designed to be deleted" and promises users that with Hinge,
you will "go on your last first date."[35] There are apps that facilitate
meeting people based on different types of information and different communication styles: OkCupid "matches you on what matters
to you," based on an algorithm that crunches data from an extensive questionnaire about your preferences, politics, and pastimes.
The app called Match facilitates a more investigative-journalist approach to date selection, allowing users to provide detailed profiles
that include several free-writing sections and up to twenty-six photos. Azar, on the other hand, involves minimal screening but allows
people to jump right into live conversations in video chats. Other
apps focus on demographic communities: BLK is a dating app for
Black singles, Chispa is for Latinx singles, Meetic is for French
speakers, and The League is for people who are regularly told by
friends and family that their standards are too high—they are
reaching "out of their league." The League assures you that you are
not. Joining The League requires an application process and being
placed on a wait list while you are vetted. Oh, and it also requires
that you provide it with your LinkedIn page, so it can actively
screen potentials to create a community that is "well-balanced,
highly engaged, and full of high-powered (and empowered)
people."[36]

Could the Match Group have tried to serve all these various
constituencies through a single brand? Sure. But it could not simultaneously serve them all well. Could it have used sub-brands

(Tinder by Match; BLK by Match; Chispa by Match)? Yes, but with so many brands, that's a recipe for confusion and possible identity conflict. Also, the equities of one brand might not be valuable to another; knowing Tinder is a sub-brand of Match probably wouldn't make the app any more valuable or attractive to users looking for a one-night stand.

Dating apps might seem to be a straightforward example of Connected Communities—the more people using a dating app, the more people there are to potentially match with, and the greater the likelihood that one's soulmate is also on the app. But, while statistically true, that analysis leaves out the search and evaluation costs associated with matching within a larger pool. From a customer's point of view, the ideal dating service would have only one other person in it: the person ideally suited to the customer. Everyone using the app who is not suited to the customer's preferences just imposes time, effort, and hassle costs.

Every type of conflict is reduced or eliminated by creating separate brands that focus on the preferences of specific segments of customers: functional conflict (e.g., those who enjoy finding matches by swiping based on a single picture versus those who prefer creating and evaluating long text responses to thoughtful questions), user identity conflict (e.g., there are people who would rather die alone than admit they are the type of person who could meet their future spouse on Tinder), brand image conflict (e.g., would customers believe the same app would be just as good at finding potential marriage partners as casual hookups?), and ideological conflict (e.g., there are dating apps designed to specifically serve people with particular political views, religious beliefs, and farmers—which we consider to be an ideology).

Companies routinely escape conflict, or potential conflict, by launching new brands. Black & Decker launched DeWalt to better serve the professional tradesman segment and reduce user identity conflicts with the amateur DIYers. Toyota launched Lexus to better meet the preferences of premium car buyers, avoiding the brand image conflict that likely would have arisen had the same brand that sells the Corolla also tried selling $100,000 luxury sedans. Toyota later also launched Scion as a "fighting brand" to compete with low-priced rivals like Kia and Hyundai. The new brand allowed for a fun, youthful, self-expressive positioning that probably would have caused conflicts with the preferences of traditional Toyota customers, if the models were sold under a single brand.

This book is primarily about growing a brand by adding customers. But sometimes growth within a brand risks more conflict than it's worth. Sometimes, the benefits of leveraging a known brand are not worth the intersegment friction it will create. In those cases, spinning off or acquiring a completely distinct brand may be the best path forward. Just remember: it's expensive. It's complicated. And it creates a new base of customers who will then also need to be managed based on their relationships within the brand.

Escape Conflict via Multiple Strategies

As most of the examples in this chapter suggest, brands don't need to pick just one strategy to escape conflict, especially when they have multiple segments in conflict. In fact, even within one conflict-reducing strategy, brands can—and usually should—use multiple tactics. Burberry created sub-brands, fired customers, and diversified its product line. BMW used nontraditional channels and sub-branding via its various car models to create separation between customers with different utility needs and spending power. Starbucks created Separate Communities via distribution channels and established a new Leader-Follower coffee hierarchy with its Roasteries and Reserves.

Intersegment conflict can create huge problems for brands—from an image and revenue perspective. Thus, avoiding it should be a core part of your brand strategy. Also, expect that despite your best efforts, it will occur anyway, and prepare plans to escape it. This means deploying multiple tactics across the marketing mix, quickly, decisively, and aggressively. Avoiding or escaping conflict is no time for delicacy and precision. Use a hatchet, not a scalpel.

13

Embracing Conflict

Porsches for Soccer Moms,
Swifties for the NFL

Conflict between customer segments is bad for brands and should be avoided. Usually.

Occasionally, however, deliberately and carefully wading into conflict can be the best strategy for long-term growth. Nike put on a master class in embracing conflict when it partnered with retired NFL quarterback Colin Kaepernick for the thirtieth anniversary of its "Just Do It" campaign. Several years earlier, Kaepernick had sparked a national conversation when, after consulting a veteran on the appropriateness of his protest, he started kneeling during the national anthem before games. These silent protests against racial injustice and police brutality expanded across the NFL, and eventually spread to collegiate and high school athletes. Kaepernick's activism made him a central figure in debates about racial equality and activism in the United States. Responses ran the gamut. Kaepernick's kneeling protests drew support from fans who saw his actions as a sincere and reasonable exercise of free speech to draw attention to important issues. Others claimed to support his aims, but criticized the specific form of the protest, admitting that the issues he was highlighting were real, but that kneeling during the anthem was disrespectful. And others were outright hostile, either because they rejected the social justice causes at the heart of the protests or because they saw the demonstrations as unpatriotic or an affront to the US military.

It is widely believed that Kaepernick's political activism cost him his job at the end of the 2016 season. When his contract was up, no team in the NFL was willing to sign him despite an impressive on-field record. The risks of controversy seemed to outweigh the potential benefit of acquiring an objectively talented QB. He never played again.

Two years later, in 2018, Kaepernick posted to his Instagram account a dramatic black-and-white close-up of his face above the Nike swoosh and "Just Do It." The caption read: "Believe in something, even if it means sacrificing everything." It was just a teaser for a Nike campaign featuring the same close-up of Kaepernick in print ads and on billboards. Kaepernick was also the narrator of a two-minute video spot titled *Dream Crazy* featuring both amateur and professional athletes with compelling stories of having overcome challenges.

The campaign incited immediate and vociferous responses. Right-leaning political pundits referred to the Nike campaign as "an attack on the country." People filmed themselves burning their Nike sneakers in protest—solidifying destroying things that you have already purchased with your own money as America's new favorite form of registering outrage. Country music star John Rich posted a photo of one of his crew, who had angrily cut the Nike swoosh off the tops of his athletic socks.[1] Online sentiment measures of the Nike brand dropped from 90 percent positive to under 40 percent after the ad was released, and Nike's favorability rating dropped by double digits.[2]

Nike knew something like this was going to happen. This was a deliberate move to court controversy. When the ads ran, Kaepernick had already been out of the NFL for two years. This was clearly a decision to align the brand with the causes Kaepernick stood for. Nike knew that customers would be furious. Or more to the point, it knew that *some* customers would be furious. Nike did it anyway, because it wanted to reaffirm that Kaepernick's values were *Nike's* values. Offending customers who did not support Kaepernick or the movement he represented was fine by Nike. It was willing to let those customers go. As marketing expert Lucas Bean put it in a blog post directed at those who were offended: "You're not boycotting Nike. They fired you as a customer."[3]

The long-term play here was to incite conflict as a way of drawing some segments closer to the brand. Nike wanted to be a brand that some segments loved because it aligned with their beliefs and values, rather than being a milquetoast brand that tried not to offend anyone. Nike believed there were more customers who supported the values Nike was espousing via its partnership with Kaepernick than there were customers who would protest those values, particularly among younger customers, who would be with the brand longer.[4] It chose to communicate this message with a campaign it knew was very likely to cost it customers—in the hopes of winning more, and more loyal, customers in the exchange.

Nike was right. Within weeks, online sales increased by more than 30 percent, year over year. The initial dip in the company's stock was followed by a surge to its highest-ever market valuation, more than $6 billion. Overall, Nike claimed $163 million in earned media from the campaign, and Kaepernick's NFL jersey became a top seller again, years after he retired. A senior editor for *Adweek* said: "Nike conducted its due diligence prior to running the work. But the brand captured lightning in a bottle by taking a clear position on a divisive sociopolitical topic at a moment that guaranteed maximum cultural impact while accepting that the work would alienate some consumers."[5]

Nike did not need to invite conflict by inserting itself into the conversation on social justice but chose to do so, fully aware of the conflict it would create. It was a carefully calculated move based on an assessment of its customers—including which segments were most valuable and had the most growth potential. It was consistent with its brand image and the value that its core segments got out of the brand. As a result, the decision to embrace conflict ultimately benefited the brand.[6]

So, should you alienate one of your segments to goose the stock price? Probably not. Please go back and review the last couple of chapters for the numerous examples of conflict that caused serious and, at times, irreparable problems for brands. We can't restate enough that conflict is most often bad and should be avoided or swiftly de-escalated.

But if a brand is considering a strategy that invites conflict, there are a few principles that increase the chances of that strategy being successful. Successfully embracing conflict requires weighing the financial and reputational pros and cons of conflict, reinforcing brand values or equities, demonstrating commitment and consistency in response to backlash, and executing wisely. Brands that succeed via deliberate conflict excel at all four points, while brands that stumble through deliberate conflict usually fail to consider or implement one or more. We'll meet both types of brands in the coming pages.

Weigh the Pros and Cons

You should only consider a conflict strategy if you can reasonably expect it to lead to net growth *despite* the losses that almost certainly will occur. This growth could come from creating stronger bonds with an existing set of customers, who will then buy more or stick with the brand longer. It could come from bringing in new customers—either new customers from within existing segments, or new customers from new segments that are attracted to the brand because of the conflict. Nike almost certainly benefited from both sources of growth as a result of its alignment with Kaepernick. But the path forward should be clear to the brand before conflict is courted. Ideally, this analysis of pros and cons will be rooted in some hard numbers estimating the size of various segments, and their current and potential revenues.

Take Porsche. Until the launch of the Cayenne, a midsize SUV, the Porsche brand was singularly focused on expensive, high-performance sports cars, targeted mostly to wealthy men. However, as SUVs grew in popularity in the late '90s and early 2000s, Porsche saw an opportunity to diversify its product line and attract new segments to the brand. This departure from the brand's sports car heritage ignited controversy among purists, who questioned if sport utility was what Porsche should be about.

For Porsche's original customer segments, the brand represented power, prestige, and masculinity—a "true sports car" in terms of styling, functional performance, and engineering excellence. The Cayenne SUV violated that identity, at least among the Porsche devotees, who responded to the new product with hostility. Social media, car forums, and automotive publications became platforms for enthusiasts to voice their skepticism and disappointment. Porsche-philes felt the brand had *sold out*. The Cayenne was a car for impostors, for soccer moms who didn't want a minivan and who did not understand the history, heritage, and performance of Porsche. Not for real Porsche drivers. The inclusion of these drivers into the Porsche fold threatened the true sports car meaning of the brand.[7]

But Porsche management felt the introduction of the Cayenne was a necessary extension of the brand. The president of Porsche North America at the time said, "Those in the Porsche clubs of America will castigate us for the SUV decision, but they just don't know business. For them to keep having their beloved 911s, we have to find a niche elsewhere. That is modern business."[8] Porsche management anticipated the brand image conflict the SUV would create among brand purists but proceeded anyway, estimating that the rewards would be worth it in the long run.

To alleviate some concerns among traditionalists, the brand crafted its marketing and communication strategies to shape a narrative that the Cayenne was aligned with the brand's core values. Ads emphasized performance, craftsmanship, and engineering excellence. Taglines like "Another twisted branch on the family tree," and "Only one sport utility vehicle has bloodlines like these," emphasized the Cayenne's membership in the Porsche family.[9]

This bet paid off. Sales exceeded expectations. The Cayenne drew in new customers and created new Porsche fans. While some purists no doubt left the brand forever, most did not. Many believe the Cayenne saved Porsche from going under. Two decades later, the Cayenne is a mainstay, selling 80,000 units in 2021 alone, compared to 34,000 of the 911. As then-chairman of Porsche's executive board Oliver Blume put it, "With the Cayenne, we have succeeded in successfully transferring the Porsche legend to a completely new market segment."[10] Porsche successfully handled the brand image conflict and leveraged the brand equity to enter an adjacent, non-sports car category.

Porsche succeeded, in part, because the conflict that ensued was anticipated and well managed and because the brand weighed the pros and cons of rattling some cages with attracting a much larger market that would open the door for many other Porsche models down the line.

NASCAR made a similar clear-eyed assessment of the pros and cons of conflict on its path to attracting a more diverse audience in the 2020s. After years of declining viewership, NASCAR tried to grow the fan base by making decisions that it knew would alienate some of its core fans. Specifically, the organization started prohibiting Confederate flags at NASCAR events in 2020. Prior to this ban, Confederate flags were a common sight in the grandstands and infields of stock car racing stadiums. On race days, the flag could be seen all over, on T-shirts, hats, and bandannas. Not surprisingly, some fans were furious at the banning of the rebel flag, claiming it to be part of a Southern heritage that NASCAR is rooted in, rather than a symbol of racism. Those fans were not wrong about the flag having an entrenched history with NA-SCAR. In fact, during the 1960s and 70s, a character called "Johnny Reb" would ride on the hood of the winning car at Darlington Raceway in South Carolina. The character was dressed in a Confederate soldier's gray uniform and waved the rebel flag on the way to the victory lane. While many NASCAR fans celebrated the Confederate flag as a symbol of their history and heritage, its prominence—and NASCAR's reputation for having a nondiverse fan base—likely made many potential racing fans feel unwelcome at NASCAR events.[11]

So, in 2020, NASCAR banned it. African American NASCAR star Bubba Wallace, who had been urging the organization to ban the flag, said in an interview with NPR shortly after the ban, "Hats off to NASCAR. . . . [I]t was a huge, pivotal moment for the sport—a lot of backlash but it creates doors that allow the community to come together as one."[12] Peter Jung, NASCAR chief marketing officer, reiterated to the *Wall Street Journal* in 2024, "Yes, there were a handful of fans like, 'You're taking away my rights,' . . . but it also opened the door to far, far, far, far more people that are like, 'Huh, OK. Maybe I do want to learn more about NASCAR.'"[13] NASCAR knew that the pros far outweighed the cons.

NASCAR also took additional steps to be more inclusive as an organization and market more directly to diverse audiences, despite some pushback. Jung noted, "Diversity is represented throughout the entire industry starting with our company, but also team owners and sponsors and talent, content on television, pit crews and drivers. When all of that comes into play, then people see that in different ways and they're like, 'OK now I start to see myself in NASCAR.'" Its efforts started paying off quickly. Jung claims its fastest-growing fan demographics come from African American and Hispanic consumer audiences. And more than 80 percent of in-person ticket sales for the first Chicago Street Race in 2023 went to consumers who had never attended a NASCAR event before.[14] Like Nike and Porsche, NASCAR calculated that this type of growth was possible, and it far outweighed whatever fans the company alienated.

Reinforce Brand Values or Equities

Deliberate conflict should align with the values or equities of the brand. Nike was able to tie the social justice movement Kaepernick represented back to its core values: being courageous, overcoming adversity, knocking down barriers, achieving greatness. As a result, Nike's position on the issue felt like a natural extension of the brand, not a calculated ploy, and it ultimately reaped long-term benefits by embracing conflict.

The Signal Foundation is a nonprofit organization designed to "protect free expression and enable secure global communication through open-source privacy technology." The foundation is known for its text messaging app Signal, which uses end-to-end encryption, making it a top choice for security- and privacy-minded users.[15] But prior to 2023, if a Signal user sent a text to a non–Signal user, the app reverted to the terribly insecure and non-private SMS standard. By supporting both encrypted and SMS texts, Signal built up a significant user base. But supporting SMS posed a potential problem for customers who valued the security and privacy that Signal promised.

Signal worried that users might mistake SMS messaging via the app as secure and private, when it was not. It was also concerned that those communications sent via Signal could be collected by other entities and used in nefarious ways. So, Signal told users it was going to stop supporting SMS messaging.[16] Once this change was implemented, the only way to use Signal would be with other Signal users. Clearly, this change would create functional conflict for users who enjoyed the interoperability between Signal and SMS. Signal acknowledged on its blog, "We understand that this

change will be frustrating for those of you who use Signal on Android for SMS messaging in addition to sending Signal messages. It
rarely feels good to have to switch up the ways that you communicate
with the people who matter to you." But the brand added, "We did
not make this choice lightly, but we do believe it is necessary to
ensure that Signal meets the highest privacy standards for the
future. . . . With privacy and security at the heart of what we do,
letting a deeply insecure messaging protocol [SMS] have a place in
the Signal interface is inconsistent with our values and with what
people expect when they open Signal."[17]

When Signal ultimately removed SMS support, it generated relatively little fanfare. Sure, a few users expressed discontent on Reddit and GitHub forums, and it is likely that the app lost a number of
users who could no longer send and receive plain text messages in
the same places as their Signal messages, eroding some of the value
of its Connected Communities.[18] Regardless, the conflict Signal
created in removing SMS support was a reasonable and arguably
necessary means of protecting the brand's values and functional integrity for core users. The brand's position on the matter will likely
benefit Signal in the long run as it continues to strive to offer the
world's most secure communications platform.

Demonstrate Commitment and Consistency

Deliberate conflict strategies also work best when brands confi-
dently own the actions that provoked the conflict. When brands
generate controversy but then flinch and retreat, or hesitate to pick
a side, they typically lose whatever benefits they had hoped to gain
by entering the fray. Compounding that, they fail to restore the
goodwill lost by the alienated segments. The result is shooting oneself in both feet: the brand fails to endear itself to the customers it
was hoping to attract and fails to recover any customers it lost
through the controversy.

Nike leaned into its conflict, no matter how contentious or uncomfortable it might have felt as the stock price fell and people cut up their socks. It inked a multiyear deal with Kaepernick—it was committed to this strategy. When the protests came, Nike just kept doing what it had always done. In the years since the Kaepernick ads, Nike has continued to support social justice causes more broadly, including equal pay in women's soccer and anti-racism initiatives.

On the other hand, not only did Bud Light appear to vastly underweight the risk of alienating a substantial segment of its current customers with its Dylan Mulvaney partnership, it made matters worse when it failed to commit to its decision. When pressed to respond to the backlash, Bud Light put out a one-page public announcement titled, "Our Responsibility to America." The statement helpfully reminded readers of the company's long history (more than 165 years), its many employees (18,000, plus another 47,000 independent distributors), its "Americanness" ("founded in America's heartland" "part of the fabric of this country," "a proud history of supporting our communities, military, first responders, sports fans and hard-working Americans everywhere"), and its values ("freedom, hard work and respect for one another"). The only part of the statement pointing in even the general direction of one of the largest marketing controversies in decades: "We never intended to be a part of a discussion that divides people. We are in the business of bringing people together over a beer."[19]

Perhaps not surprisingly, a response of "we never intended to be a part of a discussion" pleased approximately no one. This is the kind of flinch you can't have if you're going to deliberately embrace conflict. Those offended by the hiring of a trans influencer were likely looking for an apology and a promise to never do anything like that again. The trans community and its allies were looking for the brand to stand behind the partner that Bud Light had accidentally dragged into a major national controversy. Bud Light could have used the backlash as an opportunity to cite its decades of support for the LGBTQ+ community and double down on its support for the trans community. Instead, Bud Light's attempt at a hasty retreat just left everyone mad.

Lands' End had a similarly capricious response to a conflict of its own making during its failed rebrand in the 2010s. In addition to stirring up brand image and functional conflict in her attempts to win over customers to the brand, then-CEO Federica Marchionni also managed to spark ideological conflict during her time as CEO. Specifically, Marchionni introduced the "Legend Series," which were to be one-on-one interviews between the CEO and celebrities and thought leaders "who have made a difference in both their respective industries and the world at large."[20] The interviews were featured as articles in the brand's catalogs.

The first Legend to be interviewed? Feminist icon Gloria Steinem. There was an immediate uproar from Lands' End's many conservative customers, who disagreed with many of Steinem's views, especially her long-standing, vocal support of abortion rights. Interviewing Steinem seems like an intentional choice to make a statement and gin up some controversy, especially as a first interview in the planned series. It seems like an obvious decision made to affirm a new set of values for a new set of customers. But Lands' End reacted as if it had no idea anyone would object. Rather than stand by Steinem, and its choice to wade into discussions on women's rights, the Equal Rights Amendment, and abortion, Lands' End immediately backtracked, removing the Steinem interview from its catalog and its website, and issuing a wishy-washy apology stating it never meant to be "divisive." The apology led to an equally angry reaction from left-leaning Lands' End customers, who were upset that the brand walked away from Steinem and the causes she supports.

Too often, brands seem to make deliberatively provocative moves that they reasonably should have foreseen would incite conflict, then respond as if they had no idea the conflict was coming. This sometimes happens because brands are not thinking about what they're doing as creating conflict but instead as "being edgy" or "pushing the envelope." They overfocus on the potential upsides of such a strategy (Going viral! Increasing engagement!), then seem shocked by the downsides (Protests! Boycotts! Negative press!). They don't weigh the pros and cons in earnest. And then, when they feel the heat, rather than clearly choosing a side, they shrink away, alienating everyone as a result.

Execute Wisely

How brands wade into conflict is just as important as whether they choose to embrace conflict or not. An unfortunate example of a misstep in implementation is when Gillette joined the #MeToo conversation in 2019 with an ad encouraging men to be less toxically masculine. The ad, titled "We Believe," included such cringe-worthy vignettes as a line of dozens of suburban dads standing in front of identical backyard grills chanting, "Boys will be boys!" in unison over and over. There was also a clip of one man apparently about to catcall a woman walking past, when his friend shakes his head and puts a hand on his chest to stop him. The ad swapped out Gillette's traditional tagline, "The Best a Man Can Get," for "The Best a Man Can Be." The sentiment was well intentioned and certainly in line with the major dialogue happening at that time. Adapting the tagline to fit its stance was also a clever way of trying to create brand alignment. But it did not resonate with all of Gillette's customers.

Some consumers were offended that Gillette seemed to characterize many, if not all, men as misogynistic. Others agreed with the message but did not appreciate it coming from the brand that sold them toiletries. Further, there was nothing in Gillette's brand history that resonated with this new anti-toxic-masculinity stance. The extent of Gillette's previous contribution to gender relations seemed mostly limited to including beautiful young women in its ads ready to approvingly stroke the faces of freshly shaved men. Gillette was also known for applying a "pink tax" to its products, charging more for razors and shaving creams designed for women than it did for equivalent men's products. For many, Gillette's new ad was not seen as embracing its core values but instead as being cynically opportunistic. If Gillette hadn't realized the ad would generate conflict, it probably should have.

The solitary ad had no measurable impact on sales one way or the other, but Gillette's parent company, Procter & Gamble, declared the campaign a success.[21] Company representatives said the ad generated significant conversation and supported the brand's efforts to connect more meaningfully with younger consumers.[22] Outside of corporate HQ, it's less clear that the impact on "conversation" was perceived as positively by customers. As Laura Wasson wrote in *Ad Age*, "Consumers are smart, and you underestimate your audience at your own peril. While Gillette's (and ultimately, Procter & Gamble's) desire to promote positive attitudes towards gender equality is admirable, their audience is massive and diverse. They assumed their target would be receptive to the message, but it was delivered in a bizarre fashion, towing the line between humor and earnestness. While the message clicked for some (including many women), it made others feel uncomfortable or downright angry. And who can blame them? No one likes being told they're bad and then asked to buy something."[23]

Gillette seemed to needlessly court intersegment conflict by lowering the boom in a way that felt threatening or demeaning to many of its loyal customers. As another article by Jack Neff in *Ad Age* put it, "Many of the customers for Gillette, a 117-year-old brand, are older white males less likely to be attuned to the #MeToo movement . . . and it was that core shaving demographic that disliked Gillette's ads most."[24] Gillette could have reasonably added its voice to the conversation, taken a progressive position on #MeToo, and started connecting more meaningfully with the values of younger customers, without drawing so much negative attention and scrutiny to the brand. A less aggressive execution might have done the job better.

Conflict as Growth Strategy: The National Football League

When Nike hired Kaepernick as a spokesperson, it intentionally provoked an intense conflict among some customer segments, a deliberate choice that worked out well for the brand in the long run. But strategically inviting conflict doesn't just mean lobbing firebombs. There are also cases where brands can invite less intense conflict as a means of facilitating growth: more like intentionally allowing friction between segments, and less like locking them together inside the Thunderdome, as seen in the earlier example of Signal. The NFL provides an interesting example of a brand that has repeatedly provoked conflict—mostly mild, but occasionally intense—as a part of its growth strategy.

The NFL is the biggest sports league in America, by a wide margin. In 2023, a staggering 69 percent of Americans described themselves as fans of the NFL, with 37 percent claiming to be "avid" fans. It's hard to imagine 70 percent of Americans agreeing on anything, but they agree on the NFL. (For reference, the fan and avid fan numbers for Major League Baseball are 58 percent and 51 percent, and the National Basketball Association are 22 percent and 21 percent.[25]) So it's not like the NFL needed help. But midway through the 2023 football season, a deus ex machina in the human form of Taylor Swift started regularly showing up at Kansas City Chiefs games.

Swift may not actually be superhuman, but at this point her mere mortality should probably not be assumed. She measurably affects the global economy when she goes on tour.[26] Her concert venues generate artificial earthquakes that can be measured by seismologists.[27] In the time it takes you to read this chapter, she will probably have written two more Grammy-award-winning songs. And in 2023, she suddenly ignited an interest among her many, many fans in, of all things, professional football. After the news broke that Swift had started dating Kansas City Chiefs tight end Travis Kelce, there was an estimated net increase of more than 2 million female viewers of NFL games. Viewership increased by 34 percent among women over thirty-five, 24 percent among women eighteen to twenty-four, and a whopping 53 percent among teenaged girls.[28] Travis Kelce's jersey sales increased 400 percent, and his podcast, *New Heights*, became Spotify's number-one sports podcast globally.

This was obviously an opportunity for the NFL, but also a potential source of conflict. The sudden influx of new fans skewed younger, more female, and definitely less steeped in the history and nuances of the game than the NFL's core fans. They were also less interested in the game itself. Swift disciples made T-shirts showing the Chiefs' game schedule under the title "TAYLOR SWIFT, KC Chiefs Tour, with special guest Travis Kelce."

Should the NFL lean into this opportunity and emphasize Swift's presence through its media channels? Should it speak to Swift's fandom directly? And how would the league's core fans respond to any efforts by the NFL to welcome in these interlopers? This seems like a recipe for conflict. User identity conflict if Swifties started to crowd out traditional fan segments, and functional conflict if the NFL adjusted the game-watching experience to overaccommodate the cult of TS.

The NFL didn't turn away from these potential conflicts. Instead, it waded into the conflict using the protocols we outlined in this chapter. First, it weighed the pros and cons: the upside potential of millions of new fans was obvious. But the benefits of those legions of Swiftie-KC fans needed to be measured against any potential dissatisfaction or defection among current fans. A part of the NFL's decision calculus was anticipating just how much friction the new fans would generate among NFL diehards. The answer was not zero, but the NFL assessed it was likely to be relatively small and manageable.

The second and, arguably, most important issue to address was whether and how this conflict would align with the NFL's brand values or equities. Conflict should only be courted when it reinforces the brand for existing customers or indicates a clear position for the brand moving forward. When we asked Tim Ellis, executive vice president and chief marketing officer of the NFL, about this, he was quick to point out that broad-based inclusion was one of the NFL's core values: "Our fan base is evenly distributed across the country. Across demographics. Across the political spectrum. We represent America." The NFL firmly believes that football is for everyone, that core to its mission is creating experiences that bring people of all types together. That sometimes means annoying the self-appointed gatekeepers within the NFL fandom, and even letting some go if they refuse to play nice with new fans.

The third step in growing via strategic conflict is demonstrating commitment to the planned course of action, and consistency to the values at the core of the conflict. Unlike Bud Light and Lands' End, the NFL stuck to its plan, which might best be summarized, at least initially, as more Taylor. A lot more Taylor. During Swift's second appearance at a Chiefs game, there were seventeen televised cutaways to Swift in the stands and two commercials for her concert film. That same week, the NFL's official social media accounts posted about Swift thirty times, resulting in more than 170 million impressions. Many people, probably including Swift herself, felt that this was too much—and the NFL quickly turned down the volume. But this was an adjustment, not an abandonment. According to Ellis, "We saw some disgruntlement by some of our most avid core fans because of the way we emphasized Taylor Swift in our mainstream marketing. And we responded to that. We decreased the pressure a bit—but we didn't move away from it completely. We knew that it was much more important to us to welcome in these new fans than it was to worry about somebody who saw too many Instagram posts of Taylor Swift." The NFL was committed.

The final step in making this conflict serve the NFL was to execute well on its plan. The NFL never lost track of its goal: the goal was to make these new fans feel welcomed and to help them develop a love for the game. Would a constant stream of Taylor posts on Instagram and continuous cutting to her box seats during games help with that? Yes, probably, to some extent. But the NFL also focused on meeting the needs that were unique to this group of fans. One hurdle for new potential fans of a sport is just getting up to speed on the rules and strategy. The average NFL game lasts more than three hours. That is a long time to endure a game one doesn't really understand just to catch a few candid moments of Taylor Swift sharing a joke with Blake Lively. To address this, the NFL started a low-key educational campaign to help these new fans enjoy the game more by understanding it better. "We knew that we could identify and connect with a lot of the fans who followed Taylor on TikTok. And those are channels where most of our main core audience aren't hanging out. So, we welcomed them with a different style of communication, less about the games itself, more about the fun and the excitement of the NFL," Ellis told us. "But there was a lot of material that we created and shared about understanding the game. An education strategy. A lot of these fans that came in didn't really understand football. They were fascinated by it, but they didn't really understand it." The goal was to use this window of engagement to educate these new fans so that whatever ends up happening with this particular celebrity relationship, the NFL can "bring them in as part of the NFL family, so they will stick around and be lifelong fans."

The conflict between Swifties and traditional fans was admittedly pretty minor. There were some obstreperous NFL purists that made the rounds on social media and in the press, but there were many more viewers who were either indifferent or delighted by the NFL's embrace of Taylor. Still, the NFL took the appropriate steps to manage it.

A more dramatic example of the NFL's commitment and consistency on inclusion and social justice can be found in its "Football Is for Everyone" TV ad, which aired in 2021. The ad starts with the statement "Football is gay" in white text on a black background. "Gay" is replaced with other words the NFL claims are associated with football: "beautiful," "heart," "freedom," "American," "for Everyone." The words flashing on the screen accelerate until they are replaced with "LGBTQ+ youth with at least one accepting adult have 40% lower risk of attempting suicide." The ad was released shortly after Carl Nassib came out as the first openly gay player still active in the NFL.

As expected, the ad was controversial. The comments section below the ad on YouTube is a wall of negative reactions: "Goodbye NFL. I'll miss you." "Commercials like this are why I'm no longer an NFL fan." "NFL=No Fans Left." "I'm glad my father passed away before he saw football reduced to this." Hundreds of negative comments.

But as Ellis told us, the NFL saw it coming: "I knew there would be a lot of folks out there who wouldn't like the ad. And I knew there would be people inside the NFL, and on teams, and even players who would not like the ad. But I also knew how meaningful it would be to the LGBTQ+ community and to a lot of young fans in general. I also felt it was important for us to make a big statement to support Carl. It is important for us overall to get behind the beliefs of players and help them express themselves and be the face of the league. So, this was part of a long-term strategy that involves supporting players and what they believe. Even if not every player would have liked it in this case, it was still consistent with that general strategy."

For Ellis, the long-term strategic aim of being more inclusive, explicitly supporting players, and elevating their public profiles was more important than any immediate backlash the ad would create. The NFL knew the ad was risky. In fact, risk in furtherance of a core brand value was kind of the point. "People remember how you behave in those moments. . . . It takes time to earn trust and respect, and those have to be part—authentically part—of your brand. Making these bold moves for a company the size of the NFL, and a brand that's as big as the NFL, is important to really make a fundamental change of perception. It takes being courageous" said Ellis.

Has strategically embracing conflict been an effective strategy for the NFL? It certainly hasn't hurt. The league's revenue in 2023 was the highest ever recorded.

PART THREE

MANAGING SEGMENT RELATIONSHIPS OVER TIME

14

Combining Relationship Strategies

Fences, Bridges, and Ladders

Throughout this book, we have mostly discussed examples of brands facilitating one type of relationship between any given two customer segments—whether Separate Communities, Connected Communities, or Leader-Follower Segments—or establishing and maintaining any one of these strategies in isolation to avoid or escape conflict between Incompatible Segments. But segment relationship management can get much more complex than managing one relationship type between two segments. Brands can implement substrategies within or across segments, allowing them to tap into the benefits of the different relationship types simultaneously. For example, brands can facilitate Leader-Follower dynamics within a segment or connect Separate Communities to each other through networks or platforms, reaping some of the benefits of Connected Communities within Separate Communities.

Secondary relationship strategies can help brands provide more value to customers, such as through more-tailored experiences, creating hierarchies that keep customers engaged and motivated, or by connecting like-minded customers to each other. Secondary strategies can also help brands extract nonmonetary value from customers in the form of social influence, data, and content. To see how this can be done well, let's start by looking at how Nike manages different layers of relationships between customers.

Nike is the eight-hundred-pound gorilla of the athletic apparel world. The brand's influence is felt in virtually all sports—basketball and running, of course, but also field hockey, water polo, table tennis, and curling.[1] Nike takes in nearly twice as much revenue as the second leading global sporting goods company, Adidas, and nearly five times as much as third-ranked Puma. The iconic swoosh is one of the most recognized logos in the world. It is seen on the shoes and clothing of professional and amateur athletes, adults and children, sneakerheads and lifestyle consumers. Nike's "Just Do It" slogan appears on merchandise and in advertisements around the world. This can be a bit unsettling once you learn the phrase was inspired by the final words of a death-row inmate who, upon facing execution, said, "You know, let's do it."[2] Which, to be fair, was one of the more motivational quotes ever to come from a serial killer immediately before execution. Never mind that, though. The point is: Nike is Goliath.

There is no single factor that can account for Nike's dominance. But one of the key advantages that Nike has cultivated over its competitors is its expertise in managing the relationships between its various customer segments. We restrained ourselves from using Nike examples in every chapter of this book, but we could have. It has artfully executed nearly every customer segment relationship principle we have articulated.

From the outside, Nike's primary segmentation strategy appears to be Separate Communities built around different sports and special interests: runners, basketball players, soccer players, tennis players, golfers, fitness and training enthusiasts, sneakerheads, everyday athletes, and more. Consumers in each Separate Community share a love for Nike and what it stands for as an umbrella brand. But they also all seek divergent value from Nike—in terms of products and content—as a function of their sport or fitness orientation.

Part of Nike's broad appeal comes from the fact that it treats each Separate Community like a discrete business and facilitates different types of relationships between customers within those segments. For example, the running business markets its own Nike Running app and focuses on selling running shoes and apparel with content featuring professional runners, such as Galen Rupp, English Gardner, or Mo Farah. Meanwhile, the sneakerheads business gives its customers the SNKRS app to buy limited-edition shoes, watch behind-the-scenes content, and use virtual try-on technology. Products for sneakerheads are less about performance and more about iconicity, art, and fashion. Nike's basketball division, on the other hand, has the Nike X HomeCourt app, which recommends products and gear, and can be used to learn basketball skills through interactive, motion-tracking game play. Nike runs basketball-specific campaigns featuring legends like Michael Jordan, LeBron James, and Caitlin Clark.

It is likely that these various segments would not be fundamentally incompatible. They are aware of each other and mostly indifferent to the fact that athletes of other sports use the brand. If anything, seeing the swoosh at every corner of the sports world further legitimizes its status as *the* brand for all athletes. But they do want divergent value from the brand, and they benefit from being treated as Separate Communities. It is nearly certain that Nike would create a poorer experience for all of these segments by trying to serve them together simultaneously. (More on that in the next chapter.) By breaking each sport segment into its own Separate Community, Nike can tailor the experience of the brand to each group's needs and provide nonoverlapping value to each segment. In fact, some of the brilliance of Nike's strategy is in exaggerating the differences between these groups, giving the brand the room to create customized, unique brand experiences for each segment.

The differences in the marketing mixes between segments make each group feel like it lives in its own Nike world. The brand is still a unifier, but the tone, manner, and swagger of the brand feels a little different depending on the customer's sport of choice.

These Separate Communities are all still very much Nike communities. The Nike brand is cohesive across all of its segments under the general umbrella of *inspired performance* and the idea that "if you have a body, you're an athlete." This overarching positioning encourages inclusion of all types of athletes and indifference between the presence or use of the Nike brand by other segments—athletes of one sport are no more or less "true Nike" athletes compared to athletes of another sport. It also means that if some customers see themselves as Nike runners, the passion they share for the brand will make sense to and resonate with other customers who see themselves as Nike tennis players. The brand meaning is consistent, even if it comes to life in distinct ways for each sport community.

But where Nike has created a real depth of value for each of those communities is by applying the lessons of the Segment Compatibility Matrix at a more granular level, within each community. The most common relationship strategy Nike facilitates within segments is Leader–Follower. Within each sport community, the brand cultivates and serves an aspirational group of customers to attract the segment of consumers who aspire to be like them. Many amateur athletes prefer Nike because they know it is the brand preferred by the elite athletes in their sport. Nike wins the loyalty of these elites through extensive sponsorship deals, yes, but also by consistently being one of the most innovative brands in each of its categories.

Take distance running as an example. In 2017, Nike launched Breaking2, an ambitious new running project designed to help elite marathoners finish a race in under two hours. Nike pulled in the world's top distance runners and had them work with scientists and designers to create a shoe that would enable what had previously seemed impossible. Breaking2 went beyond sponsorships and influencer marketing to create something truly innovative. *National Geographic* aired a one-hour documentary about the project.

Nike set out to create shoes specifically designed for the small but important segment of ultra elite runners. Shoe engineering was a crucial aspect of Breaking2. The runners needed the right shoes to run a marathon in less than two hours. The shoes resulting from this work can cost nearly $600—four times as much as Nike's other running shoes—and are seen on the feet of runners in some of the most competitive marathons in the world. The project served as a reminder that Nike serves a Leader segment, namely, ultra elite runners, with specific shoes. So, if casual and aspirational runners want to perform like record-breaking runners such as Eliud Kipchoge—who did, by the way, eventually break the two-hour-marathon barrier wearing a version of those special Nikes—well, they should also wear Nike.[3]

Given that Nike serves athletes at all levels and abilities, there is always a risk the brand could become overly associated with amateurs or wannabes, which might create brand image or user identity conflict for elite or professional athletes. One of the ways Nike stays well ahead of potential conflict within and across segments is by creating clear hierarchies between the elite athletes who wear its shoes and the much larger segments of Followers who dream of greatness. Both are celebrated, but they are clearly not the same. Nike does this in nearly every sport it serves by sponsoring professional and elite amateur athletes (and featuring them across its communications channels), to form the core of a Leader segment. But it also creates real functional value for those Leaders by consistently producing some of the highest-performing, most innovative shoes, apparel, accessories, and equipment in nearly every sport. A much larger segment of Followers who span the spectrum from ever so slightly less elites hoping to break into the big leagues down to wishful amateurs, who emulate whatever the stars in the sport are wearing.

To help facilitate this dynamic, the brand also incorporates design innovations discovered by working with elite athletes to improve the designs of casual athletic gear. For example, Nike released both elite and consumer versions of the Vaporfly shoe Kipchoge wore for Breaking2. The consumer shoes, called the Vaporfly 4%, are similar in terms of style, geometrics, and materials as the Vaporfly Elite model but are not customized and have a slightly less clunky shape. They arc also less than half the price of the Elites at $260. But the commercially available Vaporflys are not necessarily for mainstream runners either—they are released in limited quantities and mostly bought up by obsessive runners who are willing to shell out hundreds of dollars. A third shoe called the Zoom Fly also came out of the Breaking2 project. This shoe features a similar design and aesthetic to the Vaporfly but weighs a few ounces more and uses more standard foam materials that are slightly less responsive. It also lasts a lot longer. Vaporfly 4% shoes start deteriorating at about a hundred miles (yes, you're paying about $2.60 a mile), while the Zoom Flys last for closer to three hundred to four hundred miles before showing noticeable wear and tear.[4] Newer models of Zoom Flys go for about $150, a quarter of the price of the elite models and comparable in price to other high-end, commercial running shoes. Zoom Flys tend to attract anyone from casual to serious runners, but not obsessive or elite runners.

The hierarchy is clear: Vaporfly Elites for the Eliud Kipchoge's of the world, Vapor Fly 4%s for the serious marathon runners, and Zoom Flys for the rest of us who want to feel like Eliud Kipchoge when we're "zooming" around the suburbs at a nine-minute-mile pace. This Leader-Follower hierarchy allows runners of all speeds to wear Nike shoes without introducing any meaningful risk of brand image or user identity conflict.

In addition to establishing Leader-Follower sub-segments within its separate sport communities, Nike orchestrates Connected Communities within its sport-specific segments too. The Nike Run Club app allows runners to connect to each other, share performance metrics, and participate in running challenges together. Nike X HomeCourt lets basketball players compete in drills and challenges and share their progress, analytics, and videos. These apps provide additional value to consumers who can connect (or compete) with other users to make fitness—and the Nike brand—more appealing. Nike pulls invaluable data from these networks that it pours back into product and customer experience innovation. For example, when the brand noticed that many of its most-engaged SNKRS app users were from Dominican neighborhoods, it created a new Air Force 1 shoe to pay homage to Dominicans. The shoe was called the "De Lo Mio," a term of endearment that roughly translates to "of my people." For its release, Nike worked with Dominican photographers who took photos of Dominicans wearing the shoes.[5] Meanwhile, Nike Studios are physical spaces the brand created to be used for working out, workshops, and events to bring its general workout segment together. Nike Studios are typically located in urban areas to attract a high volume of visitors, facilitating interaction and connections.

By creating Leader-Follower dynamics and Connected Communities within and across its Separate Communities, Nike makes its brand more valuable to each of its customer segments. Consumers don't just want to consume Nike for its functional value, but also because of its association with Leaders in their respective sports and access to like-minded communities. Put simply, Nike maintains its dominance in the athletic footwear and apparel space, in part, because of its savvy layering of different customer-to-customer relationship types to maximize value and minimize conflict, both across and within segments.

Nike reinforces the core premise of this book: brands need to understand how their overarching customer segments relate to one another—or could relate to one another—to keep customer segments happy and prevent conflict between them (see all of the preceding chapters). At the same time, what Nike also demonstrates is the value of pursuing secondary customer segment relationship strategies. The primary relationship between customer segments of Nike is Separate Communities. But the brand also uses secondary relationship strategies that are layered over, or nested within, those Separate Communities.

Of course, you're probably thinking, *Sure, layering customer relationship strategies works well for large brands like Nike in sexy consumer categories with virtually unlimited marketing budgets. But what about agricultural commodities?* We're so glad you asked.

The Milk Processors Education Program (MilkPEP)—the organization behind the famous "Got Milk?" and Milk Mustache ad campaigns—adeptly and efficiently allocates its relatively modest marketing budget by layering multiple segment relationship management (SRM) strategies. MilkPEP is funded by milk processors and is tasked with increasing dairy milk consumption through category-level consumer marketing. This is a formidable goal. Milk consumption has been decreasing for decades, and there are deep regulatory and perceptual challenges working against the consumption of dairy milk. Milk is also a product that allows for relatively limited innovation around the offering itself. But when Yin Woon Rani took the reins as CEO and chief marketing officer of MilkPEP in 2019, she decided she was going to help milk "get its mojo back." To do this, Rani worked with the advertising agency GALE to launch a new national campaign called "You're Gonna Need Milk for That" to reclaim milk's swagger.

Nearly every American household drinks milk—its household penetration is approximately 93 percent—even if the amount each household drinks has been declining. Given its ubiquity, there are naturally many different segments of milk buyers that MilkPEP could target in any particular campaign. Rani chose to focus on two specific groups of consumers to regain milk's cultural relevance and drive reconsideration of milk as a performance drink—moms and youth—and to treat these segments as Separate Communities. It chose to target moms because they are usually the primary household shoppers and youth because that's where some of the biggest declines in milk consumption have been observed, particularly as the kids transition into teenagers and start making more of their own beverage decisions.

One way that MilkPEP reached moms was by tapping into the running community. MilkPEP observed that there was high overlap between runners and the types of moms it wanted to target. Athletes had also long been a customer segment of focus for MilkPEP because of their aspirational value and the clear link between the benefits of milk and performance via maintaining a strong body. In its new campaign, MilkPEP elevated runners as Leaders within the mom segment, a group many other moms, even non-runners, would admire and desire to emulate. To reach the youth segment, it tapped into the gaming community using a similar strategy of attaching itself to a group that kids and teens admired, listened to, and aspired to be like.

The organization worked with highly influential runners and gamers, both professional and amateur, to highlight the role of milk as a performance drink. MilkPEP sponsored women runners at several marathons, from New York to Boston to Chicago, and various other local races. It also hosted its very own Every Women's Marathon in Savannah, Georgia, in November 2024. MilkPEP used an analogous strategy within the gaming community to reach youth consumers by advertising chocolate milk as *the* performance drink for gamers. MilkPEP sponsored gaming events such as TwitchCon and VidCon, created new *Fortnite* games, and hosted a female-only gaming tournament (the Milk Cup) with a $250,000 prize pool. It also partnered with prominent gamers like Extra Emily, who was shown slurping down a glass of chocolate milk in a Twitch ad.

The intention, according to Rani, was to associate itself with Leaders in the running and gaming communities to change perception and drive interest for Followers within those communities. The primary relationship strategy for MilkPEP was serving moms and youth via Separate Communities, but running and gaming were used as the vehicles for reaching those segments and facilitating secondary Leader-Follower dynamics within each Separate Community. Rani told us, "When you have a small budget, you have to think about how to multiply the value of each dollar. Associating with Leaders can create a halo effect within the community to attract Followers." MilkPEP helps drive this dynamic by elevating Leaders within each community, showcasing them across their communications channels. Importantly, MilkPEP also has a policy that everyone it sponsors or partners with must actually be a milk drinker. This helps ensure they are viewed as members of a true Leader segment versus simply paid influencers or endorsers. So far, Rani says the campaign has proven effective in improving positive perceptions of milk as "extremely healthy" and "culturally relevant" across all customer segments, and adding to incremental milk sales.

As demonstrated in the cases of Nike and MilkPEP, brands can reap more value, and provide additional value to customers, by combining SRM strategies. Practically speaking, this often results in a multilayered segmentation strategy, with brands using SRM to manage the relationship between its primary customer segments (e.g., the Separate Communities that use Nike, including basketball players, runners, sneakerheads, etc.) and to manage the relationships between sub-segments of customers within each segment to create more value for customers (e.g., creating Connected Communities and Leader-Follower relationships within the runners customer segment).

Layering Segment Relationship Management Strategies

Once a brand identifies the ideal relationship for managing customer segments, it should consider whether there are benefits to cultivating a secondary relationship across or within segments too. In what follows, we elaborate on how brands can think about using the three compatible customer segment relationship quadrants as secondary

FIGURE 14-1

Segment Compatibility Matrix

The value that segments get from the offering

		Divergent	Collaborative
Orientation toward other segments	Indifferent	Separate Communities	Connected Communities
	Influenced	Incompatible Segments	Leader-Follower Segments

strategies for managing customer-to-customer relationships. As a reminder, see our Segment Compatibility Matrix in figure 14-1.

Separate Communities as a secondary strategy

One of the most common places to see Separate Communities used as a secondary strategy is for brands that use Connected Communities as their primary strategy. Connected Communities can often benefit from imposed divisions between groups of users over time—or the creation of Separate Communities within them. At inception, products and brands that rely on Connected Communities usually must prioritize fast growth to establish a minimum viable network as fast as possible. Remember, if early Uber users logged in to the app and couldn't find any drivers, or drivers didn't receive any ride requests, they would quickly leave the platform. If early YouTubers logged on and there was no content, they'd likely look elsewhere for their cat videos. In the mad dash to establish the minimum volume for a viable new network, exactly *which* customer segments are joining can be a secondary concern for many brands and even for users as the value they derive is primarily a function of the size of the network or community.

But once a Connected Community is sufficiently large, the creation of some boundaries between users who want different things from the offering can ease tensions and increase overall value for customers. Once YouTube was bursting with content (as of 2024, an estimated 3.7 million new videos were uploaded *each day!*), it was important to reduce the functional conflict that might arise if, for example, someone looking for videos of cats playing the piano have to wade through endless streams of Excel tutorials to find it. And you want to ensure that not only can users find what *they want* quickly, but once the video of a cat playing piano concludes, the subsequent recommended content on the platform is also appealing and keeps them engaged, such as a video that shows you how to make a helmet for your cat out of a watermelon rind.

So as YouTube reached the point where users can find videos on nearly any topic, it refined the user experience in a way that clustered customers into smaller communities or content streams in the platform. YouTube creates these Separate Communities within its network in several ways. First, it provides categories of video content in tabs on its website and app, including music, sports, gaming, and news, which allow users to self-select into the content "communities" that match their interests. YouTube also allows users to subscribe to channels that align with their interests. And creators and users can organize videos into playlists that make it easier to find related content. The result is that users can access and create the content they value on YouTube without eroding the experience for users and creators with dissonant content preferences, which could result in functional conflict for some or all users. The overall customer base still operates as a Connected Community of users, but users with different preferences select into experiences they prefer without enduring experiences that might make them rebel against the brand or lead to conflict over the brand image or who it is for. YouTube's algorithm further reinforces the boundaries between the Separate Communities. Its tailored recommendations effectively establish invisible barriers between segments, based on viewing history, likes, channel subscriptions, shares, and on the behavior of viewers with similar imputed preferences. The siloed YouTube experiences of customers with different political interests, for example, is well documented.[6]

Uber has similarly created Separate Communities within its Connected Communities by allowing room for riders and drivers to segregate according to what kind of experience they would like to have. UberX, UberBlack, and UberPool can all be accessed via the same app and will all facilitate getting one from point A to point B. But carving off Separate Communities within the network allows the platform to serve everyone better.

Brands can also create Separate Sub-Communities within Separate Communities. For example, the North Face serves two primary customer segments as Separate Communities: wilderness enthusiasts and fashionable urbanites. But there are distinctions within each of these segments, based on their tastes and interests. The brand's main account (@thenorthface) mostly serves wilderness enthusiasts, with curated content centering on sponsored athletes and performance technology. But even looking at the handles of some of the other accounts helps you see how it has nested communities within the wilderness community: @thenorthface_climb and @thenorthface_snow. Its other segment, fashionable urbanites, is served by the city account (@thenorthface_city), but also has its own sub-communities, including the purple label (@thenorthface.purplelabel), a collab with the Japanese label Nanamica.

Leader-Follower as a secondary strategy

Years after they were launched, Facebook, Instagram, YouTube, Twitter, and LinkedIn all migrated toward status markers of some kind to indicate that an account is owned by an authentic public figure, celebrity, or global brand (i.e., a Leader). Along with serving as a means of distinguishing authentic from inauthentic accounts, the checkmark badges have become highly sought-after status symbols for aspiring creators, influencers, and other noncelebrity users (i.e., Followers). Earning a checkmark not only provides users with access to different tools and features on some platforms, but is a marker of legitimacy, influence, or importance.

Brands also elevate leaders in the community by providing them with special designations (similar to the blue checkmark) and featuring them in social media and promotional materials. A common approach to this is an ambassador program. For example, Athletic Brewing Company's ambassador program encourages customers across its different segments to become brand advocates through events as well as personal and branded communications. Ambassadors are tasked with projecting the brand's values, including having a positive orientation toward health, fitness, and the environment— as well as enjoying nonalcoholic beer, of course—and helping to spread the word about Athletic. Ambassadors are a separate group from the brand's sponsored athletes, which includes J.J. Watt, Malia Manuel, Jordan Burroughs, Carlin Isles, and Alex Johnson. Ambassadors are customers, who can earn rewards and merch, and who represent Athletic at various events and on its website and social pages. The ambassadors serve as a Leader group that makes the brand more desirable to Followers within the Athletic community.

Connected Communities as a secondary strategy

Even for brands that don't sell products or services that naturally rely on Connected Communities, brands can create more value for customers by connecting customers to each other through networks. For example, Apple's Developer Network and Roblox's Creator Hub connect each brand's consumers, giving participants the opportunity to learn from each other and contribute higher-quality creations for all users to enjoy. These opportunities for connection enable customers within Separate Communities to create value within their segment. In turn, the brand can stoke stronger loyalty and use networks and communities as data sources for research and product development. The primary strategy for these brands is that of Separate Communities, but they layer Connected Community dynamics within and over these larger segments.

American Express added a Connected Community strategy to its primary strategy of Separate Communities when it created the OPEN forum. OPEN is an online platform that provides resources for Amex's small-business owners segment and connects them to each other through educational and networking initiatives. Members can use the forum to access content and contributions from experts and peers, post questions, share experiences, and learn from other business owners facing similar challenges or pursuing similar goals. The forum is also a sales and advice platform: owners can list what they can offer to other businesses, and what they need from them. OPEN provides additional value to small businesses, which want to use Amex because being a customer provides access to this larger network of similar customers. While small-business owners represent one of several Separate Communities that use Amex (alongside affluent individuals, corporate clients, travelers, and merchants), the brand created a connected relationship within this segment to increase customer acquisition, retention, and loyalty for small-business owners.

Hosting in-person events and experiences can also be opportunities for brands to create connected relationships with other customers. Berkshire Hathaway is a multinational conglomerate holding company led by "the oracle," Warren Buffett. Berkshire serves a wide range of customer segments through its subsidiaries and investments in insurance, retail, utilities, manufacturing, railroads, financial services, and media and entertainment. Primarily the brand serves Separate Communities. But one segment in particular drives much of the fanfare around Berkshire Hathaway: shareholders. Berkshire Hathaway's shareholders include sub-segments of both individual retail investors and institutional investors, and they vary in terms of the types of shares they tend to buy and the amount they have invested. But within this community, shareholders value Berkshire

Hathaway for overlapping reasons, including Buffett's investing philosophies, his track record of success and celebrity, and the long-term growth potential of the stock.

Often referred to as the "Woodstock for Capitalists," Berkshire Hathaway hosts an annual shareholders' meeting to connect shareholders to each other and reaffirm the organization's values and purpose. Attendees can use the event to hear Buffett's wisdom first-hand and mingle with like-minded investors and industry professionals. Participants can build relationships and swap insights and advice during workshops and panel discussions, while shopping for Warren Buffett merch (for example, you can buy boxer shorts with Buffett's face on them) or while running the annual "Invest in Yourself 5K" road race sponsored by Brooks Running Company, a Berkshire Hathaway company.[7]

Connected Communities can be used to provide new sources of value for entirely new external stakeholders, too. A small, family-owned paper-craft company headquartered in Arizona provides an interesting example of this. It developed a nontraditional two-sided market to create connected value between its customers and a group of charities. Scrapbook.com sells colorful card stock, stickers, punches, and dies to hobbyists, who turn them into handmade cards, intricate scrapbook pages, and mixed-media artwork. The retail website is built around a social network, custom built to allow paper crafters of all kinds to share their creations. Unlike most social media networks, the goal is not to facilitate conversation among members. As CEO Drex Davis told us, "When people are talking, they aren't scrapbooking." Instead, the goal is inspiration: members of the community share new designs, new ways to use various supplies and tools, and provide support and encouragement.

More recently, Scrapbook.com created an additional, novel network to solve a problem for their customers. Like other pastimes that involve making things (e.g., quilting, painting, woodworking), much of the joy in paper crafting is in the creation, after which the hobbyist is left to cope with a growing pile of that creative output. These hobbyists often give away this excess to friends and family, but there are simply not enough special occasions on the calendar to keep up with the yield of avid card makers. For many crafters, that pile of unused cards stuffing drawers, filling boxes, and crowding counters can start to dissuade these amateur artists from making more. Scrapbook.com sought to solve this problem for its customers by creating a unique two-sided market: a nonprofit that collects cards from makers and delivers them to charities, which complete them with handwritten messages and share them with those they serve.

More than two hundred organizations participate in the program. Ronald McDonald House in Arizona includes some of these handmade cards in the welcome baskets prepared for the families it houses while a child is receiving medical care. Dignity Health gives cards to doctors, nurses, volunteers, and patients. Some charities give the cards to cancer patients, others to the elderly, to soldiers deployed overseas, and to children in need on holidays and birthdays. In the five years since its inception, the Cards for Kindness program has given more than 2 million cards to charities all over the country.

Within this volunteer-driven, nonprofit, two-sided market, the card makers are the "sellers" and the charities are the "buyers." As in more traditional markets, both sides receive value from the transaction, and the market becomes more valuable the more creators and charities participate, in terms of both the volume of cards gathered and the number of charitable causes that might inspire a creator. The value in this case is measured more in warm fuzzies than in dollars, but that makes the value no less real and no less compelling. As evidenced by the overwhelming response from the paper-crafting community, this program lets participating crafters continue to do what they love—which includes buying more paper-craft supplies—and to feel good about doing it.

Fences, Bridges, and Ladders

SRM can get complicated, particularly when you start applying the principles at different levels of the brand or its segments and implementing primary and secondary relationships between customers. So, perhaps a simplifying metaphor would help. If you ever find yourself lost in the weeds of all the decisions required to serve multiple customer segments, remember that growth through acquiring new customers ultimately comes down to the simple decision of selecting which segments to pull apart, which to push together, and which to vertically segregate. Or when to construct fences, bridges, or ladders between customers.

Fences keep groups of customers who want distinct things from the brand away from each other. As the Robert Frost poem goes, "Good fences make good neighbors." Fences give brands the ability to create more value for groups of customers within a larger user base by creating more-tailored brand experiences for each segment or subgroup. They can be subtle—as seen with YouTube's algorithms that create more-tailored content experiences—or they can be explicit—such as Nike creating separate apps for runners and sneakerheads or Starbucks creating different store formats for third placers and on-the-goers. In each of these cases, the segments of customers are OK coexisting within the brand ecosystem, but they benefit when they are given their own space—whether real or conceptual. Any time customers would benefit from having less interaction with each other, or less interaction with what other customers want from the brand, create a fence.

Bridges, meanwhile, bring customer segments together. They create links between and within various communities. A brand should build bridges whenever there is opportunity for customers to create more value by collaborating with each other. For some brands and customers, facilitating relationships between customers can provide additional value to customers and enrich their brand experience. This is evident in how Nike creates more value for customers by inviting them to join networks of runners, athletes, and sneakerheads through its various apps, how Amex uses the OPEN forum to connect small-business owners, and how Berkshire Hathaway brings shareholders together at its annual meeting. Connecting customers to each other can also remove the burden of certain functions off the brand's shoulders and place it into consumers' hands, as seen with Apple's Developer Network and Roblox's Creator Hub. Brands can cut costs significantly by connecting willing consumers to each other for support and troubleshooting. Bridges can be created through digital platforms, through the establishment of brand communities, and through virtual and physical events or community spaces. Any time it would be valuable for customers to interact with each other— collaboratively or competitively—you should build a bridge of some sort.

Ladders also connect customer segments, but in a way that vertically differentiates the segments. Ladders emphasize that one segment has more status, expertise, power, coolness, credibility, or authenticity than the other. These segments are connected but not on an equal footing. Ladders give the brand an opportunity to use a group of its own customers to signal or reinforce brand attributes to other customer segments, which is often more efficient and more effective than when brands try to get the same message across directly in their communications. The brands benefit from a halo effect of reflected glory by being associated with the segment at the top of the ladder. When Nike uses its segments of elite athletes to attract amateur athletes, it is constructing ladders within the brand or sport segment. So are social media platforms when they dole out blue checkmarks to some users and not others. If you serve a group of customers that others admire or want to emulate, it might be time for a ladder.

TABLE 14-1

Layered SRM strategies

Layered SRM strategy

Primary strategy	Secondary strategy	Brand examples	Techniques
Separate Communities	+ Separate Communities	The North Face Nike	Create subcommunities
Separate Communities	+ Leader-Follower	Athletic Brewing Nike MilkPEP	Elevate a group of customers within a segment
Separate Communities	+ Connected Communities	Apple Roblox American Express Berkshire Hathaway Nike	Connect customers within or across segments via digital platforms, social media, events, or physical or virtual gathering spaces, or members clubs
Connected Communities	+ Separate Communities	YouTube Uber	Create separate spaces, physical or symbolic, for different segments within the network
Connected Communities	+ Leader-Follower	Facebook Instagram YouTube Twitter LinkedIn	Create hierarchies within a network by providing status markers to aspirational segments
Connected Communities	+ Connected Communities	Scrapbook.com	Connect networks to each other via marketplaces

If you're ever in a pinch in deciding how to manage the relationship between, within, or across customer segments, just ask yourself, Would these groups benefit from a fence, a bridge, or a ladder? Secondary strategies rely on just asking that question again, one level down. (See table 14-1.)

15

SRM Is Never Done

Why Marketing Is Exhausting

Segment relationship management (SRM) is not a box to check or a task to complete. It is a discipline that should be baked into every strategic decision a brand makes. Every year, a brand's customer base changes, even if only by a matter of degrees. Some customers leave, and new customers come in. New competitors enter the market, providing your customers with new reference points against which to value your offerings. The needs and wants of customers evolve, as do the goals of the brands that serve them. The meaning of a brand will change as it grows and stretches to serve new customer segments or shifts away from existing segments. Customer segment relationships that had been brought into equilibrium can suddenly be disrupted. Or a change made to one part of the business can have ripple effects on the ability for any two segments to coexist as customers of a brand. As a result, managing customer segment relationships is not like building a fortification to protect a brand. It is more like charting the course of a ship on roiling seas. You will have to make constant adjustments as the ocean shifts below you and new sources of conflict continuously rise from the depths of the marketplace.

One Eternal Round

Earlier, we cited Starbucks as an example of a brand that has managed the relationships between its segments well, adeptly avoiding or managing conflict as it popped up. Starbucks has done remarkably well in this regard, especially given its staggering growth. But this should not be misunderstood as Starbucks having permanently solved the problem of conflict between its customer segments.

Starbucks invested heavily in its mobile app to fuel its rewards program and streamline orders. The app was ideal for the on-the-go segment, which could order ahead and not have to wait in line for the order. As the app grew in popularity, it also became popular among Starbies, who were more easily able to order elaborate TikTok-inspired specialty drinks. The app created real benefits for certain segments. But with the success of the app came new problems and subsequent conflict. As more drinks were preordered before customers reached the store—a whopping 30 percent of all orders are processed through the mobile app—this has increased the burden on baristas and wait times for all segments. During busy periods, Starbucks counters are overcrowded with mobile orders waiting for pickup, even as the surrounding area is teeming with in-store customers impatiently waiting for their name to be called. These in-store traffic jams create frenetic store environments and lead some customers to walk in and turn right around when they see the chaos.[1] The success of the app has created functional conflict for customers who want to order coffee in stores the old-fashioned way or heaven forbid, relax and enjoy their coffee in a third-place environment.[2]

Thanks mostly to the Starbies and on-the-go segments, by the 2020s, Starbucks was also selling more than twice as many cold drinks as hot drinks in the United States. This would be fine, if not for the fact that many cold drinks, particularly frozen drinks, need to be made by hand at the time they are ordered. They also usually require a blender. That's a lot of noise, especially for customers looking to get some work done over the free Wi-Fi, or for those stuck not so patiently waiting for their flat white to arrive as the pickup counter overflows with iced matcha lattes.[3] In many locations, Starbucks also replaced much of its more comfortable seating with wooden stools.[4] Unsurprisingly, customers grew frustrated with noisy coffee shops, uncomfortable seats, long lines, and congested stores. Starbucks also leaned more aggressively into noncoffee drinks, such as by introducing fruity refreshers or matcha "moon drinks," the latter of which weren't technically on the menu but went viral among young consumers. To lure price-conscious consumers back to the brand, Starbucks rolled out deep discounts and promotions.[5] Needless to say, discounted fruity drinks clearly clash with Starbucks's image as a premium coffee purveyor.[6]

In response to these mounting frustrations, Howard Schultz—who had again taken the reins as CEO of the brand for the third time—announced at the 2022 Investor Day that Starbucks would be "reinventing" and "reimagining" the third place.[7] Schultz said, "The third-place environment which has been such a foundational aspect of the Starbucks Experience all over the world is now somewhat confined by the fact that people are not using our stores in the same way."[8] Schultz then went on to report that the brand would be installing drive-throughs in 90 percent of new locations and rolling out machinery across locations that would make drink preparation, particularly for cold and frozen drinks, less complex and more efficient for baristas.[9] The brand has also been testing faster and quieter blenders as well as new store formats designed to better manage acoustics. When the brand brought in Brian Niccol as its new chairman and CEO in 2024, Niccol announced that the brand would be focused on reinvigorating coffeehouse culture at Starbucks by adding more premium coffee drinks to the menu, promoting seasonal drinks, and reclaiming Starbucks's place as a gathering space.[10] He also announced the brand would be scaling back discounts and promotions.[11] Starbucks continues to make bold, sometimes contradictory moves to balance the often-incompatible needs of different customer segments. But all this effort emphasizes the point: it is, and will continue to be, hard work for Starbucks to keep these divergent segments happy. When you serve as many large and diverse customer segments as Starbucks does, any move that improves things for one group of customers risks inciting conflict with another.

Burberry also found itself grappling with new conflict between customer segments in the 2020s after resolving its "chav" conflict a decade earlier. Starting in 2017, Burberry targeted a more upscale, wealthier clientele than it had been serving. To attract this segment, the brand raised prices and leaned into avant-garde styles, first under the direction of Riccardo Tisci and then Daniel Lee.[12] Burberry released leather goods and handbags with sky-high price tags, charging 58 percent more on average than the bags they replaced, and de-emphasized classic features and legacy designs.[13] Changes to pricing and creative design generated brand image and functional conflict as the brand strayed from its heritage and made many of its flagship offerings unaffordable to its core customers of affluent but aspirational customers.

And while Burberry was pushing toward higher luxury with new designs and refurbished flagship stores, it continued to operate dozens of discount outlets, through which it sold roughly $1 billion of goods at steep price cuts. In fact, Burberry generated the majority of its profit from factory stores, a greater proportion than all European luxury brands.[14] Madeline Berg wrote in *Business Insider*, "The result is a series of contradictions: a British heritage brand known for its trench coats trying to become a high-end *maison*, and a label with increasingly expensive products that has had to turn to outlets and steep discounts when those products didn't move."[15] It wasn't clear who Burberry was for anymore except that it didn't seem to appeal either to the affluent but aspirational consumers it historically served or to the ultra-wealthy customer segment it wanted to attract.

Arguably, part of why the upscaling growth strategy failed was because of the preexisting incompatible relationship between ultra-wealthy customers and outlet shoppers that the brand didn't resolve before attempting to take itself higher upscale. The ultra-wealthy were unlikely to ever be attracted to the Burberry brand so long as outlet shoppers continued to be the brand's dominant customer segment, no matter how much the brand tried to convince wealthy audiences it was haute couture. As Carol Ryan wrote for the *Wall Street Journal*, "If Burberry really wants to move upmarket, it needs to go cold turkey on outlets and take a painful hit to its bottom line. . . . Another option would be to change course and follow the lead of Coach or Michael Kors, who run many of their flagship stores at a loss and make their profit from outlets. This would allow Burberry to cut costs, double down on its off-price business and boost profit. The trade-off would be a lower stock-market valuation than its European peers and an end to any hope of being a high-end luxury brand."[16]

In 2024, Burberry brought in a new CEO, Joshua Schulman, to steer the brand back on course.[17] Doing so will require SRM: resolving the conflict between the current and sought-after target customers. Primarily, Schulman will have to decide whether to continue pushing upmarket, and whether to make goods accessible to aspirational customers and outlet shoppers or find a way to serve those segments in conjunction with the ultra-wealthy, without generating conflict. Schulman will also need to decide which direction the brand will go in design-wise: reemphasize iconic and classic Burberry aesthetics and products, continue to experiment with edgier styles and a modernized brand identity, or somehow balance both. Burberry may be able to look at its own recent history for some helpful tips on strategies that can manage the relationships between segments with different preferences and different amounts of social capital.

And remember when we told you how Nike's dominance in the athletic world can be partly explained by the brand's brilliance in managing the relationships between and within customer segments? Well, it turns out even giants can stumble if they stop actively managing the dynamics between and within customer segments. Between 2021 and 2024, Nike's stock price fell from an all-time high of over $172 to about $75, its lowest closing price since its IPO in 1980.[18] Much of this decline was attributed to adjustments made by John Donahoe, who took the helm as Nike's CEO in 2020. When Donahoe joined Nike, he made a number of changes that proved regrettable. These changes included: (1) reorganizing the firm into men's, women's, and kids' categories instead of divisions dedicated to specific sports; (2) ending wholesaler relationships to boost direct-to-consumer sales; and (3) reorienting the brand's marketing from a storytelling focus to a data-driven and digitally led performance marketing focus.[19]

By eliminating sport-specific categories within Nike's management structure, Donahoe effectively took a bulldozer to the fences between the Separate Communities of athletes that Nike had so beautifully built up over decades of corporate history. To streamline operations, the firm merged functions and teams, laying off hundreds of employees, and ceasing to run each sport community as a distinct business. Sure, reorganizing the firm by gender was a useful cost-cutting measure—it was an efficient way to justify cutting jobs and reducing apparently redundant roles and teams—but it also meant the company did away with many of its employees with sport-specific experience and expertise. The new structure meant that many products were created for cross-category use rather than to satisfy the needs of athletes of a given sport. The brand tried to offer similar solutions for athletes with divergent wants and needs. This led to functional and brand image conflict as Nike started to lose its edge as an innovator and product designer for each specific sport community. Product failures—such as when Nike sent Major League Baseball teams cheap-looking, see-through uniforms for the 2024 season—were attributed to the elimination of focused teams for each sport.[20]

Nike was also losing its monopoly on Leader segments in the 2020s. Tennis legend Roger Federer left Nike in 2018, track star Allyson Felix left the brand in 2019, and gymnast Simone Biles moved on from Nike in 2021.[21] Nike's once dominant grip in the running category was weakening too. While the number of gold medals won by Nike athletes (which totaled seventeen) at the World Athletics Championships in 2019 far outweighed those of non-Nike athletes (who won only five), non-Nike athletes won more gold medals (twelve) than Nike athletes (ten) in the 2024 running events.[22] Some of Nike's marquee athletes were also not as resonant with young consumers—Gen Zers were still in diapers when Michael Jordan and Tiger Woods were at the pinnacles of their careers.[23]

Nike's emphasis on data-driven and digitally led performance marketing over brand-building and storytelling had a corrosive effect on its brand image. Massimo Giunco, a former Nike branding executive, told *Adweek*, "Nike became a machine to produce content to feed this digital ecosystem. It was all resources that it took away from brand-building. . . . The main objective was to drive people to Nike.com, not to resonate with or inspire people to play sport."[24] Resources were diverted away from Nike's traditional focus on bold, brand-heavy campaigns featuring sport legends and Leader segments and toward uninspiring and ineffective programmatic ads designed for sales conversion. *GQ* writer Noah Johnson aptly summarized this misstep, saying, "Big data strikes again. Word to the wise: Never leave your brand in the hands of the algorithm. It won't go well. Making a brand is like cooking a soufflé. It cannot be automated. There are too many factors. Every oven is different. It requires the watchful eye of a dedicated, intuitive chef."[25] By over-relying on data and prioritizing operational efficiencies over understanding the value customers derive from a brand and managing relationships between and within segments, Nike drove itself into brand image and identity conflict to its own peril.

Nike also overproduced some of its top-selling shoes, including its retro lifestyle sneakers and Air Jordans, despite signals suggesting consumers were losing interest in them. Between 2019 and 2023, the brand released more than double the number of Air Jordan 1 Highs and more than triple the number of Nike Dunk Lows through its SNKRS app. And because the brand stuffed the market with Dunks and Jordans to make them more available to mainstream consumers, the shoes lost their cachet with collectors and style mavens. By 2024, retailers were slashing prices on Nike products to try to move inventory, chipping away at the Nike veneer and exacerbating brand image conflict.[26]

Once Nike's problems became painfully obvious, Donahoe changed tack. In a 2024 earnings call, he said Nike would be making four adjustments to reinvigorate the brand and its customer base: (1) sharpen its focus on sport and reinvest in sport-focused teams; (2) drive a continuous flow of new product innovation; (3) create bolder and more distinctive brand marketing that would specifically feature storytelling that leveraged athletes and sport moments; and (4) reengage with wholesale partners. Or, pretty much go back to what Nike was doing before Donahoe mucked things up.[27] The brand even renamed its categories "fields of play," to reflect a return to sport-based segmentation.[28]

If any brand is poised to capitalize on an underdog narrative, it's Nike. And in theory, the adjustments Donahoe promised should help restore sport-based Separate Communities and reestablish Leader-Follower relationships through storytelling and product innovations. In anticipation of the 2024 Olympics, Nike released a campaign called "Winning Isn't for Everyone." Advertisements featured elite athletes overcoming extreme struggles and displaying unapologetic competitive attitudes as they relentlessly pursue their athletic ambitions.[29] The campaign appeared to be an explicit attempt to restore Nike's image as a champion of athletic excellence and mental toughness and to realign the Nike brand with a Leader segment of elite athletes. Time will tell whether Nike can recapture its own greatness.

The point—for Starbucks, Burberry, and Nike—is that it is never possible to permanently resolve the growth dilemma. Even the most successful brands must *constantly* monitor and manage the relationships between customer segments. Relationships between customer segments are dynamic. How segments relate to each other changes as the wants and needs of customers evolve, as the cultural and social context morphs, and as brands make decisions to try to attract new and different segments. Just as your friend groups change as a function of where you live, work, and what your interests are at any given stage of life, so do the customers within a brand's ecosystem. Managing the relationships between customer segments is an ongoing job, not a single decision made at a single point in time. If you try to grow by acquiring new customer segments, you will need to grapple with how to manage different customers with different wants and needs. And you'll have to engage in increasingly complex negotiations between your various customer segments and stakeholders over how your brand should be used, what it means, whom it serves and doesn't serve, and what ideologies it supports.

Monitoring Customer Segments

Brands commonly track their performance and reputation over time. Brands monitor how aware customers are of them, what they think of the brand, and how much they trust it. Brands also track consumers' likelihood of trying the brand, of abandoning the brand, or of recommending the brand to others. But organizations often look at brand performance in aggregate, evaluating feedback based on a representative sample of their customer base or of the market generally. It is less common, in our experience, for brands to analyze brand metrics at the segment level. Sure, organizations sometimes consider brand performance by subgroups or demographics, perhaps because they want to see what young people think of their brand, or LGBTQ+ consumers, or whatever other demographic profile they might be interested in at the moment. But, as you already know from our discussion in chapter 11, profile-based categories don't make for great segments. And rarely do brands track their reputation—or even financial outcomes for that matter—as a function of their value-based segments.

Continuously monitoring brand sentiment and performance for each value-based segment is essential for detecting emerging conflict between customer segments. Timberland should monitor brand performance for workers and hip-hop fans; Crocs should monitor brand performance for the feel goods, explorers, and fashion followers; and Nike should monitor brand performance for each sport community or athlete type it serves. They should analyze metrics at the segment level because aggregate or demographically defined metrics can conceal meaningful patterns or interactions between customer segments. It is possible for a brand to have one customer segment that perceives the brand in an increasingly positive way, driving an increase in revenue from that segment, while another segment views the brand in an increasingly negative way, and so is spending less on the brand. Traditional brand-tracking surveys would likely show stable sentiment. Traditional sales-tracking methods would show that revenues are unchanged. But neither metric would give an accurate picture of the underlying tension, which could have provided an opportunity to fix the conflict between segments before one abandons the brand entirely. Aggregate metrics frequently belie a more nuanced reality.

Value Tracking

Ideally, brands should also monitor the extent to which segments perceive that the brand is able to deliver on the functional image, identity, and ideological value they seek from it. For example, if what customers value from the Timberland brand is its authentic image, the durability of its products, its association with blue-collar workers, and its relevance to hip-hop culture, then Timberland should track the brand's performance on these attributes over time. In other words, it should monitor the extent to which segments—both current customer segments and future potential target segments—see the Timberland brand as authentic, durable, associated with workers, and relevant to hip-hop culture. Tracking each of the components of the value proposition for each segment would give Timberland insight into how the brand is performing on the dimensions its customers care about. This offers more clarity than, say, an overall brand liking or net promoter score, because it can indicate which sources of value the brand should prioritize or invest in. For example, if the authentic image of the brand is suffering for hip-hop fans, and Timberland wants to maintain this customer segment, then it would need to give more attention to reinforcing authenticity in a way that would resonate with that segment.

Measuring performance based on sources of value for the brand can also help managers determine whether there are relationships between sources of value. If Burberry becomes more valuable for outlet shoppers, does it lose its prestige for wealthier segments? And brands can glean whether actions they take affect any given segment's perception and its ability to get what it wants from the brand. If Weight Watchers tries to reposition around wellness or Lands' End takes a political stance, will it affect current customers' relationship with the brand? Finally, brands can track whether changes in the composition of the customer base erode value across segments too. If too many drunk adults vacation at Disney World, will families no longer see a Disney vacation as a magical or wholesome experience? If too many people start posting sappy stories about how they proposed to their partners on LinkedIn, will it undermine the functional value for those who want LinkedIn to remain a strictly professional networking site? Implicit in the notion of value tracking is the idea that organizations should not overly rely on sales data as an indicator of brand health or segment relationship harmony. As we saw with Supreme, Tiffany, Burberry, Ray-Ban, and others, the same actions or patterns that caused short-term spikes in revenue can yield destructive conflict between customer segments in the long run. For example, in the mid-1980s, the luxury sports fashion company Lacoste, in a desperate grasp for revenue, lowered prices and broadened distribution for many of the brand's mainstay products. Lacoste polos were even being sold at Walmart. At first, sales increased as more consumers could get their hands on the coveted crocodile logos. But unsurprisingly, over-exposure and over-discounting eventually led to brand image conflict, and wealthy customers lost interest in Lacoste's fitted tennis shirts and sunglasses. The brand was close to being shuttered until it hired Robert Siegel as CEO in 2002. Siegel aggressively raised prices, limited distribution again, and got cool or sophisticated celebrities like Natalie Portman, Katie Couric, and the cast of *The O.C.* to sport the brand. The immediate impact of this reversal on revenue was minimal, but between 2002 and 2005, sales grew 800 percent and the brand was valued at $1.8 billion globally.[30] The brand moves under Siegel's direction resolved the key conflicts that almost put it out of business by effectively firing the customers who contributed to the cheapening of the brand and establishing a new Leader segment.

What the Lacoste roller coaster illustrates is the importance of monitoring more than just short-term sales and brand metrics to diagnose the health of the business. The short-term sales gains in the 1980s, and the initial lack thereof under Siegel's new direction, were poor indicators of the long-term impact these changes caused. The very actions that drove a spike in sales created the conflict between customer segments that almost drove the brand into the ground. In contrast, actions that had minimal short-term impact helped resolve conflicts and grew the brand to new heights.

Revenue and sales are obviously essential indicators of performance—they're sort of the entire point of a business—but brands also need to pay attention to how customers relate to the brand and to each other. Attending to these metrics can help brands see the writing on the wall *before* it shows up in their bottom line.

Operational Checkpoints

Sometimes, the structure of an organization encourages decisional myopia. When a middle manager owns only a small piece of the overall brand strategy, it is natural for them to seek out local maxima, making decisions that are optimal within their limited purview, even if that is not what is best for the long-term growth of the brand. A marketer whose only job is to grow new segments of customers may reasonably not even consider the impact of new customers on existing segments in their strategizing. And a marketer focused only on nurturing the brand's relationships with one particular customer segment may not be incentivized to attend to how creating more value for those customers might affect other segments. Outside of marketing, a manager whose job is to streamline the business and cut costs may implement changes that have the unintended side effect of destabilizing segment communities or the relationships between customer segments. Unfortunately, this operational tunnel vision becomes more pronounced as organizations grow and become more matrixed, and roles are increasingly specialized. Those who have the vantage point of seeing activity occurring across the organization must take responsibility for ensuring the brand doesn't erode value for current customers in the process of trying to acquire new segments. This responsibility might reasonably fall on upper-level managers and executives, though we envision a day when an SRM perspective is adopted across organizations and by all employees.

As a best practice, brands should regularly gut check their plans to attract or grow a target segment. This doesn't need to be complicated. It can be as simple as sketching out the answers to a few simple questions. Start by identifying the primary customer segment you want to target for growth. Next, define the tactics you plan to implement and why, specifically, you think they will work to grow the target segment. Then, answer the following questions:

1. What are the relationships between the segment targeted for growth and the other segments?

2. If the target segment grows, what will be the effect on other segments?

3. What is the predicted effect of the specific tactics for growing the target segment on the nontarget segments?

The answers to questions one and two can help brands determine whether generally growing the target segment is likely to provoke conflict—regardless of the way that growth is achieved. Sometimes, segments can peacefully coexist only as long as one of them doesn't get too large. It's OK if there are a few drunk adults at Disney World, or a small fraction of Burberry shoppers buy their goods at outlet stores, but if there are herds of drunk adults walking around Disney parks, or if most consumers buy their Burberry goods through off-price channels, or if LinkedIn becomes a site predominantly for trauma dumping, then it can become a problem for other customer segments. If the mere growth of one segment could create conflict, then the brand might want to revisit the decision to target that segment for growth.

The answer to question three can then help the brand see whether the specific tactics for growing the target segment could result in conflict for any other segment. It's possible that the strategy of growing a particular segment would not be problematic for other segments, but the way in which the brand attempts to grow that segment could stir up conflict. Indeed, conflict is often generated between customer segments, not necessarily because a brand tries to create more value for one customer segment at the expense or neglect of another, but because of *how* it went about creating value.

For Burberry, growing the ultra-wealthy-customer segment probably could have had a positive effect on the affluent but aspirational customers. A greater number of ultra-wealthy customers would enhance the prestigious image of Burberry for its less wealthy customer segments. However, the way Burberry tried to attract new customers—which involved effectively pricing out the affluent but aspirational customers—created functional conflict for those who could no longer afford flagship products.

The answers to these questions can be organized into a simple table, as we will demonstrate using Nike's 2024 "Winning Isn't for Everyone" campaign as an example (see table 15-1). (We have included a blank back-of-the-napkin SRM table for you to use and reference in assessing growth strategies for your brand at the end of the chapter.) Nike would begin the analysis by indicating the target growth segment: elite athletes. Next, Nike would define the tactics it will implement to grow this segment: the "Winning Isn't for Everyone" campaign. At this point it would want to articulate why it thinks this tactic would work to promote growth in the target segment: elite athletes will probably be more drawn to Nike if the brand more strongly and clearly aligns itself with the elite athletes and their competitive mindset. This campaign would help realign the brand with the values of the elite athlete segment.

Then, Nike would want to ask how other segments relate to the target growth segment. For the sake of this example, we will construct segments based on athletic ability and interests: elite athletes, semi-elite athletes, aspirational athletes, casual athletes, low-performing athletes, and fashion mavens. Given these segments, we could reasonably assume that semi-elite athletes, aspirational athletes, and casual athletes all have a Leader-Follower relationship with the elite athletes, wherein they are the Followers and the elites are the Leaders. Meanwhile, low-performing athletes and fashion mavens likely relate to the elite athletes as Separate Communities—both segments consume the brand for divergent reasons from the elite athletes, with whom they have an indifferent relationship.

TABLE 15-1

Nike's "Winning Isn't for Everyone" campaign

Target growth segment: Elite athletes

Growth tactic: "Winning Isn't for Everyone" campaign

Anticipated effect on target: Elite athletes will prefer Nike if we align the brand image more strongly and clearly with an elite athlete customer and mentality.

	Semi-elite athletes	Aspirational athletes	Casual athletes	Low-performing athletes	Fashion mavens
How do other segments relate to the target growth segment?	Leader-Follower (Followers)	Leader-Follower (Followers)	Leader-Follower (Followers)	Separate Communities	Separate Communities
How will other segments react if the target segment grows?	**Positive:** Leader segment provides brand image and user identity value	**Positive:** Leader segment provides brand image and user identity value	**Positive:** Leader segment provides brand image and user identity value	**Neutral:** Largely indifferent to elite athlete segment	**Neutral:** Largely indifferent to elite athlete segment
What is the predicted effect of the specific growth tactics on each segment?	**Positive:** Reminds them Nike is for who they want to be	**Positive:** Reminds them Nike is for who they want to be	**Negative:** Tells them Nike might not be for them, inconsistent with historic Nike egalitarian image (brand image conflict)	**Negative:** Tells them Nike might not be for them, inconsistent with historic Nike egalitarian image (brand image conflict)	**Neutral:** Doesn't affect them

Next, Nike would want to evaluate how each of the nontarget segments would react to the growth of the target segment. As their segment relationships suggest, the semi-elite athletes, aspirational athletes, and casual athletes would all probably react positively to the growth of the elite athlete segment. This is because the elite athlete Leader segment provides positive brand image and user identity value to these Follower segments. Meanwhile, because they are Separate Communities, the low-performing athletes and fashion mavens will likely be indifferent if the elite athlete segment grows. This first analysis suggests the general brand strategy of increasing the elite athlete segment would likely be positive for the Nike brand and have a neutral to positive effect on its different segments. This is a good sign.

Next, Nike can move on to evaluating the effect of the specific tactics it plans to implement as part of the growth strategy on each of the nontarget segments. In particular, what is the predicted effect of the specific growth tactics—the "Winning Isn't for Everyone" campaign—on each nontarget segment? We recommend qualitative assessments of positive, negative, or neutral. One could reasonably predict the campaign would have a positive effect on the semi-elite and aspirational athletes because it serves as a reminder that Nike is for the type of athlete they want to be. For the casual and low-performing athletes, however, the "Winning Isn't for Everyone" campaign would likely have a negative effect if it feels like Nike is telling them that the brand isn't for them, eliciting brand image and user identity conflict. The particulars of the ads were jarringly aggressive. The voice-over text implicitly claimed to reflect the mindset of athletes who put winning above anything else: "I have no empathy. I don't respect you. I have an obsession with power. I think I'm better than everyone else. I have no remorse. I have no sense of compassion. What's mine is mine. I want to take what's yours and never give it back." Where elite athletes and their Follower segments might resonate with the extreme dedication, to some other segments, this might feel unrelatable and maybe even off-putting.[31] The campaign flew in the face of Nike's long history of promoting itself as a brand for *all* athletes. Its implied exclusivity risked stirring up brand image conflict and even user identity conflict for the casual athletes who had always felt welcomed by the Nike brand. The fashion mavens segment, on the other hand, was likely unaffected by the campaign, given its interest in Nike is largely unrelated to its athletic narrative.

From this perspective, it's clear that trying to attract a more elite athlete segment by positioning the brand as only for the most dogged and brutal of competitors has the reasonable potential to create positive value for multiple Nike segments. However, it also could reasonably create some brand image or user identity conflict for lower-performing athletic segments within Nike. In our classes, we have observed that most of the students who identify as serious athletes love the campaign, while most of those who don't identify as serious athletes do not like the campaign; they feel it conflicts with their idea of what Nike means or stands for as a brand. Nike would now need to go through the calculus of whether this potential conflict is worth the risk relative to the potential upside of growing its elite athletes segment. Whether the campaign was worth it or not, this quick SRM analysis can allow Nike to make a more informed decision on the full potential scope of its potential to spur growth. This short, back-of-the-napkin exercise can offer a bird's-eye view of the customer ecosystem, refocusing the brand on the entire customer base, not just on the segment or segments it aims to grow.

TABLE 15-2

Assess your brand's growth strategies and tactics

Target growth segment:

Growth tactics:

Anticipated effect on target:

	Segment 1	Segment 2	Segment 3	Segment 4	Segment 5
How do other segments relate to the target growth segment?					
How will other segments react if the target segment grows?					
What is the predicted effect of the specific growth tactics on each segment?					

Cats with Smartphones and Strong Opinions

Growing up, one of your authors (Annie) belonged to a beach club in Connecticut called Roton Point. This beach club was unique from other country clubs in that it was known for its friendly and informal atmosphere. People who belonged to Roton Point could sail, swim, play tennis, buy snack bar food, and enjoy waterfront views. But unlike other clubs in the area, which typically also had golf courses, a bar and restaurant, and areas that required jackets or dinner wear, Roton Point was intentionally more laid-back. There was no golf, no sit-down restaurant, no specific attire requirements. There was also no bar; the club was strictly BYOB. It was common for families to set up picnic dinners on long summer nights in the club's picnic area. Roton Point was special in its casualness. It was a place for people who wanted to enjoy views of the Long Island Sound over a cocktail they mixed themselves, from booze they brought with them, without straining to keep their pinkies up. For a long time, things at the club ran smoothly: the members who bought in chose Roton Point because they were aligned with the club's values.

Some of the unique club atmosphere was driven by its governance structure. For many country clubs, people apply to join and, if they are accepted, pay gobs of money for access to the club's grounds, amenities, and hobnobbing benefits, but they don't have any say in how the club is run. In contrast, Roton Point was organized like a condominium association. Membership was limited to four hundred people, who each had a voice in the club's management. New members could only join when an existing member sold their share of the beach club.

As each generation sold its ownership share on to the next, however—capitalism being what it is—the price of buying into Roton Point steadily increased. Between the mid-'90s and the mid-2020s, the price of membership went up by more than ten times. And with that shift in price came a shift in the types of people wanting to use the club. For these higher prices, newer members started expecting a lot more out of humble Roton Point. They wanted to spiff up the place: update the architecture of the buildings, cut down some trees, and add a bar—which would limit members' ability to bring their own alcohol to the club. These changes would start to bring the club's amenities more in line with the price of the membership, and more in line with what other country clubs in the area were offering. The result was conflict between the long-term club members, many of whom had bought memberships back when they sold for low five figures, and the new members, who had bought in more recently for something in the low six figures. There was brand image conflict between members who appreciated Roton Point's unpretentious values and those looking for a more prototypical country club experience. Functional conflict between those who wanted a full-service bar and those who liked being able to bring their own beverages to the club. User identity conflict between those who saw themselves as *not* being stereotypical country club people and those who aspired to be exactly that. Ideological conflict between those who coveted country club life and those who were fundamentally opposed to snooty country club culture. Board meetings became vociferous, lawyers got involved, jobs were threatened. A billboard popped up in the picnic area with Xs over the faces of board members. As of this writing, the conflict at Roton Point has yet to be resolved. But it's clear there will be winners and losers, and the club will probably lose members from one faction or the other.

Any time two or more groups of people seek value from a brand—or from a community-owned beach club—there is the potential for conflict. But although conflict has always been a risk for brands, it feels like it is becoming more common, and like the breadth of actions or situations that can trigger conflict is widening. If heated conflicts can spring up over whether pickleball should be allowed at a beach club, or over a change in the footwear of the green M&M, or over Elmo getting a vaccine, it is reasonable to ask, Why do we all seem so prone to conflict now? Are brands just doomed to cope with customers in conflict? Unfortunately, the answer is probably yes.

We believe four marketplace shifts, driven by changes in technology, culture, and consumerism, are contributing to the increased risk of conflict for brands:

- Increasing consumer expectations

- Porous communication channels

- Consumers using brands as a means of self-expression

- An increased pace of consumerism

Brands have always grappled with the dilemma of managing different customers with different preferences, but these trends have elevated the risks of conflict.

Increasing Consumer Expectations

Generally speaking, consumers today have more choice than in the past. This tips the balance of power in favor of customers, who expect more from brands—in terms of the experiences they offer, their customer service, and their ability to provide instant gratification. Brands must work hard to earn customers' loyalty. And customers are much less tolerant of offerings that don't meet their expectations entirely or suit their particular preferences or value systems on all dimensions. This dramatically increases the risks of conflict as brands grow and new customers come in, bringing their idiosyncratic preferences and expectations with them. Brands serving multiple segments who all have exacting demands that their own needs be met above those of any other segments is an environment ripe for conflict. Any deviations from what a customer thought they were buying, or any pull in new directions by other customer segments, can provoke discontent.

Porous Communication Channels

It is easier than ever to provide a customized message or target marketing to a niche group of consumers, but it is harder than ever to keep that message contained to that audience. In the past, brands could speak to different segments of customers via separate communication channels relatively easily, without those communications being easily observed across segments. Joe Six Pack wouldn't have seen Bud Light banners at a Pride parade unless he was also at the Pride parade. Today, however, Joe and millions of his friends can unintentionally stumble upon a social media post intended for a more progressive slice of Bud Light's customer base. Perhaps someone in Joe's network shares the post with him, or perhaps it is surfaced in his feed by an algorithm that knew he liked Bud Light.

The participatory nature of communication on social media has contributed to the breakdown of message control. Where brands could traditionally decide which outlets would carry their messaging, and to whom, it is now trivially easy for customers themselves to diffuse messages broadly—including those a brand might prefer stayed siloed. Any customer who is unhappy with a brand embracing another customer segment can immediately share the offending content, as well as their own hot take on the matter. In the case of Bud Light, it wasn't merely Dylan Mulvaney's initial post that ignited a cultural firestorm. It was the subsequent reposting by people hostile to Bud Light's actions that poured gasoline onto the fire.

Even for noncontroversial issues, digital communications and social media make it more likely that customers will see what brands are saying to other customer segments, for better or worse. There's nothing stopping you from going on Instagram and looking at any of Nike's various account pages including @nike, @nikebasketball, @nikerunning, @nikewomen, @nikesb, @nikefootball, @jumpman23 (Air Jordan), @nikesportswear . . . you get the idea. Nike might intend to deliver different messaging to its different sport segments. But realistically, it is less able to gatekeep that information than was possible in the past.

Brands as a Means of Self-Expression

Consumers are using brands as vehicles for value expression and self-definition more than ever. And because brands are more commonly used as extensions of the self, customers are more sensitive to the values and sociopolitical orientations of the brands, and to the identities, values, and sociopolitical orientations of any customer segments associated with the brand. These concerns are exacerbated by increased polarization of beliefs around the world. The deepening division between social and political groups cultivates an "us versus them" approach to . . . well, almost *everything*. Anecdotally, a colleague recently told one of us that he bought a hybrid Ford F150 instead of the all-electric F150 Lightning that he had preferred. His reason? The hybrid looked like a regular truck, while the Lightning had a distinctive design, trumpeting its zero-emission motor. This colleague was afraid that an electric vehicle would create conflict with his more politically conservative relatives and neighbors.

The Pace of Consumerism

To make matters more chaotic for brands, the world is moving faster than ever. Social media, fast fashion, and technological innovation mean that trends can move from niche to mainstream with shocking speed. One implication of this is that brands associated with trends can rapidly spread beyond their initial customer bases. As Jonah Weiner of the *New York Times* put it in reference to fashion, "Information that once moved at the relatively manageable pace of movies, magazines and seasonal runway collections can now travel from 'early adopters' to latecomers in the span of a few weeks, if not days."[1]

On the one hand, this is good news for brands. It means they can accelerate trends or broaden their brand's influence by becoming popular with the "right" kind of people. This is partly how Crocs and Stanley turned squishy clogs and metal water bottles into cultural obsessions. In these cases, brands turned customers into collaborators for creating value, allowing them to grow at a faster speed and to a greater height than may have been possible in the past.

On the other hand, the rapidity with which trends explode into ubiquity can be problematic for brands if the relationships among adopters are not anticipated and carefully managed. Brands can grow too fast for their own good. If the time from niche to mainstream is faster than ever, so too is the time from mainstream to cringe, and from fashionable to "cheugy." Quick, widespread adoption can lead to quick, widespread conflict over what the brand means, who it represents, or what it stands for.

In a World Full of Conflict, Learning to Manage Conflict Is an Opportunity

In today's marketplace, managing relationships between different customer segments can be like trying to herd cats—except these cats have smartphones and strong opinions. Given the trends we have outlined, it seems likely that conflict between customer segments will only become more likely for brands. As technology races ahead and consumer culture evolves, the risks of conflict will increase, but so will the benefits of coordinating positive relationships between customer segments.

The good news is that if you have made it this far, you now have the tools you need to anticipate and avoid conflict where possible. You also have the tools to coordinate relationships between customer segments to create more resilient and self-perpetuating customer ecosystems. In a world where all brands face increased risks of friction between customer segments, those with the skills to steer customer segments toward relationship types that facilitate growth and away from relationship types that generate conflict will have a sustainable strategic advantage over the brands that lack those skills. By understanding and applying the principles of segmentation relationship management, brands can turn the growth dilemma into a growth opportunity.

NOTES

Introduction

1. Suzanne Kapner, "New Lands' End CEO Delivers High Fashion—and a Culture Clash," *Wall Street Journal*, May 6, 2016, https://www.wsj.com/articles/new-lands-end-ceo-delivers-high-fashionand-a-culture-clash-1462547397.

2. Parija Kavilanz, "Retailers Are Tripping over Themselves for Millennial and Gen Z Shoppers. But Not This One," CNN, January 21, 2023, https://www.cnn.com/2023/01/21/business/lands-end-gen-x-customers/index.html.

3. Lara Ewen, "Why Lands' End Parted Ways with Its CEO—and Why It's Still in Deep Trouble," Retail Dive, October 11, 2016, https://www.retaildive.com/news/why-lands-end-parted-ways-with-its-ceo-and-why-its-still-in-deep-troubl/428074/.

4. Kapner, "New Lands' End CEO Delivers High Fashion."

5. Kapner, "New Lands' End CEO Delivers High Fashion."

6. Suzanne Kapner, "Lands' End CEO Federica Marchionni Is Pushed Out," *Wall Street Journal*, September 26, 2016, https://www.wsj.com/articles/lands-end-ceo-federica-marchionni-steps-down-1474890464.

7. Marshall Fisher, Vishal Gaur, and Herb Kleinberger, "Curing the Addiction to Growth," *Harvard Business Review*, January–February 2017, https://hbr.org/2017/01/curing-the-addiction-to-growth.

Chapter 1

1. Erin Carlyle, "Under New CEO, Crocs May Have a Biting Chance," *Forbes*, July 29, 2015, https://www.forbes.com/sites/erincarlyle/2015/07/29/crocs-bites-back-its-gotta-be-the-shoes/.

2. "Crocs—See Those Little Holes? That Is Where Your Dignity Leaks Out," Know Your Meme, https://knowyourmeme.com/photos/1069950-crocs.

3. Daniel Rodgers, "It's High Time the Divisive Havaiana Flip-Flop Made a Comeback," *Vogue*, August 7, 2023, https://www.vogue.com/article/haviana-flip-flops-comeback.

4. Ayelet Israeli and Anne V. Wilson, "Crocs: Using Community-Centric Marketing to Make Ugly Iconic," Case 524006 (Boston: Harvard Business School, July 25, 2023).

5. Israeli and Wilson, "Crocs."

6. "Crocs, Inc. Expects Record Annual Revenues of ~$3.95B, Up Over 11% Year-Over-Year," Crocs Inc. press release, January 8, 2024, https://investors.crocs .com/news-and-events/press-releases/press-release-details/2024/Crocs-Inc.-Expects -Record-Annual-Revenues-of-3.95B-Up-Over-11-Year-Over-Year/default.aspx.

Chapter 2

1. Warby Parker, "History," https://www.warbyparker.com/history.
2. Daryl Austin, "The Inside Story of How a 'Band of Misfits' Saved Lego," *National Geographic*, July 21, 2021, https://www.nationalgeographic.com/culture /article/adult-legos.
3. Jack Yates, "LEGO Isn't Just for Kids: More Sales Than Ever Go to Adults," Brick Fanatics, October 1, 2021, https://www.brickfanatics.com/lego-isnt-just-for -kids-more-sales-than-ever-go-to-adults.
4. Alysha Webb, "How Hip Hop's Love of the Iconic Yellow Workboot Helped Make Timberland a Billion-Dollar Company," CNBC, December 20, 2020, https:// www.cnbc.com/2020/12/20/how-timberland-became-billion-dollar-company.html.
5. Robert Klara, "How Timberland Went from Dirty Work Boots to Hip-Hop Drip," *Adweek*, June 15, 2023, https://www.adweek.com/brand-marketing/how -timberland-went-from-dirty-work-boots-to-hip-hop-drip/; Emmy Liederman, "Timberland Honors Hip-Hop Trailblazers Who Made Blue Collar Boots Cool," *Adweek*, March 15, 2023, https://www.adweek.com/creativity/timberland-hip-hop -trailblazers-who-made-blue-collar-boots-cool/.

Chapter 3

1. Wikipedia, "FarmVille," https://en.wikipedia.org/wiki/FarmVille.
2. Alexander Gladstone, Alexander Saeedy, and Konrad Putzier, "WeWork, Once Valued at $47 Billion, Files for Bankruptcy," *Wall Street Journal*, November 7, 2023, https://www.wsj.com/articles/wework-files-for-bankruptcy-5cd362b5.

Chapter 4

1. "Apple's Final Cut Pro Wins Emmy Award," Apple, press release, August 20, 2002, https://www.apple.com/newsroom/2002/08/20Apples-Final-Cut-Pro-Wins -Emmy-Award/.
2. S. Irene Virbila, "Review: At Michael Cimarusti's Providence, Each Bite Is a Revelation," *Los Angeles Times*, October 28, 2010, https://www.latimes.com/archives /la-xpm-2010-oct-28-la-fo-review-20101028-story.html.
3. Daniel Modlin, "Why You Need This Classic Dutch Oven, According to a Michelin-Starred Chef," *Food and Wine*, February 8, 2023, https://www.foodand wine.com/le-creuset-michelin-star-chef-amazon-7106678.
4. Le Creuset, "About Le Creuset," https://www.lecreuset.com/about-le-creuset /about-le-creuset.html.
5. "Bose Quiet Comfort 20 TV Spot, 'Stay Focused' Featuring Rory McIlroy," iSpot.tv, August 18, 2014, https://www.ispot.tv/ad/7rR5/bose-quiet-comfort-20 -stay-focused-featuring-rory-mcilroy; "Bose QuietComfort 35 TV Spot, 'Get Closer' Featuring J.J. Watt," iSpot.tv, October 14, 2016, https://www.ispot.tv/ad /AEWc/bose-quietcomfort-35-get-closer-featuring-jj-watt; "Music Deserves Bose

Featuring Russell Wilson and Macklemore," YouTube, November 10, 2015, https://www.youtube.com/watch?v=now50oSfSHQ.

6. Stuart Kemp, "London 2012: Dr. Dre at Center of Olympics Marketing Controversy," *Hollywood Reporter*, July 31, 2012, https://www.hollywoodreporter .com/news/general-news/london-2012-dr-dre-beats-marketing-olympics -356349/.

7. Jeff Beer, "How Beats Tapped the Stories of Sport to Sell the Emotion of Sound," *Fast Company*, February 11, 2015, https://www.fastcompany.com/3042176 /how-beats-tapped-the-stories-of-sport-to-sell-the-emotion-of-sound.

8. Louis Bien, "NFL Bans Players from Wearing Beats Headphones on Camera," SB Nation, October 4, 2014, https://www.sbnation.com/nfl/2014/10/5/6913767/nfl -beats-dre-headphones-ban-camera-players.

9. Robert J. Dolan, "Bose Corporation: Communication Strategy for Challenging Apple's Beats by Dr. Dre," Case 518036 (Boston: Harvard Business School, November 2, 2017); Brian X. Chen, "Apple to Pay $3 Billion to Buy Beats," *New York Times*, May 28, 2014, https://www.nytimes.com/2014/05/29/technology/apple -confirms-its-3-billion-deal-for-beats-electronics.html.

10. Cheddar, "How Hipsters Saved PBR—Cheddar Examines," YouTube, August 28, 2018, https://www.youtube.com/watch?v=HrCgtCYgTkw&list =WL&index=39&t=328s.

11. "Hipster Style: A Blueprint to Embrace This Eclectic Fashion," FashionBeans, https://www.fashionbeans.com/article/hipster-style/?http://ignorenitro=854acb57e5 c011877e30abaa029eff63.

12. Cheddar, "How Hipsters Saved PBR."

13. Laura Rysman, "Ferrari Is Racing into Fashion," *New York Times*, June 16, 2021, https://www.nytimes.com/2021/06/16/style/ferrari-fashion-collection.html.

Chapter 5

1. Elizabeth Segran, "Old Navy's Plus-Size Experiment Failed. It Didn't Have To," *Fast Company*, June 9, 2022, https://www.fastcompany.com/90759394/old -navys-plus-size-experiment-failed-it-didnt-have-to; Elizabeth Segran, "Old Navy Is Overhauling How It Designs Clothes. Here's Why," *Fast Company*, August 19, 2021, https://www.fastcompany.com/90667244/old-navy-is-overhauling-how-it -designs-clothes-heres-why.

2. Grace Dobush, "How Etsy Alienated Its Crafters and Lost Its Soul," *Wired*, February 19, 2015, https://www.wired.com/2015/02/etsy-not-good-for-crafters/; Cade Metz, "Etsy Lost Its Soul, But That Doesn't Matter to Its IPO," *Wired*, March 4, 2015, https://www.wired.com/2015/03/etsy-lost-soul-doesnt-matter-ipo/.

3. Cory Doctorow, "The 'Enshittification' of TikTok," *Wired*, January 23, 2023, https://www.wired.com/story/tiktok-platforms-cory-doctorow/.

4. Peter Sucio, "Social Media Isn't Really All That Social Anymore—Can It Be Again?," *Forbes*, November 16, 2023, https://www.forbes.com/sites/petersuciu /2023/11/16/social-media-isnt-really-all-that-social-anymore-can-it-be-again/?sh =4f04aad42bbe.

5. Doctorow, "The 'Enshittification' of TikTok."

6. Danielle Abril, "LinkedIn Is Getting Weirdly Personal and Not Everyone Likes It," *Washington Post*, August 31, 2023, https://www.washingtonpost.com /technology/2023/08/31/linkedin-personal-posts/.

7. Rob Price, "It's Not Just You. LinkedIn Has Gotten Really Weird," *Business Insider*, September 25, 2023, https://www.businessinsider.com/how-linkedin-got-weird-work-life-blurred-lines-of-oversharing-2023-9.

8. Price, "It's Not Just You."

Chapter 6

1. "New Starbucks Opens in Rest Room of Existing Starbucks," *The Onion*, June 27, 1998, https://theonion.com/new-starbucks-opens-in-rest-room-of-existing-starbucks-1819564800/.

2. Youngme Moon and John A. Quelch, "Starbucks: Delivering Customer Service," Case 504016 (Boston: Harvard Business School, July 31, 2003).

3. Janet Adamy, "McDonald's Takes on a Weakened Starbucks," *Wall Street Journal*, January 7, 2008, https://www.wsj.com/articles/SB119967000012871311.

Chapter 7

1. Kaitlyn Tiffany, "How Pedialyte Got Pedialit," Vox, September 10, 2018, https://www.vox.com/the-goods/2018/9/10/17819358/pedialyte-hangover-marketing-strategy-instagram-influencers.

2. Reed Alexander, "How 'Child-Free' Adults Are Transforming the Company's Theme Parks as Disney Pours $60 Billion into the Division," Business Insider, September 19, 2023, https://www.businessinsider.com/why-disney-parks-top-destinations-millennials-gen-z-2023-9.

3. Sara McOmber, "Disney Adults vs. Families: The Battle for Disney World," *Disney Food Blog*, https://www.disneyfoodblog.com/2022/10/14/childfree-millennials-vs-families-the-battle-for-disney-world/.

4. Disney Weddings, https://www.disneyweddings.com/; Adult Exclusive Adventures, Adventures by Disney, https://www.adventuresbydisney.com/adult-exclusive-experiences/.

5. Ali Wunderman, "How Disneyland Stayed Dry for Almost 65 Years," SFGate, August 15, 2020, https://www.sfgate.com/disneyland/article/disneyland-alcohol-history-galaxys-edge-15485242.php.

6. Alexander, "How 'Child-Free' Adults Are Transforming the Company's Theme Parks."

7. Krysten Swensen, "Guest Calls Epcot Festival a 'Festival of Drunks,'" Disney Fanatic, March 24, 2024, https://www.disneyfanatic.com/guest-calls-epcot-festival-of-drunks-ks1/.

8. Julie Tremaine, "The Ultimate Guide to Drinking Around the World at Epcot," *Delish*, April 20, 2023, https://www.delish.com/just-for-fun/g43658734/best-epcot-drinks/.

9. Alexander, "How 'Child-Free' Adults Are Transforming the Company's Theme Parks."

10. Andria Cheng, "Ron Johnson Made Apple Stores the Envy of Retail and Target Hip, but This Startup May Be His Crowning Achievement," *Forbes*, January 17, 2020, https://www.forbes.com/sites/andriacheng/2020/01/17/he-made-apple-stores-envy-of-retail-and-target-hip-but-his-biggest--career-chapter-may-be-just-starting/.

11. Elie Ofek and Jill Avery, "J.C. Penney's 'Fair and Square' Pricing Strategy," Case 513036 (Boston: Harvard Business School, September 12, 2012).

12. Stephanie Clifford, "J.C. Penney to Revise Pricing Methods and Limit Promotions," *New York Times*, January 25, 2012, https://www.nytimes.com/2012/01/26/business/jc-penneys-chief-ron-johnson-announces-plans-to-revamp-stores.html.

13. Ofek and Avery, "J.C. Penney's Pricing Strategy."

14. Nathaniel Meyersohn, "How It All Went Wrong at JCPenney," CNN, September 27, 2018, https://www.cnn.com/2018/09/27/business/jcpenney-history/index.html.

15. Meyersohn, "How It All Went Wrong at JCPenney"; Sapna Maheshwari, "J.C. Penney Lowest Sales in Decades Show Johnson Stumbles," Bloomberg, February 28, 2013, https://www.bloomberg.com/news/articles/2013-02-27/j-c-penney-posts-wider-fourth-quarter-net-loss.

16. Meyersohn, "How It All Went Wrong at JCPenney."

17. Uri Friedman, "SunChips: A Brief History of a Packaging Disaster," *Atlantic*, February 24, 2011, https://www.theatlantic.com/business/archive/2011/02/sunchips-a-brief-history-of-a-packaging-disaster/342114/.

Chapter 8

1. Leigh Gallagher, "How Airbnb Found a Mission—and a Brand," *Fortune*, December 22, 2016, https://fortune.com/longform/airbnb-travel-mission-brand/.

2. "Airbnb Launches New Products to Inspire People to 'Live There,'" Airbnb, April 16, 2016, https://news.airbnb.com/airbnb-launches-new-products-to-inspire-people-to-live-there/.

3. Michele Hermann, "Airbnb Offers Once-in-a-Lifetime Chance to Spend Night at the Louvre," *Forbes*, April 4, 2019, https://www.forbes.com/sites/michele herrmann/2019/04/04/airbnb-sleep-over-at-the-louvre/.

4. Alexa Lisitza, "These Former Airbnb Guests Screenshot the Most Ridiculous Fees and Checkout Lists They've Ever Seen, and Yikes, Some Hosts Have the Audacity," BuzzFeed, November 24, 2022, https://www.buzzfeed.com/alexalisitza/checklist-fees-screenshots-airbnb.

5. Rebecca R. Ruiz, "Luxury Cars Imprint Their Brands on Goods from Cologne to Clothing," *New York Times*, February 20, 2015, https://www.nytimes.com/2015/02/21/automobiles/luxury-cars-imprint-their-brands-on-goods-from-cologne-to-clothing.html.

6. Ellen Byron, "To Refurbish Its Image, Tiffany Risks Profits," *Wall Street Journal*, January 10, 2007, https://www.wsj.com/articles/SB116836324469271556.

7. Byron, "To Refurbish Its Image, Tiffany Risks Profits."

8. "Not Your Mother's Tiffany: Tiffany & Co.'s Controversial Rebranding Campaign," TFR, August 3, 2021, https://tfr.news/news/not-your-mothers-tiffany-tiffany-amp-cos-controversial-rebranding-campaign.

9. Ryan General, "New Tiffany Co. x Pokémon Collab Features $29,000 Pikachu Necklace," Yahoo News, November 17, 2023, https://www.yahoo.com/news/tiffany-co-x-pok-mon-005348561.html.

10. "Not Your Mother's Tiffany."

11. Byron, "To Refurbish Its Image, Tiffany Risks Profits."

12. "Puma Ditching Hipsters in Return to Athletic Roots," *New Zealand Herald*, September 21, 2014, https://www.nzherald.co.nz/business/puma-ditching-hipsters-in-return-to-athletic-roots.

13. Maghan McDowell, "Puma's Returning to the Fashion Arena—This Time, with a Web3 Layer," *Vogue Business*, October 25, 2022, https://www.voguebusiness.com /technology/pumas-returning-to-the-fashion-arena-this-time-with-a-web3-layer.

14. Nilofer Merchant, "When TED Lost Control of Its Crowd," *Harvard Business Review*, April 2013, https://hbr.org/2013/04/when-ted-lost-control-of-its-crowd.

15. "TED-Ed Student Talks Celebrates 10 Years," *TED blog*, October 9, 2024, https://blog.ted.com/ted-ed-student-talks-10-years/.

16. Gopa Praturi and Can Uslay, "The WW Wellness Journey: The Rebranding of Weight Watchers," Case W20611 (Ivey Publishing, July 30, 2020).

17. Jess Miller, "Weight Watchers Isn't Fooling Anyone," *Slate*, March 8, 2021, https://slate.com/business/2021/03/weight-watchers-name-change-ww-dieting -culture.html.

18. Avi Dan, "The Weight Watchers Rebrand Points to the Risk of Chasing Trends," *Forbes*, April 11, 2019, https://www.forbes.com/sites/avidan/2019/04/11/ the-weight-watchers-rebrand-points-to-the-risk-of-chasing-trends/; Dearbail Jordan, "What's Gone Wrong at Weight Watchers?" BBC, March 1, 2019, https:// www.bbc.com/news/business-47392730; Lindsey Rupp, Lauren Coleman-Lochner, and Inyoung Hwang, "Weight Watchers Tumbles as Rebranding Fails to Wow Investors," Bloomberg, January 2, 2015, https://www.bloomberg.com/news/articles /2015-01-02/weight-watchers-tumbles-as-rebranding-fails-to-impress-investors.

19. Dan, "The Weight Watchers Rebrand"; Lipi Roy, "Oprah's 2020 Vision for Connection and Clarity: A Physician's Perspective," *Forbes*, March 10, 2020, https://www.forbes.com/sites/lipiroy/2020/03/06/oprahs-2020-vision-for -connection-and-clarity-a-physicians-perspective/.

20. Erich Schwartzel, "The Company That Defined Dieting Is Sorry It Told Us to Have More Willpower," *Wall Street Journal*, October 7, 2023, https://www.wsj.com /health/pharma/oprah-winfrey-ozempic-weightwatchers-new-formula-1ec4e706.

21. Schwartzel, "The Company That Defined Dieting"; Moira Forbes, "Inside Weight Watchers' Bold Pivot to Dominate the Ozempic Era," *Forbes*, August 19, 2024, https://www.forbes.com/sites/moiraforbes/2024/08/19/inside-weightwatchers -bold-pivot-to-dominate-the-ozempic-era/.

22. Edward Segal, "The Sudden Departure of Weight Watchers' CEO Is Latest Jolt for Company," *Forbes*, September 29, 2024, https://www.forbes.com/sites /edwardsegal/2024/09/29/the-sudden-departure-of-weightwatchers-ceo-is-latest -jolt-for-company/.

23. Andrea Chang, "Patagonia Shows Corporate Activism Is Simpler Than It Looks," *Los Angeles Times*, May 9, 2021, https://www.latimes.com/business/story /2021-05-09/patagonia-shows-corporate-activism-is-simpler-than-it-looks.

24. 1% for the Planet, "Our Story," https://www.onepercentfortheplanet.org /about/story.

25. Uri Neren, "Patagonia's Provocative Black Friday Campaign," hbr.org, November 23, 2012, https://hbr.org/2012/11/patagonias-provocative-black-f.

26. Patagonia, "Our Core Values," https://www.patagonia.com/core-values/.

27. David Gelles, "Billionaire No More: Patagonia Founder Gives Away Company," *New York Times*, September 14, 2022, https://www.nytimes.com/2022 /09/14/climate/patagonia-climate-philanthropy-chouinard.html.

28. Jacob Gallagher, "How the Fleece Vest Became the New Corporate Uniform," *Wall Street Journal*, July 24, 2018, https://www.wsj.com/articles/how-the -fleece-vest-became-the-new-corporate-uniform-1532442297.

29. Megan Cerullo, "Patagonia Will No Longer Sell Vests with Finance Firm Logos on Them," CBS News, April 3, 2019, https://www.cbsnews.com/news/midtown-uniform-patagonia-will-no-longer-sell-vests-with-finance-firms-logos-on-them/; Elizabeth Segran, "Pour One Out for the Tech Bro Uniform: Patagonia Ditches Corporate Logos on Its Vests," *Fast Company*, April 19, 2021, https://www.fastcompany.com/90626274/pour-one-out-for-the-tech-bro-uniform-patagonia-ditches-corporate-logos-on-its-vests.

30. Katie Notopoulos, "Patagonia Is Refusing to Sell Its Iconic Power Vests to Some Financial Firms," BuzzFeed News, April 2, 2019, https://www.buzzfeednews.com/article/katienotopoulos/patagonia-power-vest-policy-change.

31. Theresa Hegel, "Patagonia Once Again Allows Direct Branding on Apparel," ASI, March 21, 2023, https://members.asicentral.com/news/newsletters/promogram/march-2023/patagonia-once-again-allows-direct-branding-on-apparel/.

Chapter 9

1. Jonah Berger and Chip Heath, "Who Drives Divergence? Identity Signaling, Outgroup Dissimilarity, and the Abandonment of Cultural Tastes," *Journal of Personality and Social Psychology* 95, no. 3 (2008): 593.

2. "VF Corporation Buys Lifestyle Brand Supreme for $2.1 Billion," Retail Insight Network, December 29, 2020, https://www.retail-insight-network.com/news/vf-corporation-supreme/.

3. Marko Ristic, "'Supreme' Sell Out: How the Brand Lost Its Edge," Daily Nexus, January 16, 2020, https://dailynexus.com/2020-01-16/supreme-sell-out-how-the-brand-lost-its-edge/.

4. "Supreme Reports Decreased Revenue in Financial Year Ending March 2023," Hypebeast, June 12, 2023, https://hypebeast.com/2023/6/supreme-revenue-decline-financial-report-results-vf-corp.

5. Beth Berselli, "Retooling at Black & Decker," *Washington Post*, February 9, 1998, https://www.washingtonpost.com/archive/business/1998/02/09/retooling-at-black-decker/ecbccdb3-09d9-4fb3-b65f-e7dcf4f33fbe/.

6. Katie Mather, "TikTok Reveals Why Fashion Company Used to Allegedly Send 'Cheap and Tacky' Reality Stars Products," Yahoo, September 18, 2020, https://www.yahoo.com/lifestyle/turns-high-fashion-brands-very-191154873.html; Shankar Vedantam and Tara Boyle, "Snooki and the Handbag," NPR, July 9, 2018, https://www.npr.org/2018/07/09/627403187/snooki-and-the-handbag.

7. Chris Jordan, "Snooki Puts to Rest Louis Vuitton and Gucci Bag Intrigue During 'Jersey Shore' Special," App, May 19, 2023, https://www.app.com/story/entertainment/television/2023/05/19/snooki-louis-vuitton-gucci-bags-jersey-shore-urban-myth/70236485007/.

8. Franki Rudnesky, "'Jersey Shore' Stars Munch Wawa Pizza in New Commercial Filmed in Cape May County," Philly Voice, September 18, 2023, https://www.phillyvoice.com/wawa-jersey-shore-pizza-commercial-cape-may-county/.

Chapter 10

1. Chris Morris, "Delta, REI, and Now Yeti Coolers. Here's a List of Brands Cutting Ties with the NRA," Yahoo Finance, April 23, 2018, https://finance.yahoo.com/news/delta-rei-now-yeti-coolers-140050877.html.

2. Meagan Flynn, "NRA Supporters Are Blowing Up Yeti Coolers. Yeti Says It's All a Big Mistake," *Washington Post*, April 24, 2018, https://www.washingtonpost .com/news/morning-mix/wp/2018/04/24/nra-supporters-are-blowing-up-yeti -coolers-yeti-says-its-all-a-big-mistake/.

3. Eric Levenson, "NRA Supporters Are Blowing Up Their Expensive Yeti Coolers over a Canceled Discount," CNN, April 25, 2018, https://www.cnn.com /2018/04/24/us/yeti-coolers-nra-explode-trnd/index.html; Flynn, "NRA Support- ers Are Blowing Up Their Coolers."

4. Morris, "Delta, REI, and Now Yeti."

5. "NRA Supporters Are Blowing Up Their Expensive Yeti Coolers," Fox 6 Milwaukee, April 24, 2018, https://www.fox6now.com/news/nra-supporters-are -blowing-up-their-expensive-yeti-coolers.

6. Morris, "Delta, REI, and Now Yeti"; Daniella Genovese, "Former Dick's Sporting Goods CEO Defends Stance on Gun Restrictions Despite Backlash," Fox Business, January 15, 2024, https://www.foxbusiness.com/lifestyle/former-dicks -sporting-goods-ceo-defends-stance-gun-restrictions-despite-backlash; Kate Gibson, "Walmart Returns Guns and Ammo to Store Floors, Saying Civil Unrest Was 'Isolated,'" CBS News, October 30, 2020, https://www.cbsnews.com/news /walmart-returning-firearm-guns-ammo-store-displays; "L.L. Bean Will No Longer Sell Guns or Ammo to Anyone Under 21," CBS News, March 2, 2018, https://www.cbsnews.com/boston/news/ll-bean-guns-ammunition-sales-21 -rifles.

7. "Sen. Ted Cruz Calls Big Bird Vaccine Tweet 'Government Propaganda for Your 5-Year-Old,'" CBS News, November 8, 2021, https://www.cbsnews.com/texas /news/ted-cruz-big-bird-vaccine-tweet-government-propaganda/; Samira Asma- Sadeque, "Ted Cruz Bashes New Sesame Street Video Discussing Covid Vaccine for Children," *Guardian*, June 29, 2022, https://www.theguardian.com/tv-and-radio /2022/jun/29/ted-cruz-sesame-street-video-covid-vaccine-children.

8. Martin Pengelly, "Ted Cruz Condemns Big Bird for Advocating Covid Vaccines for Kids," *Guardian*, November 7, 2021, https://www.theguardian.com/tv -and-radio/2021/nov/07/ted-cruz-condemns-big-bird-covid-vaccines.

9. "Sesame Street's Elmo and His Dad Louie Star in New PSA Informing Parents of Young Children About Covid-19 Vaccines," Ad Council, June 28, 2022, https:// www.adcouncil.org/press-releases/sesame-streets-elmo-and-his-dad-louie-star-in -new-psa-informing-parents-of-young-children-about-covid-19-vaccines.

10. Christopher Rosa, "Billy Porter Had an Epic Response to People Who Are Mad That He's Wearing a Dress on Sesame Street," *Glamour*, February 7, 2020, https://www.glamour.com/story/billy-porter-had-an-epic-response-to-people-who -are-mad-hes-wearing-a-dress-on-sesame-street.

11. Adam Gabatt, "Fox News Host Talks Race by Calling Out the Real Enemy: Sesame Street's Elmo," *Guardian*, June 10, 2020, https://www.theguardian.com /media/2020/jun/10/fox-news-sesame-street-elmo-tucker-carlson.

12. "Firestorm over Houston Rockets GM's Tweet Backing Hong Kong Protes- tors over China," CBS News, October 7, 2019, https://www.cbsnews.com/news /daryl-morey-tweet-firestorm-houston-rockets-gm-tweet-backing-hong-kong -protesters-over-china/.

13. Ohm Youngmisuk, "LeBron James: Daryl Morey Was 'Misinformed' before Sending Tweet about China and Hong Kong," ESPN, October 14, 2019, https://www

.espn.com/nba/story/_/id/27847951/daryl-morey-was-misinformed-sending-tweet
-china-hong-kong.

14. Petrana Radulovic, "Disney Replaces FastPass with Paid Line-Skipping
Replacement Disney Genie Plus," Polygon, April 19, 2021, https://www.polygon
.com/22632224/disney-genie-plus-cost-disneyland-disney-world-app-fastpass.

15. Nathaniel Meyersohn, "The Wealthy Are Cutting the Line at the Airport,
Disney World, and Ski Resorts," CNN, February 8, 2024, https://www.cnn.com
/2024/02/08/business/line-skipping-clear-disney/index.html.

16. Craig LeMoult, "New Balance on Damage Control after Trump Statement
'Taken out of Context,'" NPR, November 19, 2016, https://www.npr.org/2016/11
/19/502685437/new-balance-on-damage-control-after-trump-statement-taken-out
-of-context-across.

17. Hannah Jane Parkinson, "Does New Balance Really Support Trump?,"
Guardian, November 15, 2016, https://www.theguardian.com/fashion/2016/nov/15
/does-new-balance-really-support-trump-trainers-trade-plans.

18. Parkinson, "Does New Balance Really Support Trump?"

19. Ryan Beehler, "New Balance Reeling from Trump Endorsement," FSU
News.com, November 28, 2016, https://www.fsunews.com/story/life/2016/11/28
/new-balance-reeling-trump-endorsement/94510644/.

20. Katie Mettler, "We Live in Crazy Times: Neo-Nazis Have Declared New
Balance the 'Official Shoes of White People,'" Washington Post, November 15, 2016,
https://www.washingtonpost.com/news/morning-mix/wp/2016/11/15/the-crazy
-reason-neo-nazis-have-declared-new-balance-the-official-shoes-of-white-people/.

21. Danielle Wiener-Bronner, "M&M's Beloved Characters Are Getting a New
Look," CNN, January 20, 2022, https://www.cnn.com/2022/01/20/business/mms
-characters-logo/index.html.

22. Dani De Placido, "Tucker Carlson Widely Mocked after Criticizing 'Less
Sexy' M&Ms," Forbes, January 22, 2022, https://www.forbes.com/sites/danidiplacido
/2022/01/22/tucker-carlson-widely-mocked-after-criticizing-less-sexy-mms/.

23. "M&Ms Replacing Spokescandies with Comedian Maya Rudolph," BBC,
January 23, 2023, https://www.bbc.com/news/world-us-canada-64380510.

24. "Protestors Rally Against Supreme Court Ruling at Burbank Hobby Lobby
Store," CBS News, July 7, 2014, https://www.cbsnews.com/losangeles/news
/protesters-to-hand-out-condoms-at-burbank-hobby-lobby-store/; Clint Rainey,
"Chick-fil-A Nears $19 Billion in Sales: Inside the Evolution of a Controversial
Brand," Fast Company, November 29, 2023, https://www.fastcompany.com
/90978735/chick-fil-a-okay-to-like-boycott-right-left.

25. Elizabeth Culliford, "SoulCycle, Equinox Face Boycott Calls over Investor's
Trump Fundraiser," Reuters, August 7, 2019, https://www.reuters.com/article
/business/soulcycle-equinox-face-boycott-calls-over-investors-trump-fundraiser
-idUSKCN1UY00K/.

26. John Paul Brammer, "The M&M's Changes Aren't Progressive. Give Green
Her Boots Back," Washington Post, January 21, 2022, https://www.washingtonpost
.com/opinions/2022/01/21/mm-candy-mascot-redesign-not-woke-capitalism/.

27. Christopher Zara, "Who Actually Boycotts Brands? More Liberals and
College Grads, It Turns Out," Fast Company, September 20, 2019, https://www
.fastcompany.com/90407051/who-boycotts-brands-liberals-and-college-grads
-says-study.

Chapter 11

1. Hank Berrien, "'One Single Can': Anheuser-Busch Sends Letter to Minimize Disastrous Mulvaney Backlash," Daily Wire, May 4, 2023, https://www.dailywire .com/news/one-single-can-anheuser-busch-sends-letter-to-minimize-disastrous -mulvaney-backlash.

2. Danielle Wiener-Bronner, "Bud Light Wanted to Market to All. Instead, It's Alienating Everyone," CNN, May 1, 2023, https://www.cnn.com/2023/05/01 /business/bud-light-marketing/index.html.

3. Danielle Wiener-Bronner, "Anheuser-Busch Facilities Face Threats after Bud Light Backlash," CNN, April 20, 2023, https://www.cnn.com/2023/04/20/business /bud-light-threats/index.html.

4. "Bud Light Boycott," Wikipedia, https://en.wikipedia.org/wiki/2023_Bud _Light_boycott.

5. Daniel Neman, "A-B Responds to Bud Light Controversy: 'One Single Can' Sent to One Influencer," *St. Louis Post Dispatch*, May 3, 2023, https://www.stltoday .com/news/local/a-b-responds-to-bud-light-controversy-one-single-can-sent-to -one-influencer/article_12db8c52-e90f-11ed-be5d-338d88dc3a41.html.

6. Yael Halon, "Anheuser-Busch Blames 'Third Party Ad Agency' for Dylan Mulvaney Partnership, Cuts Ties Amid Marketing Shakeup," Fox News, May 8, 2023, https://www.foxnews.com/media/anheuser-busch-blames-third-party-ad -agency-for-dylan-mulvaney-partnership-cuts-ties-amid-marketing-shakeup.

7. YouTube, "Alissa Heinerscheid, VP, Bud Light," March 23, 2023, https://www .youtube.com/watch?v=UnsSoS8s6Ok&t=1556s.

8. Philip Bump, "What the Bud Light Backlash Has in Common with the Republican Party," *Washington Post*, April 10, 2023, https://www.washingtonpost .com/politics/2023/04/10/bud-light-beer-ad-transgender-dylan-mulvaney/.

9. Analisa Novak, "Anheuser-Busch CEO Brendan Whitworth Says Financial Assistance Is Being Sent to Wholesalers, Beer Distributors Impacted by Boycott Backlash," CBS News, June 28, 2023, https://www.cbsnews.com/news/anheuser -busch-bud-light-dylan-mulvaney-campaign-brendan-whitworth/.

10. Dailymotion, "Bud Light Party Super Bowl 2016 Commercial with Seth Rogen and Amy Schumer," video, https://www.dailymotion.com/video/x3qxq5q.

11. "Bud Light Abruptly Pulls Amy Schumer, Seth Rogen Ads," *New York Post*, November 1, 2016, https://nypost.com/2016/11/01/bud-light-abruptly-pulls-amy -schumer-seth-rogen-ads/.

12. Angelo Young, "Epic Fashion Fail: How Lands' End Tried to Be Young and Stylish—and Fell Flat on Its Face," Salon, October 2, 2016, https://www.salon.com /2016/10/02/epic-fashion-fail-how-lands-end-tried-to-be-young-and-stylish-and -fell-flat-on-its-face/.

13. Joseph Nocera, "The Selling of Everything," *New York Times*, December 11, 1994, https://www.nytimes.com/1994/12/11/books/the-selling-of-everything.html.

14. Caitlin R. Weiner, "How Subarus Became the Car for Lesbians," Medium, January 26, 2020, https://medium.com/@caitlinrweiner/how-subarus-became-the -car-for-lesbians-ec1d5f4754fa.

15. Alex Mayyasi, "How Subaru Came to Be Seen as Cars for Lesbians," *Atlantic*, June 22, 2016, https://www.theatlantic.com/business/archive/2016/06/how-subaru -came-to-be-seen-as-cars-for-lesbians/488042/.

16. Izzy Rode, "Outward Explainer What's with Lesbians and Subarus," Slate, January 2, 2014, https://www.slate.com/blogs/outward/2014/01/02/lesbians_and _subarus_why_do_lesbians_love_outbacks_and_foresters.html.

17. "The Ultimate Gay and Lesbian Cars of All Time," Car Talk, https://www .cartalk.com/content/ultimate-gay-and-lesbian-cars-all-time.

18. Alex Mayyasi, "How an Ad Campaign Made Lesbians Fall in Love with Subaru," Priceonomics, May 23, 2016, https://priceonomics.com/how-an-ad -campaign-made-lesbians-fall-in-love-with/.

19. Alex Williams, "Gay by Design, or a Lifestyle Choice?," *New York Times*, April 12, 2007, https://www.nytimes.com/2007/04/12/fashion/12cars.html?8dpc.

20. Dana Canedy, "As the Main Character in 'Ellen' Comes Out, Some Companies See an Opportunity; Others Steer Clear," *New York Times*, April 30, 1997, https://www.nytimes.com/1997/04/30/business/main-character-ellen-comes-some -companies-see-opportunity-others-steer-clear.html.

21. Sophie Cummings, "Lesbaru . . . I Mean Subaru," Medium, October 20, 2016, https://medium.com/re-write/lesbaru-i-mean-subaru-c2291dfbe333.

22. "The North Face Celebrates Exploration as a State of Mind in Global Campaign Introducing 'New Explorers,'" PR Newswire, September 18, 2018, https://www .prnewswire.com/news-releases/the-north-face-celebrates-exploration-as-a-state-of -mind-in-global-campaign-introducing-new-explorers-300714097.html.

23. "The North Face Logo," CGain, https://cgain.co.uk/the-north-face-logo -branding/.

24. Youngme Moon, "Uber: Changing the Way the World Moves," Teaching Note 316-109 (Boston: Harvard Business School, December 2015, revised June 2016).

25. Ralph I. Allison and Kenneth P. Uhl, "Influence of Beer Brand Identification on Taste Perception," *Journal of Marketing Research* 1, no. 3 (1964), https://doi.org/10 .1177/002224376400100305.

26. Eliza Phares, "You're Boycotting Wrong," *Michigan Daily*, March 22, 2024, https://www.michigandaily.com/opinion/youre-boycotting-wrong/.

27. Dee-Ann Durbin, "Bud Light Parent Says US Market Share Stabilizing after Transgender Promotion Cost Sales," AP, August 3, 2023, https://apnews.com/article /bud-light-anheuser-busch-inbev-earnings-46b6412f84b5e8884caea941fc069d2f.

Chapter 12

1. Sam Matthews, "Burberry Axes Baseball Cap Due to Football Hooligan Links," Campaign, September 10, 2004, https://www.campaignlive.co.uk/article /burberry-axes-baseball-cap-due-football-hooligan-links/221863?src_site=brand republic.

2. "Check That Burberry at the Door," *Chicago Tribune*, August 19, 2021, https://www.chicagotribune.com/news/ct-xpm-2003-11-18-0311180044-story.html.

3. Paul Sonne, "Mink or Fox? The Trench Gets Complicated," *Wall Street Journal*, November 3, 2011, https://www.wsj.com/articles/SB10001424052970203804204577 013842801187070; Youngme Moon, "Burberry," Case 504048 (Boston: Harvard Business School, 2003).

4. Moon, "Burberry."

5. Jonah Berger and Morgan Ward, "Subtle Signals of Inconspicuous Consumption," *Journal of Consumer Research* 37, no. 4 (2010), https://doi.org/10.1086/655445.

6. Youngme Moon and Kerry Herman, "BMWFilms," Case 502046 (Boston: Harvard Business School, February 11, 2002).

7. Rumble Romagnoli, "Is TikTok the Perfect Home for Luxury Brands?," The Drum, October 27, 2022, https://www.thedrum.com/opinion/2022/10/27/tiktok-the-perfect-home-luxury-brands; Joan Kennedy, "How Luxury Finally Cracked TikTok," Business of Fashion, August 9, 2023, https://www.businessoffashion.com/articles/luxury/the-luxury-brands-taking-over-tiktok/; Stéphane JG Girod, "The Metaverse Is Much More Than a Cool New Channel for Luxury Brands," Forbes, March 29, 2023, https://www.forbes.com/sites/stephanegirod/2023/03/29/the-metaverse-is-much-more-than-a-cool-new-channel-for-luxury-brands/.

8. Philip Bump, "What the Bud Light Backlash Has in Common with Today's Republican Party," Washington Post, April 10, 2023, https://www.washingtonpost.com/politics/2023/04/10/bud-light-beer-ad-transgender-dylan-mulvaney/.

9. Hanna Rosin, "Falwell Lights into Budweiser," Washington Post, May 12, 1999, https://www.washingtonpost.com/archive/lifestyle/1999/05/12/falwell-lights-into-budweiser/fb3f6516-cb70-49ab-890d-adcf31e87503/.

10. Lisa Flam, "Is Pedialyte the Ultimate Hangover Cure," Today, May 18, 2015, https://www.today.com/health/pedialyte-ultimate-hangover-cure-t21746.

11. Marina Nazario, "Starbucks Is Opening Hundreds of Premium Stores Where the Cheapest Coffee Is $4—We Visited One to See What It's Like," Business Insider, February 23, 2016, https://www.businessinsider.com/starbucks-reserve-review-2016-2.

12. Wendy Leigh, "What Is the Difference Between Starbucks and Starbucks Reserve?," TastingTable.com, June 17, 2022, https://www.tastingtable.com/899273/what-is-the-difference-between-starbucks-and-starbucks-reserve/.

13. Kamran Kashani and Inna Francis, "Xiameter: The Past and Future of a 'Disruptive Innovation,'" Case IMD-5-0702 (IMD, December 1, 2006).

14. "How Dow Corning Beat Commoditization by Embracing It," Chief Executive, https://chiefexecutive.net/facing-the-commoditization-challenge-how-dow-cornings-xiameter-brand-beats-commoditization-by-embracing-it__trashed/.

15. Bob Lamons, "Dow Targets Segment to Keep Market Share," Marketing News, June 2005.

16. Loren Gary, "Dow Corning's Big Price Gamble," Harvard Business School Working Knowledge, July 2005, https://hbswk.hbs.edu/archive/dow-corning-s-big-pricing-gamble.

17. Silvia Bellezza and Anat Keinan, "Brand Tourists: How Non–Core Users Enhance the Brand Image by Eliciting Pride," Journal of Consumer Research 41, no. 2 (2014): 397–417.

18. Amy L. Weiss-Meyer, "Tyra Banks: Dropping H-Bombs Like Nobody's Business," The Crimson, September 17, 2012, https://www.thecrimson.com/flyby/article/2012/9/17/tyra-banks-harvard-girl/.

19. Avery Hartmans, "The Rise of Carhartt, the 134-Year-Old Workwear Brand That's Beloved by Everyone from Rappers to Celebrities to Blue-Collar Workers," Business Insider, November 27, 2022, https://www.businessinsider.com/carhartt-history-popularity-workwear-fashion-trend-2022-11.

20. Tonya Riley, "What It Means to Be a Working-Class Clothing Brand in America Today," Esquire, July 14, 2017, https://www.esquire.com/style/mens-fashion/a56175/carhartt-american-workwear/.

21. Riley, "What It Means to Be a Working-Class Clothing Brand."

22. Jacob Gallagher, "Behind Carhartt's Booming Year—from Workwear to Golden Globes Fashion," *Wall Street Journal*, April 2, 2021, https://www.wsj.com /articles/behind-carhartts-booming-yearfrom-workwear-to-golden-globes-fashion -11617364798.

23. Phil Wahba, "Re-Tooled: How Ray-Ban Brought Its Brand Back from the Brink," *Fortune*, January 27, 2016, https://fortune.com/2016/01/27/ray-ban-luxottica -retooled/.

24. "Ray-Ban: Never Hide," *Ad Age*, June 7, 2007, https://adage.com/creativity /work/never-hide/4549; Joe Berkowitz, "Rebels Throughout History Are Not Hiding in Ray-Ban Ads," *Fast Company*, April 20, 2012, https://www.fastcompany .com/1680646/rebels-throughout-history-are-not-hiding-in-new-ray-ban-ads.

25. Travis Britton, "Ray-Ban—Never Hide Launch," Behance, https://www .behance.net/gallery/102568577/Ray-Ban-Never-Hide-Launch?locale=en_US; "Ray-Ban" Avvenice, https://avvenice.com/en/323_ray-ban; Luc Gninyomo, "How 'Edgy' Marketing Brought the Ray-Bans Back to Life," *Sheen*, January 13, 2022, https://www.sheenmagazine.com/how-edgy-marketing-brought-the-ray -bans-back-to-life/; Zecheng Huang and Siqing Weng, "Brand Image and Consumers: A Case Study of Ray-Ban," *Journal of Education, Humanities and Social Sciences* 1 (2022): 118–27.

26. Wahba, "Re-Tooled."

27. Michella Oré, "The Best Ray-Bans for Men Make You Feel Like a Super Star," *GQ*, March 27, 2024, https://www.gq.com/story/best-ray-ban-sunglasses -for-men.

28. Ayelet Israeli and Anne V. Wilson, "Athletic Brewing Company: Crafting the U.S. Non-Alcoholic Beer Category," Case 523021 (Boston: Harvard Business School, July 15, 2022).

29. Eric Ryan, "The Summer's Hottest Beer Doesn't Have Alcohol," *Forbes*, May 29, 2024, https://www.forbes.com/sites/cereal-entrepreneurs/2024/05/29/the -top-selling-beer-at-whole-foods-has-no-alcohol/.

30. Ben Cohen, "The Hottest Beer in America Doesn't Have Alcohol," *Wall Street Journal*, February 3, 2024, https://www.wsj.com/business/retail/athletic -brewing-non-alcoholic-beer-864caa20.

31. Lauren Thomas, "America's Biggest Nonalcoholic Beer Brand Doubles Its Valuation," *Wall Street Journal*, July 9, 2024, https://www.wsj.com/business/retail /athletic-brewing-company-nonalcoholic-beer-valuation-a743d2d6.

32. "Six Flags Entertainment: Attendance Drop on Price Increases," Seeking Alpha, May 22, 2023, https://seekingalpha.com/article/4606606-six-flags -entertainment-attendance-drop-on-price-increases.

33. Alex Rozier, "Six Flags CEO Calls Theme Park a 'Cheap Day Care for Teens,' Says Prices Are Going Up," NBC Los Angeles, August 18, 2022, https:// www.nbclosangeles.com/news/local/six-flags-theme-park-cheap-day-care-for-teens -prices-are-going-up/2967328/.

34. Lisa Fickenscher, "Six Flags Shares Soar 20% as Higher Ticket Prices Fuel Record Revenues," *New York Post*, May 8, 2023, https://nypost.com/2023/05/08/six -flags-shares-soar-20-as-higher-ticket-prices-fuel-record-revenues/.

35. Hinge, https://hinge.co/.

36. The League, https://www.theleague.com/.

Chapter 13

1. Joseph Hudak, "Big & Rich's John Rich Blasts Nike Over Colin Kaepernick Ad," *Rolling Stone*, September 4, 2018, https://www.rollingstone.com/music/music-country/big-richs-john-rich-blasts-nike-over-colin-kaepernick-ad-718648/.

2. Andrew Beaton, "Nike Risks Backlash with Colin Kaepernick Deal," *Wall Street Journal*, September 4, 2018, https://www.wsj.com/articles/nikes-colin-kaepernick-deal-puts-risk-on-display-1536081832.

3. Lucas Bean, "You're Not Boycotting Nike, They Fired You as a Customer," LinkedIn, September 11, 2018, https://www.linkedin.com/pulse/i-know-must-suck-fired-nike-theyre-just-you-anymore-lucas-bean/.

4. Erica Sweeney, "76% of Voters Age 18–34 Support Nike's Kaepernick Ad, Study Finds," Marketing Dive, September 14, 2018, https://www.marketingdive.com/news/76-of-voters-age-18-34-support-nikes-kaepernick-ad-study-finds/532326/.

5. Patrick Coffee, "How Nike's $6 Billion Colin Kaepernick Campaign Put the Focus Back on Big Creative Ideas," *Adweek*, September 30, 2018, https://www.adweek.com/agencies/the-big-payback/.

6. Jill Avery and Koen Pauwels, "Brand Activism: Nike and Colin Kaepernick," Case 519046 (Boston: Harvard Business School, December 17, 2018), https://hbsp.harvard.edu/product/519046-PDF-ENG?Ntt=kaepernick.

7. John Deighton, Jill Avery, and Jeffrey Fear, "Porsche: The Cayenne Launch," Case 511068 (Boston: Harvard Business School, February 15, 2011), https://hbsp.harvard.edu/product/511068-PDF-ENG?Ntt=porsche%20cayenne.

8. "Porsche Roars Back . . . with Fred Schwab and an SUV," Knowledge at Wharton, March 27, 2002, https://knowledge.wharton.upenn.edu/article/porsche-roars-back-with-fred-schwab-and-an-suv/.

9. Carmen Nobel, "Gender Contamination: Why Men Prefer Products Untouched by Women," *Forbes*, November 13, 2013, https://www.forbes.com/sites/hbsworkingknowledge/2013/11/13/gender-contamination-why-men-prefer-products-untouched-by-women/.

10. Porsche Newsroom press release, "20 Years of the Cayenne: The 'Third Porsche'—an Extraordinary Success Story," October 6, 2022, https://newsroom.porsche.com/en/2022/products/porsche-cayenne-anniversary-20-years-success-story-28443.html.

11. Juliet Macur, "Bubba Wallace Thankful for Flag Ban, but NASCAR's Fans Might Not Be," *New York Times*, June 13, 2020, https://www.nytimes.com/2020/06/13/sports/bubba-wallace-nascar-confederate-flag.html.

12. Vanessa Romo, "NASCAR Bans Confederate Flag," NPR, June 10, 2020, https://www.npr.org/sections/live-updates-protests-for-racial-justice/2020/06/10/874393049/nascar-bans-confederate-flag.

13. Patrick Coffee, "Nascar Targets Diverse Audiences to Expand Viewership, Despite Anti-DEI Backlash," *Wall Street Journal*, January 26, 2024, https://www.wsj.com/articles/nascar-targets-diverse-audiences-to-expand-viewership-despite-anti-dei-backlash-b6a0d14c.

14. Melody Mercado, "NASCAR Fans Brave Rain-Soaked Chicago Weekend to Watch Shortened—and Pricey—Grant Park Races," Block Club Chicago, July 2, 2023, https://blockclubchicago.org/2023/07/02/nascar-fans-brave-rain-soaked-chicago-weekend-to-watch-shortened-and-pricey-grant-park-races/.

15. Alex Hern and Dan Milmo, "'Encryption Is Deeply Threatening to Power': Meredith Whittaker of Messaging App Signal," *Guardian*, June 18, 2024, https://www.theguardian.com/technology/article/2024/jun/18/encryption-is-deeply -threatening-to-power-meredith-whittaker-of-messaging-app-signal.

16. Mitchell Clark, "Signal Is 'Starting to Phase Out SMS Support' from Its Android App," The Verge, October 12, 2022, https://www.theverge.com/2022/10 /12/23400896/signal-sms-support-ending-android-simplification.

17. Nina, "Removing SMS Supposed from Signal Android," Signal, October 12, 2022, https://signal.org/blog/sms-removal-android.

18. "Removal of SMS Support Is a Terrible Idea," GitHub, October 12, 2022, https://github.com/signalapp/Signal-Android/issues/12517; "SMS Removal Megathread," Reddit, n.d., https://www.reddit.com/r/signal/comments/yfwia4 /sms_removal_megathread/.

19. Jameson Fleming and Emmy Liederman, "Anheuser-Busch CEO Issues Statement Following Uproar over Bud Light's Partnership with Dylan Mulvaney," *Adweek*, April 14, 2023, https://www.adweek.com/brand-marketing/anheuser-busch -ceo-issues-statement-following-uproar-over-bud-lights-partnership-with-dylan -mulvaney/.

20. Ellen Brait, "Lands' End Takes Down Interview with Gloria Steinem after Customer Backlash," *Guardian*, February 26, 2016, https://www.theguardian.com /books/2016/feb/26/gloria-steinem-lands-end-interview-abortion-backlash.

21. Nathaniel Meyersohn, "Gillette Says It's Satisfied with Sales after Controversial Ad," CNN Business, January 23, 2019, https://www.cnn.com/2019/01/23 /business/gillette-ad-procter-and-gamble-stock/index.html.

22. Meyersohn, "Gillette Says It's Satisfied with Sales after Controversial Ad."

23. Laura Wasson, "Opinion: How to Avoid the Pitfalls of Gillette's 'Woke' Commercial," *Ad Age*, January 23, 2019, https://adage.com/article/opinion/avoid -pitfalls-gillette-s-woke-advertisement/316351.

24. Jack Neff, "Blowback over 'We Believe' Ad Suggests Gillette Is No Nike," *Ad Age*, January 21, 2019, https://adage.com/article/advertising/ad-blowback -suggests-gillette-nike/316308.

25. All stats via Statista.

26. Jeannie Kopstein and Mariah Espada, "The Staggering Economic Impact of Taylor Swift's Eras Tour," *Time*, August 24, 2023, https://time.com/6307420/taylor -swift-eras-tour-money-economy/.

27. "Taylor Swift Fans 'Shake It Off,' Causing Record-Breaking Seismic Activity During Seattle Shows," CNN Entertainment, July 28, 2023, https://www.cnn.com /2023/07/27/entertainment/taylor-swift-seismic-activity/index.html.

28. Alexandra Canal, "Taylor Swift Helped Boost NFL Ratings, but Her Power Extends Far Beyond the League," Yahoo Finance, October 4, 2003, https://finance .yahoo.com/news/taylor-swift-helped-boost-nfl-ratings-but-her-power-extends-far -beyond-the-league-180303062.

Chapter 14

1. Zak Maoui, "A Pair of Nike Dunks Just Won Gold at the Beijing Winter Olympics 2022," *GQ*, February 10, 2022, https://www.gq-magazine.co.uk/fashion /article/nike-dunks-matthew-hamilton-winter-olympics.

2. Manuela López Restropo, "Just Do It: How the Iconic Nike Tagline Built a Career for the Late Dan Wieden," NPR, October 6, 2022, https://www.npr.org/2022/10/06/1127032721/nike-just-do-it-slogan-success-dan-wieden-kennedy-dies.

3. Ed Caesar, "The Epic Untold Story of Nike's (Almost) Perfect Marathon," Wired, June 29, 2017, https://www.wired.com/story/nike-breaking2-marathon-eliud-kipchoge/.

4. "Nike Zoom Fly 4 Review: Legit Carbon Plates Trainer or Not?," Believe Run Club, November 9, 2021, https://believeintherun.com/shoe-reviews/nike-zoom-fly-4-performance-review/.

5. De Lo Mio, Republica De Nueva York, SNKRS, n.d., https://www.nike.com/launch/t/de-lo-mio-republica-de-nueva-york; Marc Bain, "Nike's Digital Strategy Is to Treat Everyone the Way It Treats Sneakerheads," Quartz, November 14, 2019, https://qz.com/quartzy/1747382/how-nikes-snkrs-app-community-inspired-its-digital-strategy.

6. Matteo Cinelli et al., "The Echo Chamber Effect on Social Media," PNAS 118, no. 9 (February 23, 2021), https://www.pnas.org/doi/10.1073/pnas.2023301118.

7. Zoe Fraade-Blanar and Aaron M. Glazer, "How Warren Buffett Turned Consumers into Superfans," Inc., March 24, 2017, https://www.inc.com/zoe-fraade-blaner-and-aaron-m-glazer/how-warren-buffett-turned-consumers-into-superfans.html.

Chapter 15

1. Bryan Wassel, "Starbucks' Mobile Ordering Is So Popular, It's Slowing Some Orders Down," CXDive, May 1, 2024, https://www.customerexperiencedive.com/news/starbucks-mobile-ordering-is-so-popular-its-slowing-some-orders-down/714915/.

2. Wassel, "Starbucks' Mobile Ordering Is So Popular."

3. Jason Aten, "Company 'Lost Its Ways.' It Turns Out the Thing It Needs Most Is a New Blender," Inc., September 20, 2022, https://www.inc.com/jason-aten/starbucks-ceo-admitted-company-lost-its-way-it-turns-out-thing-it-needs-most-is-a-new-blender.html.

4. Nathaniel Meyersohn, "A Major Shift at Starbucks Is Changing Its Personality," CNN Business, July 19, 2024, https://www.cnn.com/2024/07/19/business/starbucks-mobile-orders-third-place/index.html.

5. "What Is Starbucks' Moon Drink? Inside the Viral Iced Matcha and Chai Latte Combo," EconoTimes, October 13, 2024, https://econotimes.com/What-Is-Starbucks-Moon-Drink-Inside-the-Viral-Iced-Matcha-and-Chai-Latte-Combo-1690413.

6. Julie Creswell, "Somewhere Amid the Frappuccinos, Fans Say Starbucks Lost Something," New York Times, October 30, 2024, https://www.nytimes.com/2024/10/30/business/starbucks-customers-brian-niccol.html.

7. Heidi Peiper, "Reimagining the Third Place: How Starbucks Is Evolving Its Store Experience," Starbucks Stories and News, September 13, 2022, https://stories.starbucks.com/stories/2022/reimagining-the-third-place-how-starbucks-is-evolving-its-store-experience/.

8. Heather Haddon, "Starbucks Is Having an Identity Crisis. Can Howard Schultz Fix It?," Wall Street Journal, April 22, 2023, https://www.wsj.com/articles/starbucks-can-howard-schultz-fix-it-11650631886.

9. Spencer Jakab, "At Starbucks, Third Place Is No Longer Gold," *Wall Street Journal*, May 9, 2022, https://www.wsj.com/articles/at-starbucks-third-place-is-no-longer-gold-11652094002.

10. Justin Bariso, "Starbucks's New CEO Just Announced 2 Very Big Changes. They Could Completely Change the Company," *Inc.*, September 11, 2024, https://www.inc.com/justin-bariso/starbucks-new-ceo-just-announced-2-very-big-changes-they-could-completely-change-company.html.

11. Nathaniel Meyersohn, "Starbucks Is Scaling Back Discounts and Promotions," CNN, October 14, 2024, https://www.cnn.com/2024/10/14/business/starbucks-deals-promos-endings/index.html.

12. Gregory Schmidt and Vanessa Friedman, "Burberry Replaces C.E.O. Amid 'Disappointing' Results," *New York Times*, July 15, 2024, https://www.nytimes.com/2024/07/15/business/burberry-ceo-departure.html.

13. Carol Ryan, "Why a Shabby Luxury Brand Is Hard to Fix," *Wall Street Journal*, May 24, 2024, https://www.wsj.com/business/retail/why-a-shabby-luxury-brand-is-hard-to-fix-7c675117?mod=article_inline.

14. Ryan, "Why a Shabby Luxury Brand Is Hard to Fix."

15. Madeline Berg, "How Burberry Became Fashion's Biggest Fail of the Year," *Business Insider*, August 7, 2024, https://www.businessinsider.com/how-burberry-became-fashions-biggest-fail-stock-drop-ceo-ousting-2024-8.

16. Carol Ryan, "Luxury Brands Have a Strict Hierarchy. Burberry Found Out the Hard Way," *Wall Street Journal*, April 21, 2024, https://www.wsj.com/business/retail/luxury-brands-have-a-strict-hierarchy-burberry-found-out-the-hard-way-1d5fb2c9.

17. Jennifer Creery and Angelina Rascouet, "Burberry Replaces CEO and Rethinks High-End Luxury Strategy," BNN Bloomberg, July 15, 2024, https://www.bnnbloomberg.ca/business/2024/07/15/burberry-ceo-departs-as-luxury-brand-suspends-dividend/.

18. Matthew Kish, "Nike Stock Has Worst Day on Record, Wiping Out $28 Billion in Value," *Oregonian*, June 28, 2024, https://www.oregonlive.com/business/2024/06/nike-stock-has-worst-day-on-record-wiping-out-28-billion-in-value.html; Gabrielle Fonrouge, "Nike CEO John Donahoe Comes Under Fire as Stock Sees Worst Day on Record," CNBC, June 28, 2024, https://www.cnbc.com/2024/06/28/nike-ceo-john-donahoe-under-fire-from-wall-street.html.

19. Massimo Giunco, "Nike: An Epic Saga of Value Destruction," LinkedIn, July 28, 2024, https://www.linkedin.com/pulse/nike-epic-saga-value-destruction-massimo-giunco-llplf.

20. "Nike's New Chief Runs into Trouble as Turnaround Efforts Falter," *Financial Times*, July 8, 2024, https://www.ft.com/content/4fdc1b22-246c-402b-abaf-f56e5d591cdc.

21. Simon Cambers and Simon Graf, "'Letting Roger Federer Leave Nike for Uniqlo Was an Atrocity,' Says Former Nike Tennis Director," CNN Sports, February 14, 2023, https://www.cnn.com/2023/02/14/tennis/roger-federer-nike-mike-nakajima-tennis-spt-intl/index.html; Kevin Draper, "Simone Biles Leaves Nike for a Sponsor That Focuses on Women," *New York Times*, August 7, 2021, https://www.nytimes.com/2021/04/23/sports/olympics/simone-biles-athleta-nike.html; Allyson Felix, "My Own Nike Pregnancy Story," *New York Times*, May 22, 2019, https://www.nytimes.com/2019/05/22/opinion/allyson-felix-pregnancy-nike.html.

22. "Nike Races to Keep from Losing Ground to More Nimble Rivals," *Financial Times*, January 12, 2024, https://www.ft.com/content/e83d7cf5-5752-469e-bdf2 -659bc5c92c1c.

23. "Nike's New Chief Runs into Trouble as Turnaround Efforts Falter," *Financial Times*, July 8, 2024, https://www.ft.com/content/4fdc1b22-246c-402b-abaf-f56e5d 591cdc.

24. Brittaney Kiefer and Rebecca Stewart, "Inside Nike's Race to Regain Its Marketing Edge," *Adweek*, July 31, 2024, https://www.adweek.com/brand -marketing/inside-nikes-race-to-regain-its-marketing-edge/.

25. Noah Johnson, "Is Nike Still Cool?," *GQ*, August 2, 2024, https://www.gq .com/story/is-nike-still-cool.

26. Katherine Masters and Ananya Mariam Rejash, "As Nike Bleeds Market Share, Investors Worry over Relevance," Reuters, March 21, 2024, https://www .reuters.com/business/retail-consumer/nike-its-gotta-be-shoes-could-be-thing-past -2024-03-21/; Katherine Masters, "Focus: Retailers Slash Prices on More Nike Sneakers in 2024, Data Shows," Reuters, February 2, 2024, https://www.reuters.com /business/retail-consumer/retailers-slash-prices-more-nike-sneakers-2024-data -shows-2024-02-02/.

27. "Nike Grappling with Lack of Optimism over Future amid 'Missteps' in Donahoe's Tenure as CEO," *Sports Business Journal*, September 9, 2024, https://www .sportsbusinessjournal.com/Articles/2024/09/09/nike-donahoe-comeback-plan.

28. Nike Inc., FY24 Q3 Earnings Release Conference Call Transcript, March 21, 2024, https://s1.q4cdn.com/806093406/files/doc_financials/2024/q3/NIKE-Inc -Q3FY24-OFFICIAL-Transcript-FINAL.pdf.

29. Kiefer and Stewart, "Inside Nike's Race to Regain Its Marketing Edge."

30. "Brands: Lacoste's Riposte," *Time*, September 18, 2005, https://time.com /archive/6674736/brands-lacostes-riposte/.

31. Pamela N. Danziger, "Nike Loses in the 'Winning Isn't for Everyone' Ad Campaign," *Forbes*, August 16, 2024, https://www.forbes.com/sites/pamdanziger /2024/08/16/nike-fails-in-the-winning-isnt-for-everyone-ad-campaign/.

Conclusion

1. Jonah Weiner, "Why Are Pants So Big (Again)?," *New York Times*, March 3, 2024, https://www.nytimes.com/2024/03/03/magazine/big-pants-style.html.

INDEX

Page numbers followed by *f* indicate figures; those followed by *t* indicate tables.

ACKNOWLEDGMENTS

This book would not have been possible without the support of many people. First, we are deeply grateful to our editor, Scott Berinato, for believing in this project and guiding its development. We appreciate your dedication and help in making this book the best it could be. And thank you to the entire Harvard Business Publishing team for making this book happen.

We are also very thankful for the many friends and colleagues who generously gave their time to discuss the concepts in this book and provided invaluable feedback for improving the frameworks and stories herein, especially, Heather Burgess, Eric Bradlow, Alexander Chernev, Marina Cooley, Serena Hagerty, Ayelet Israeli, Graham Jaenicke, Todd Hamilton, Barbara Kahn, Omar Rodríguez-Vilá, Brian Sternthal, and Patti Williams. A special thank-you to our students at the Wharton School and Goizueta Business School who were the first to engage with these ideas, and who, through thoughtful questions and feedback, helped us refine and improve them. And thank you to the people who provided interviews that helped bring to life the stories in this book: Ludovica Cesareo, Drex Davis, Tim Ellis, and Yin Woon Rani.

Finally, to our families: thank you for your patience and understanding while we spent many hours working on this book and for putting up with the unending Zoom and phone calls between us as we refined our ideas and writing.

ABOUT THE AUTHORS

ANNIE WILSON is a senior lecturer of marketing at the Wharton School of the University of Pennsylvania. She received a PhD in marketing from Harvard Business School and a BA in English and psychology from Georgetown University. She studies consumer psychology and marketing strategy, particularly as it relates to how brands grow and thrive. She has taught courses on advertising, consumer behavior, marketing strategy, and wellness marketing. She is an award-winning teacher, and her published case studies are taught at over two hundred universities around the world. She has given keynote talks and provided marketing consulting for companies including Vanguard, Estée Lauder, Sony Group Corporation, and Ferragamo, among others.

RYAN HAMILTON is an associate professor of marketing at Emory University's Goizueta Business School. He studies consumer decision-making, especially as influenced by pricing and branding. He has taught classes on marketing management, marketing strategy, consumer psychology, and the use of humor in business. He is an award-winning teacher and researcher whose research findings have been covered in *Harvard Business Review*, the *New York Times*, the *Wall Street Journal*, and the *Financial Times*. He has consulted on matters of pricing, branding, and customer experience with Walmart, FedEx, Home Depot, Caterpillar, ConAgra, Cigna, Visa, and Ipsos, among others, and has been a keynote speaker and trainer on various topics in marketing and consumer psychology to groups as varied as small-business owners, lawyers, advertisers, accountants, and librarians. He received his PhD in marketing from Northwestern University's Kellogg School of Management.